The Campus History Series

Chowan College

Frank Stephenson

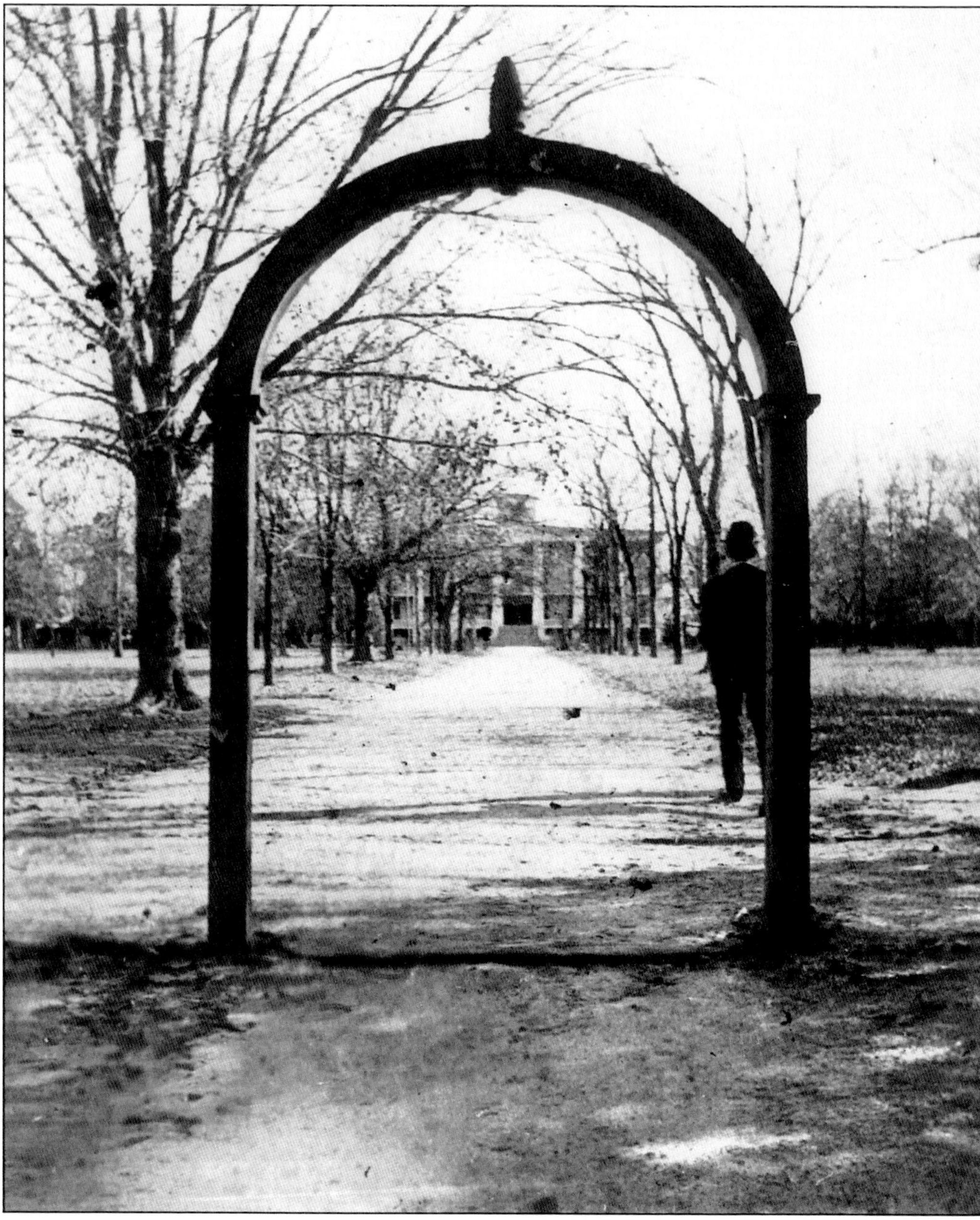

An 1890s view depicts the arch on the center walk at Chowan College.

(*cover photograph*) The signature structure on the Chowan College campus is the stately 1851 McDowell Columns Building. Listed on the National Register of Historic Buildings in the United States, it serves as the college's administration building. (Photograph by Joel C. Holland, winter 1949.)

The Campus History Series

CHOWAN COLLEGE

FRANK STEPHENSON

ARCADIA
PUBLISHING

ISBN 978-0-7385-1638-7

Published by Arcadia Publishing
Charleston, South Carolina

Printed in the United States of America

Library of Congress Catalog Card Number: 2004100873

For all general information contact Arcadia Publishing at:
Telephone 843-853-2070
Fax 843-853-0044
E-mail sales@arcadiapublishing.com
For customer service and orders:
Toll-Free 1-888-313-2665

Visit us on the Internet at www.arcadiapublishing.com

This book is dedicated to my two grandsons, Marlon Jakob Kuenstler of Como, North Carolina, and William Franklin Stephenson of Rome, Georgia.

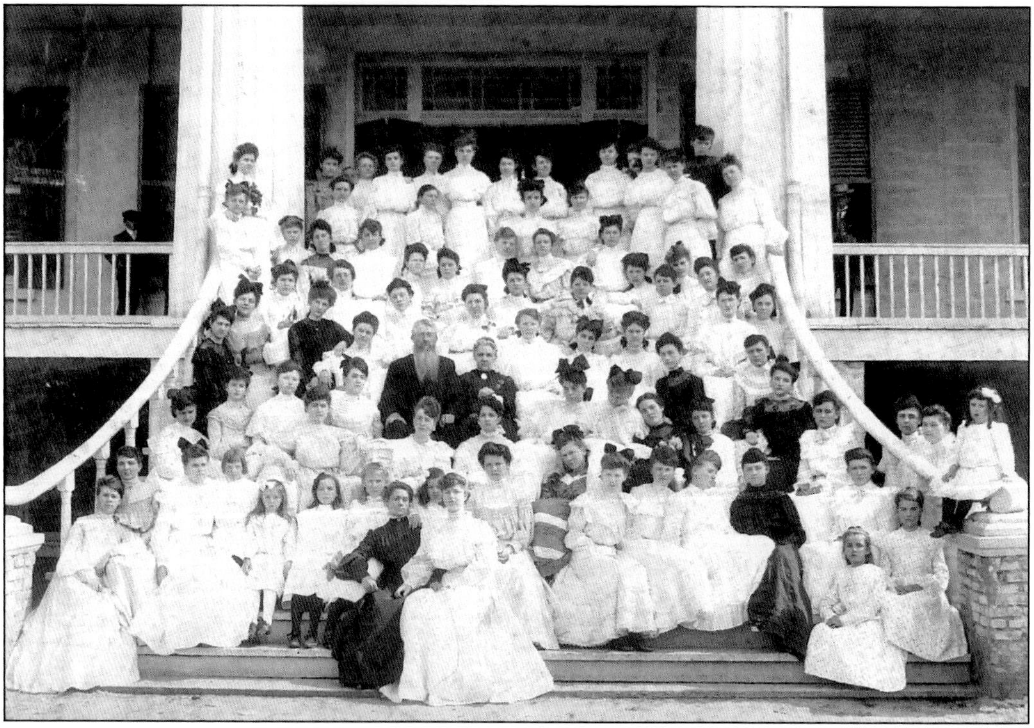

Pictured here is Chowan College president John C. Scarborough with the 1905 student body on the steps to the 1851 McDowell Columns Building, which continues to house the college's administrative offices.

Contents

ACKNOWLEDGMENTS

The author gratefully acknowledges with sincere appreciation and gratitude the assistance that made this book possible, particularly Chowan College staff members Barbara Mulder, Trudy Gibson, Kristine Mudrick, James Dewar, Linda Hassell, Mary Jo Ellis, Jane Taylor, Debbie Warren, Meredith Long, Sue Rose, Melanie Edwards, and retired Chowan College superintendent of buildings and grounds Jack Hassell. Sincere and deep appreciation is also extended to William Whitley, J.M. Jenkins, and David and Connie Day. A very special appreciation is extended to Carol Hedspeth and Peggy Davis of Conway Photo and Print Shop for their successful efforts in locating the negatives for the 1949 Chowan College reopening parade.

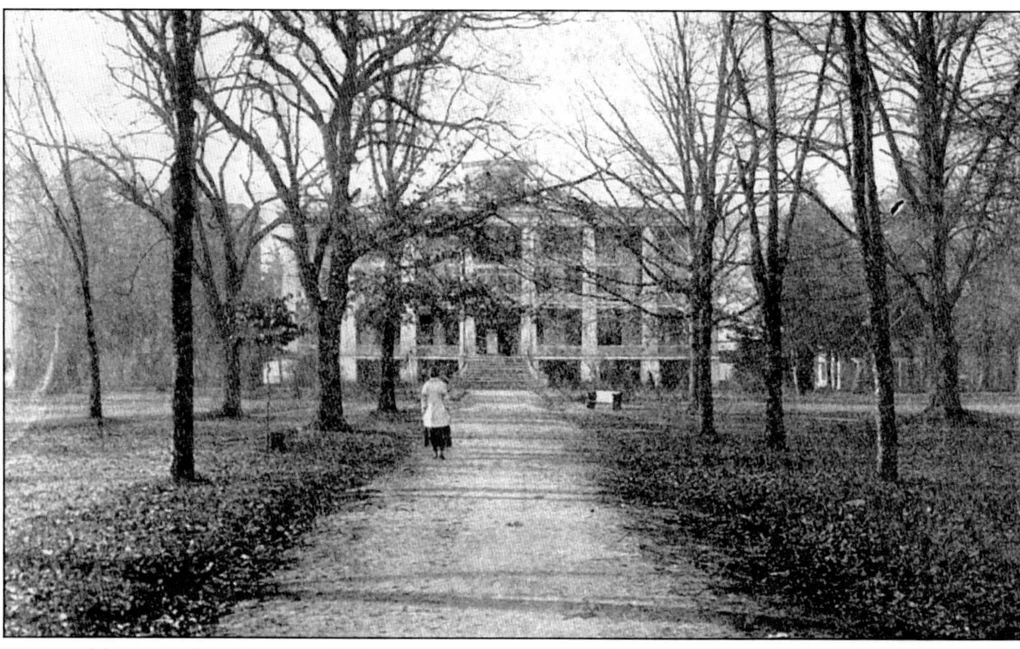

Pictured here is the Chowan College campus on a cold winter day in the early 1920s.

INTRODUCTION

I was six years old when my father and I visited the abandoned campus of Chowan College. It was a warm Saturday afternoon in May 1946. Having been closed for three years, the campus and its buildings showed signs of neglect and abuse. That visit began my lifetime association with the college. My father probably never suspected that my youngest sister and I, two of his three children, would graduate from Chowan College and that I would spend most of my adult life working there. On that visit, my father told me that he was about my age when he first visited the college as a young boy back in 1915 with my grandfather, Eugene F. Stephenson. My grandfather came to Chowan to donate food in answer to President Lineberry's plea to the area. The college had hit a financial rough spot and was low on food for students. My father said local farmers donated large quantities of salt pork, lard, flour, corn meal, molasses, potatoes, and home-canned vegetables.

I visited the abandoned Chowan College campus twice more. In the spring of 1947, my first-grade class, with our teacher Miss Bell, and Mrs. Dorothy Brown, our grade mother, went to the campus for an Easter egg hunt. I especially remember the flying squirrels on campus and climbing over downed trees and fallen limbs.

In 1848, a group of Baptist men from Eastern North Carolina, concerned about their daughters' futures, founded Chowan College. Their institution would come to have a major impact on Eastern North Carolina and Southeast Virginia, an influence that began more than 150 years ago and, on a national scale, continues today.

The original college building, the McDowell Columns, is the signature focal point of Chowan College's 289-acre campus, which is described as one of the most beautiful small college campuses in the United States. In 1856, a few years following the establishment of the college, a landscape plan was utilized to develop the grounds in front of the McDowell Columns Building. This work was completed in 1859 and much of the formal design can still be seen. The McDowell Columns Building, built in 1851, remains in use as the college's administration building. Chowan College, the second oldest of North Carolina's seven Baptist colleges, was one of a few colleges in the South that did not close during the Civil War. In 1910, the name Chowan Baptist Female Institute was changed to Chowan College.

Since 1848, Chowan College has had a proud history of producing teachers who have had a major impact on education in North Carolina and Virginia. Today, Chowan College's Department of Education is ranked as one of the best in North Carolina, and *U.S. News and World Report* named Chowan as one of the South's premier third-tier comprehensive colleges and ranked it ninth in diversity.

Until 1931, Chowan College remained a four-year college for women. Then the decision was made to admit men and, in 1937, it became a two-year institution. Chowan remained a two-year college until 1943, when it closed due to the shortage of students during World War II. Between 1943 and 1948, there were a number of attempts to reopen Chowan College, but not on its campus in Murfreesboro; however, in 1948, 100 years after its opening, another group of men from Murfreesboro and the surrounding region launched a successful effort to reopen the college on its original campus. Opened in 1949, the co-ed junior college experienced unparalleled growth and had a great impact on North Carolina, Virginia, and the East Coast. Its football, basketball, and baseball teams from the junior college era produced graduates who later became players in the National Football League, the National Basketball Association, and Major League baseball. In 1993, Chowan College returned to four-year college status. Today, young men and women from 42 states and 21 foreign countries study here.

The story of Chowan College is a remarkable story of endurance, courage, strength, character, and survival. This venerable institution has taken powerful shots from wars, hurricanes, ice storms, thunder storms, tornados, fires, frozen pipes, broken water mains, Civil War troops, and financial hardships, not to mention student pranks such as food fights, panty raids, and mysterious small cars parked on the front porch of McDowell Columns Building. The very fact that Chowan College is alive today is a testament to the indomitable spirit of this remarkable place and its many supporters throughout the years.

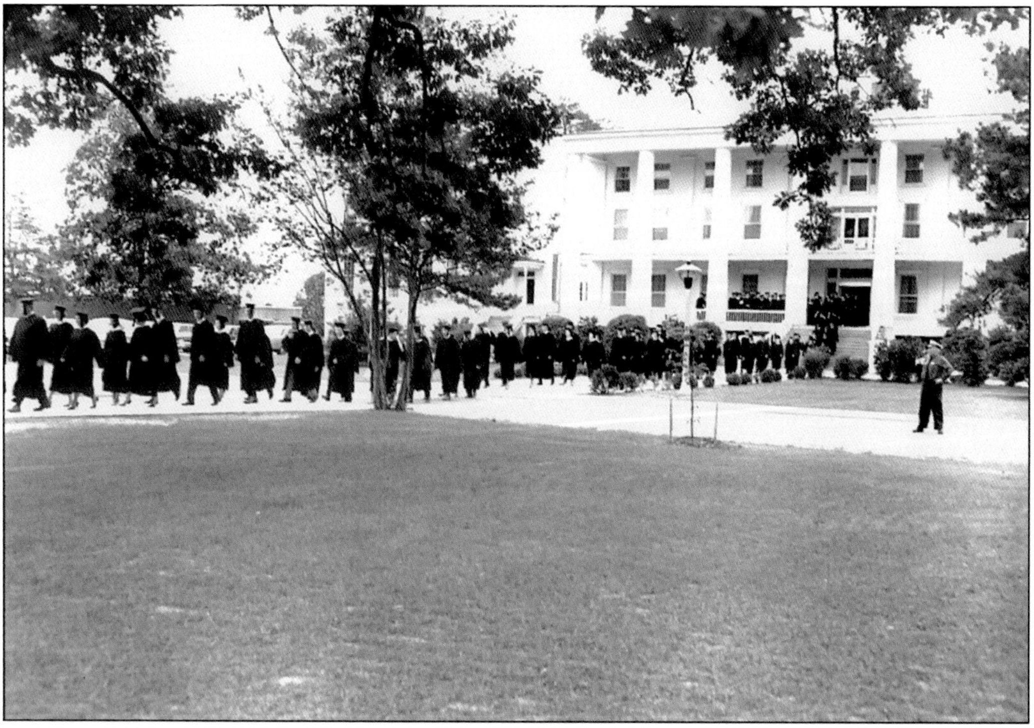

This is the May 1965 graduation on the front lawn.

One

The Formative Years 1848–1899

In 1848, the Chowan Baptist Female Institute was founded by Eastern North Carolina and Virginia Baptists who sensed the need for an upscale school of higher education and culture for their young women. The founders erected and furnished a beautiful brick building that was four stories high, on a one-acre lot, and located in a sedge field in Murfreesboro, North Carolina. Additional land in front of the four-story McDowell Columns Building was purchased shortly after the building's completion in 1852. Today, this mighty structure stands as a testament to the foresight and artistic tastes of the college's founders. The college, which formally opened on October 11, 1848, with 11 students, began to supply well-trained teachers to meet North Carolina and Eastern Virginia's educational needs.

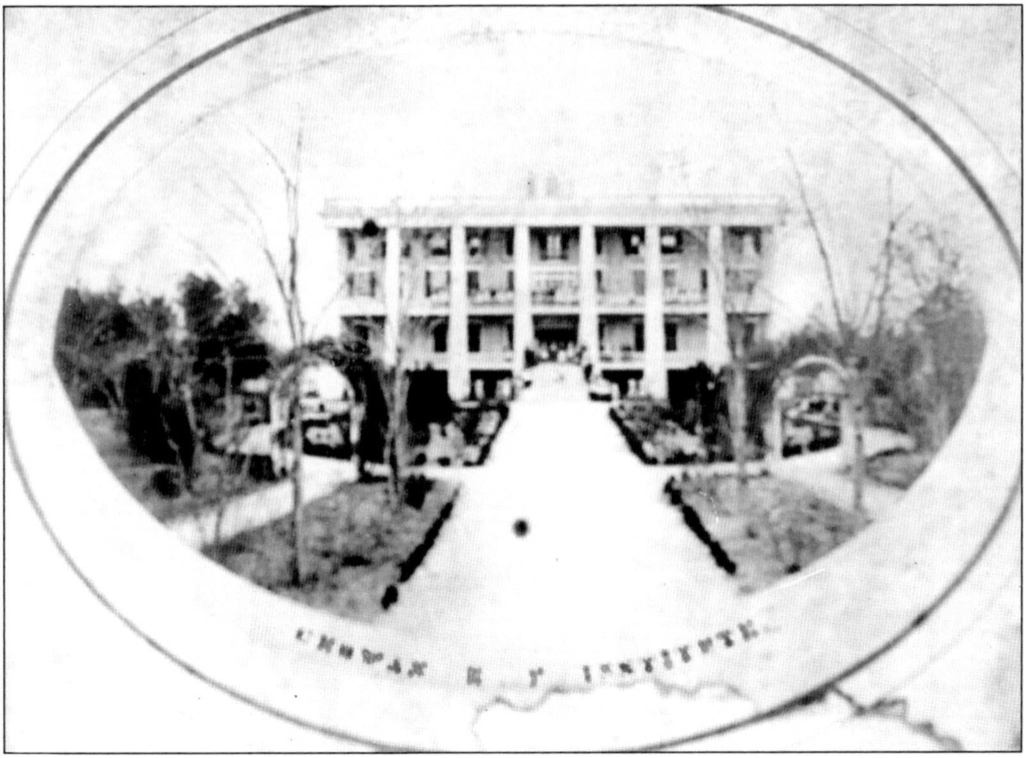

This is one of the earliest known views of the 1851 McDowell Columns Building. Judging from the size of the landscape plantings, it is believed that the photograph dates from the 1860s.

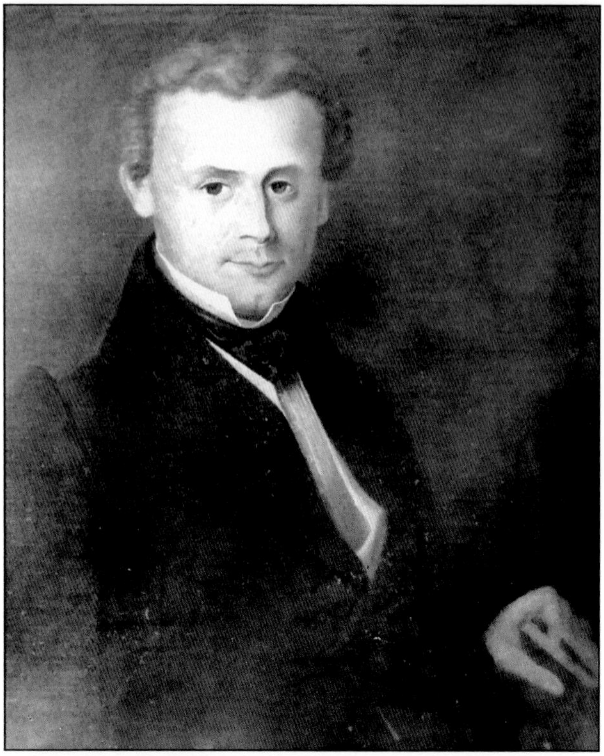

In April 1848, Dr. Godwin Cotton Moore of the St. John's section of Hertford County invited influential Bertie Union Baptists to his home at Mulberry Grove for dinner. At this dinner meeting, Chowan College was proposed and the seeds were planted that made Dr. Moore the future founder of this female college. Dr. Moore was educated at Hertford Academy in Murfreesboro, the University of North Carolina, and the University of Pennsylvania, where he studied medicine. Dr. Moore's attendance at Hertford Academy played a major role in the final decision to locate Chowan College in Murfreesboro.

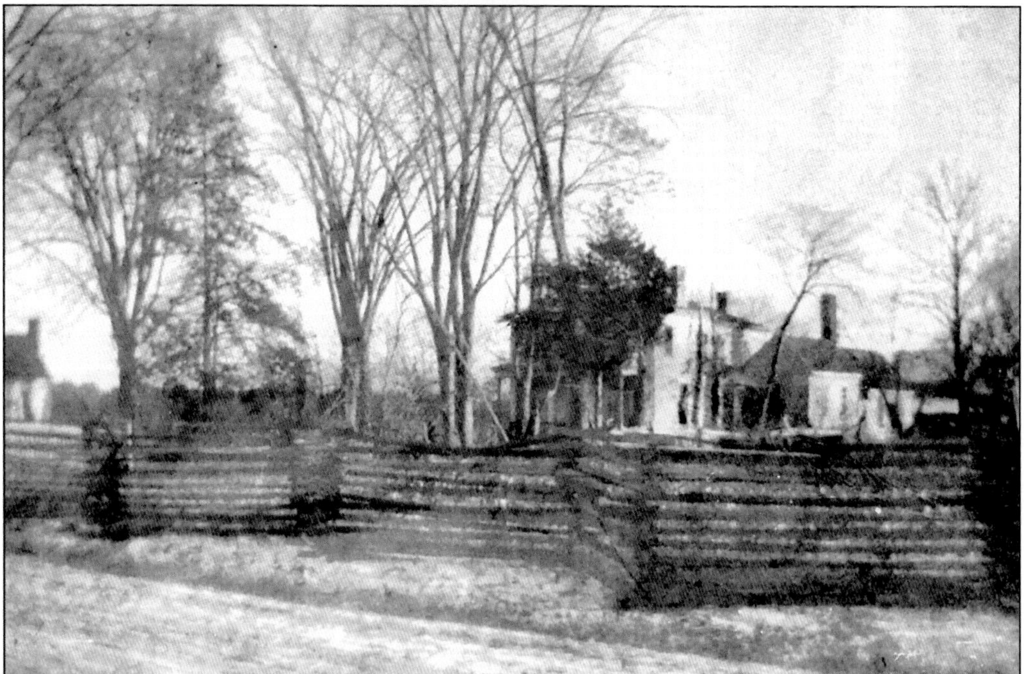

This is Mulberry Grove, the birthplace of Dr. Godwin Cotton Moore, founder of Chowan College. The site was first settled in 1730 by Dr. Moore's great-grandfather, Capt. Arthur Cotton, who served in the English Navy. Unfortunately, the house does not survive today.

When Chowan College opened in 1848, Archibald McDowell, a native of South Carolina and a Wake Forest graduate, became its first president. Archibald McDowell served as president of Chowan College on two separate occasions, from 1848 to 1849 and from 1862 to 1881.

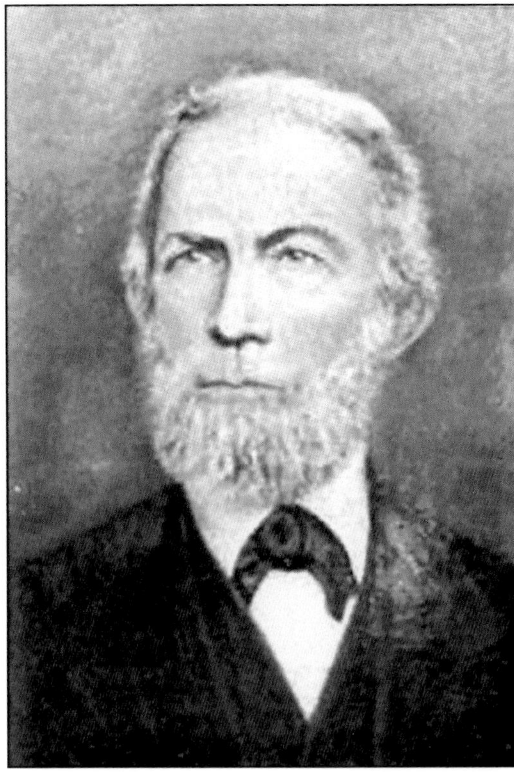

This is the Hertford Academy Building, the first home of Chowan College. When the decision to build a new college for girls was made, a site, staff, and equipment had to be secured. Murfreesboro was selected and the Hertford Academy Building for boys, later home to the Banks School for girls, was purchased. Chowan College operated in this building from the fall of 1848 to the fall of 1852, when the four-story Columns Building was completed. The Hertford Academy Building was built in 1811 and still stands on its original site on Broad Street in Murfreesboro's historic district. It is owned by the Murfreesboro Historical Association.

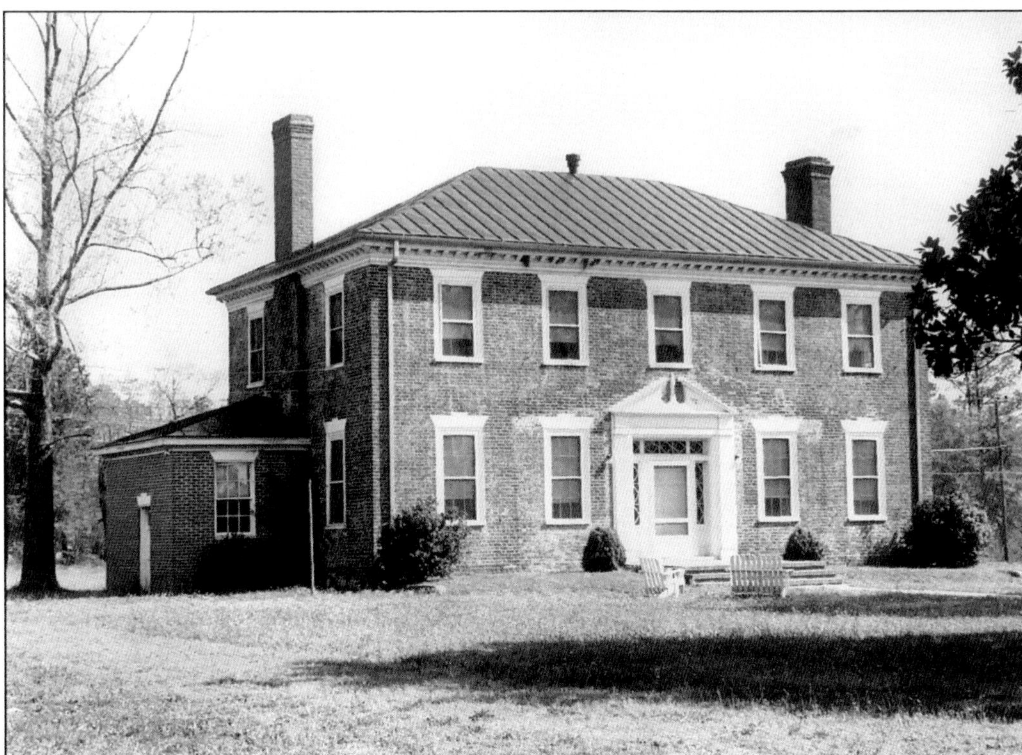

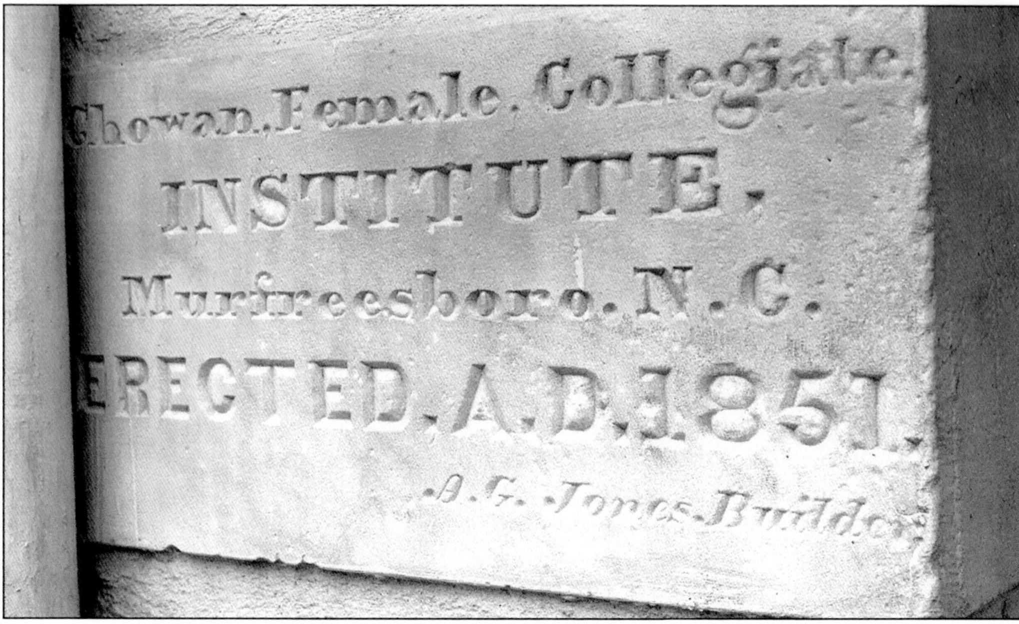

In August 1851 the Chowan College trustees, following the purchase of one acre of land from Murfreesboro merchant Perry Carter, signed a building contract with Albert G. Jones for the construction of a four-story building 106 feet long and 46 feet wide. Shortly thereafter this cornerstone was set in place and can still be seen today in the northeastern corner of the Columns Building. Jesse A. Jackson of Murfreesboro made the bricks for the building, which was completed and occupied in November 1852.

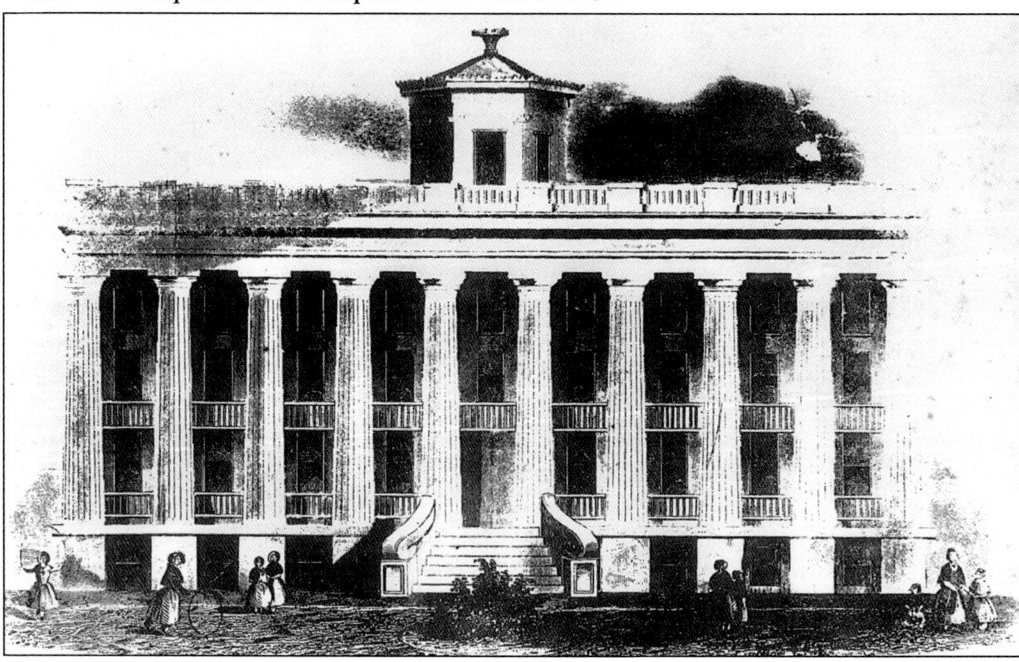

When the 1853–1854 Catalogue for Chowan Female Collegiate Institute was published in 1854, it contained this drawing of the Columns Building. This is probably the earliest known depiction of the Columns Building.

In 1939 the North Carolina State Historical Commission, forerunner of the North Carolina Department of Cultural Resources, erected this highway historical marker at the corner of Main and College Streets in Murfreesboro. In the early years, the street leading from Main Street to the Chowan campus was originally known as Seminary Avenue. It is not known when it changed to College Street.

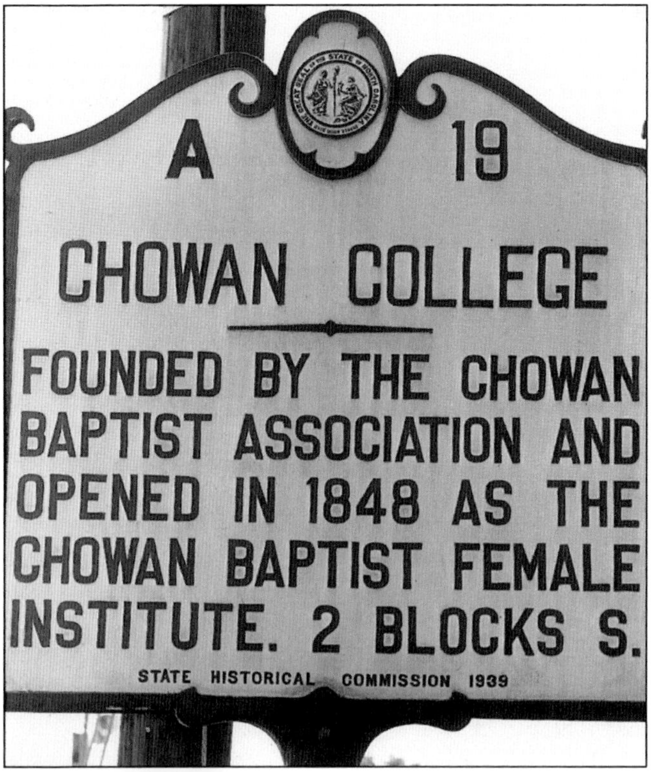

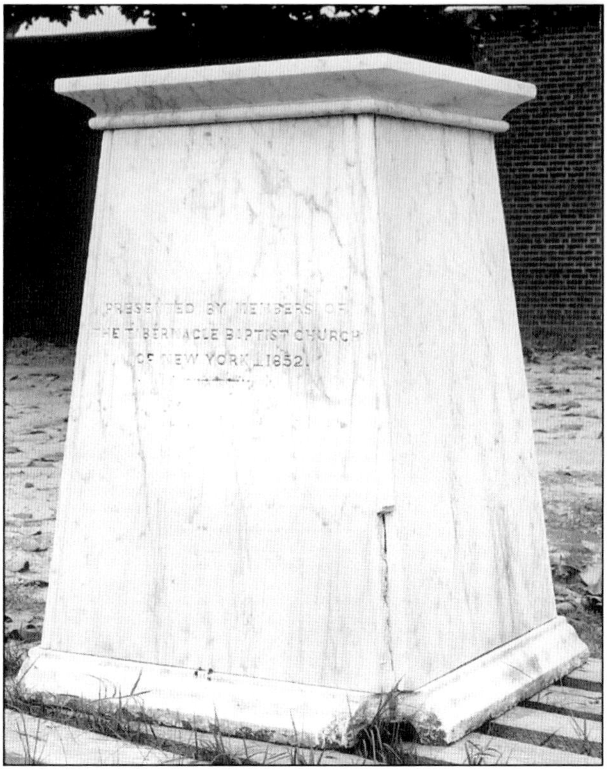

This marble stand was presented to Chowan College by members of The Tabernacle Baptist Church of New York in 1852. There is no information available concerning the circumstances surrounding this donation.

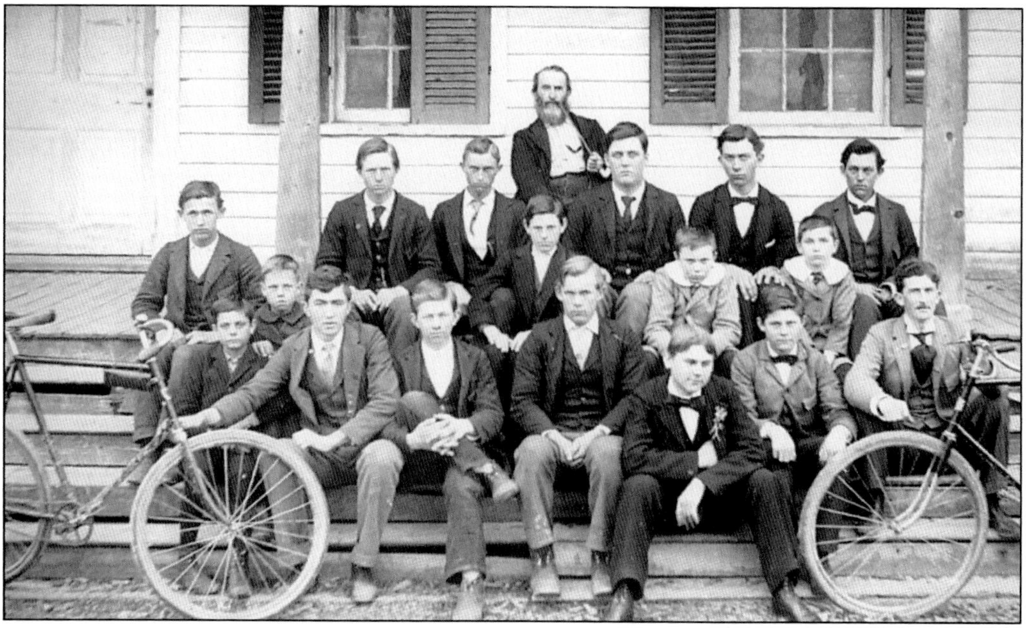

The decision to locate Chowan College in Murfreesboro was influenced by the educational, cultural, and intellectual atmosphere of the town. This atmosphere seems to have been fostered by maritime families from Northern cities who came to the region via the Meherrin and Chowan Rivers, bringing with them culture and education that had a high impact on the region. There were also local residents who fostered the same ideals, leading to the establishment of an unusually high number of educational facilities in and around Murfreesboro. Buckhorn Academy was one such school, located about four miles north of Murfreesboro and established around 1810 by Samuel Nickelson of Boston. This is an 1880s view of Buckhorn Academy principal Julian Picot and his students.

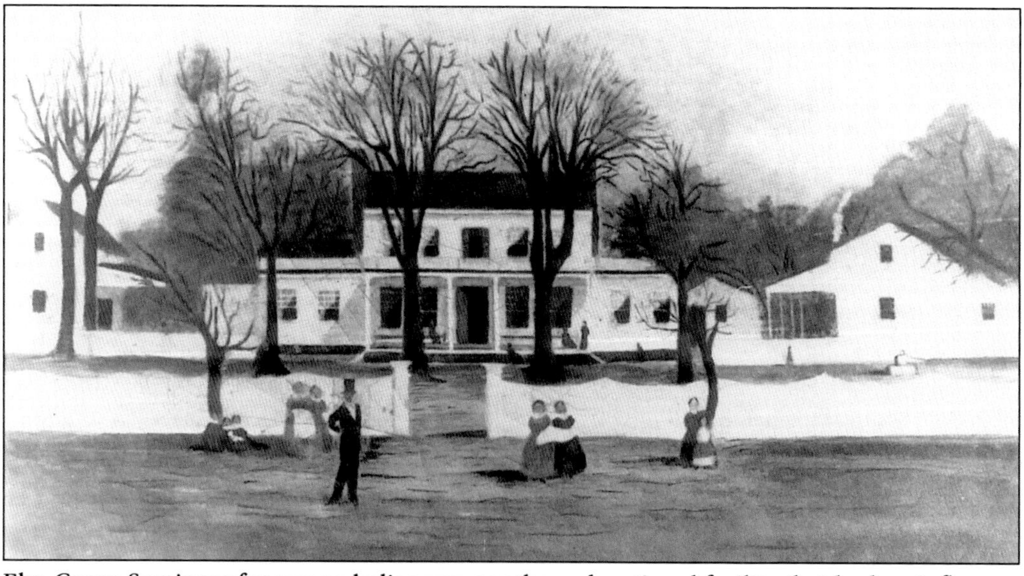

Elm Grove Seminary for young ladies was another educational facility that had an influence on locating Chowan College in Murfreesboro. This school was located in nearby Mapleton and was directed by Alfred W. Darden from the 1840s into the 1890s.

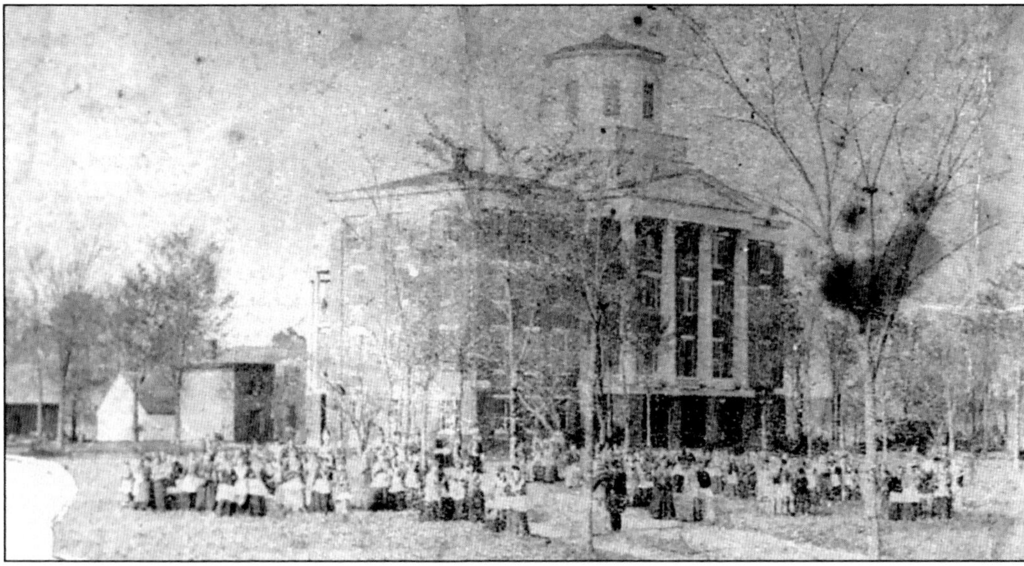

The strong educational and cultural influence of Murfreesboro and the establishment of Chowan College prompted the building of another female college in the town. Wesleyan Female College, supported by Methodists from North Carolina and Virginia, was located next door to Chowan College. Here is the first Wesleyan College building, which was erected in 1853 and destroyed by fire in 1877. In 1881 Wesleyan College reopened on the same site but was again destroyed by fire in 1893. The college did not reopen following the second fire.

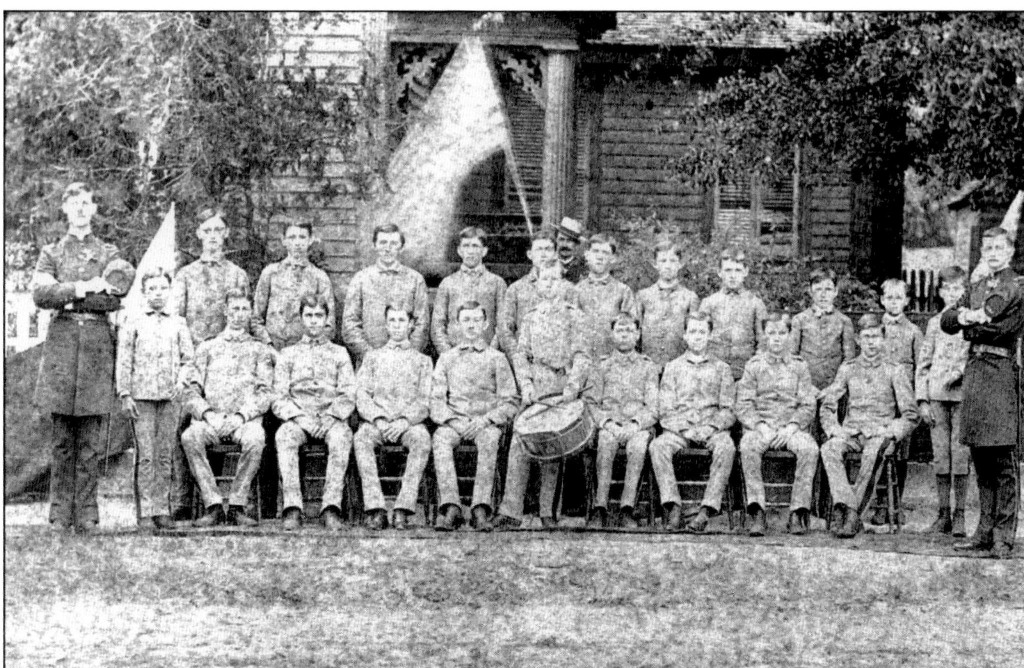

Established before Chowan College, the Murfreesboro Military Academy is pictured in the 1870s. While its origins are unclear, this military school operated as early as 1825 and was briefly located in the Hertford Academy building before moving to another structure.

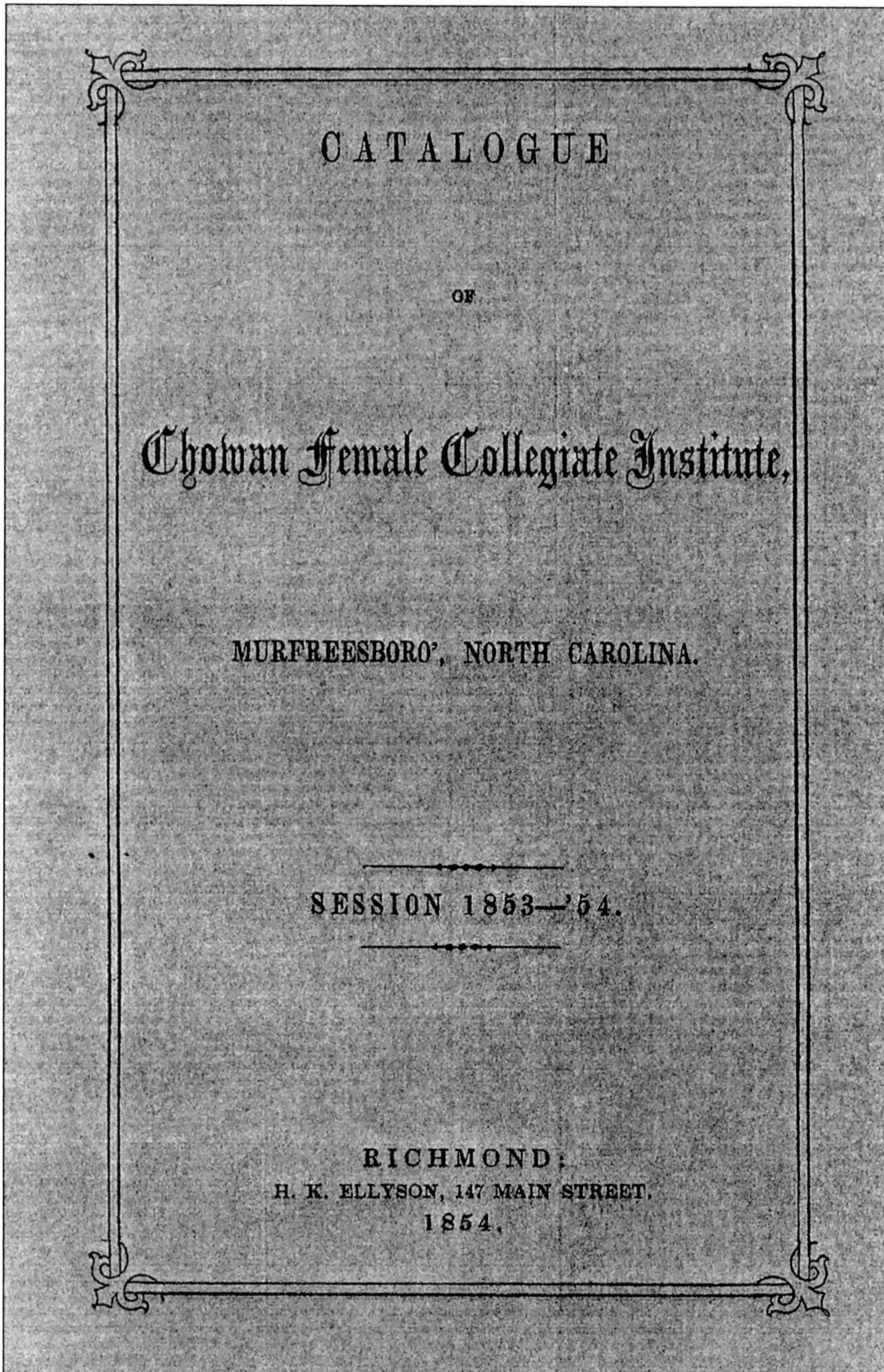

CATALOGUE

OF

Chowan Female Collegiate Institute,

MURFREESBORO', NORTH CAROLINA.

SESSION 1853—'54.

RICHMOND:
H. K. ELLYSON, 147 MAIN STREET.
1854.

This is the front cover to the 1853–1854 Catalogue for Chowan Female Collegiate Institute.

Rates of Tuition for a Session of Five Months.

PAYABLE ONE HALF IN ADVANCE.

Primary Department, - - - - - -	$10 00
English Studies of the Academic Department, -	15 00
English Studies of Collegiate Department, - -	15 00
French, Latin, Greek, Italian, each - - -	7 00
Drawing, Embroidery, and Crayon, each - -	6 00
Music, Piano and Guitar, each - - - -	20 00
Organ, - - - - - - - - -	25 00
Seraphine, - - - - - - - -	20 00
Use of Seraphine, - - - - - - -	3 00
Use of Piano, - - - - - - - -	3 00
Use of Guitar, - - - - - - - -	2 00
Use of Organ, - - - - - - - -	7 00
Scientific Lectures, - - - - - - -	1 50
School Room Expenses, - - - - - -	1 00
Vocal Music, - - - - - - - -	1 00
Oil, and Pastel Painting, each - - - -	12 00
Water Painting and Colored Crayon, each -	9 00

Board can be obtained in the Institute, or in respectable private families in its immediate vicinity, where all will be under the general supervision of the Faculty. Terms, $8 per month, not including the use of Bath Rooms. Washing $1 per month.

Application for admission can be made to the Principal by letter, or on the premises of the Institute. The expenses for one year, *without board*, may be thus stated:

For a full English course, without Music, Languages, or ornamental branches, - - - - - - - - -	$37 00
Music, with English branches, - - - - - - -	83 00
English branches, with Music and one of the Languages, -	97 00
English branches, with Music, Language, and Water Painting,	115 00

This page from the 1853–1854 Catalogue for Chowan Female Collegiate Institute shows a breakdown of tuition fees.

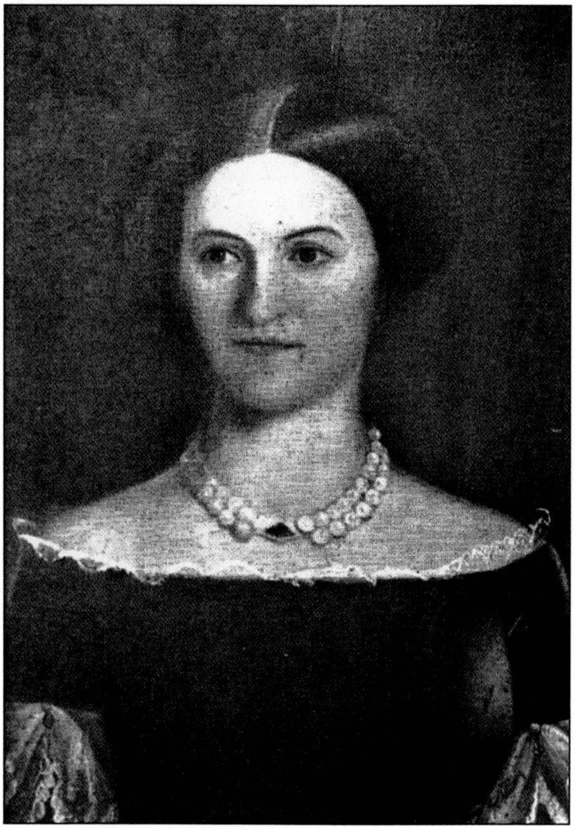

When Chowan College opened in 1848, its first class was comprised of 11 girls. Annie J. Ward, pictured here in a painting by Thomas Sully, was the only girl to graduate, becoming the first person to receive a degree from Chowan College. She later married John Wheeler Moore, the oldest son of Godwin Cotton Moore, founder of Chowan College. John Wheeler Moore became a famous North Carolina historian.

This 1870s photograph of Chowan College's front lawn provides insight into the landscape plan implemented when the front campus was developed in the 1850s. This plan can be directly attributed to landscape gardener Mr. Dennison, hired in 1856 to make improvements to the front campus. The work was completed in 1859. Unfortunately, hurricanes, tornados, and ice storms have taken a heavy toll on the original front campus plantings through the years.

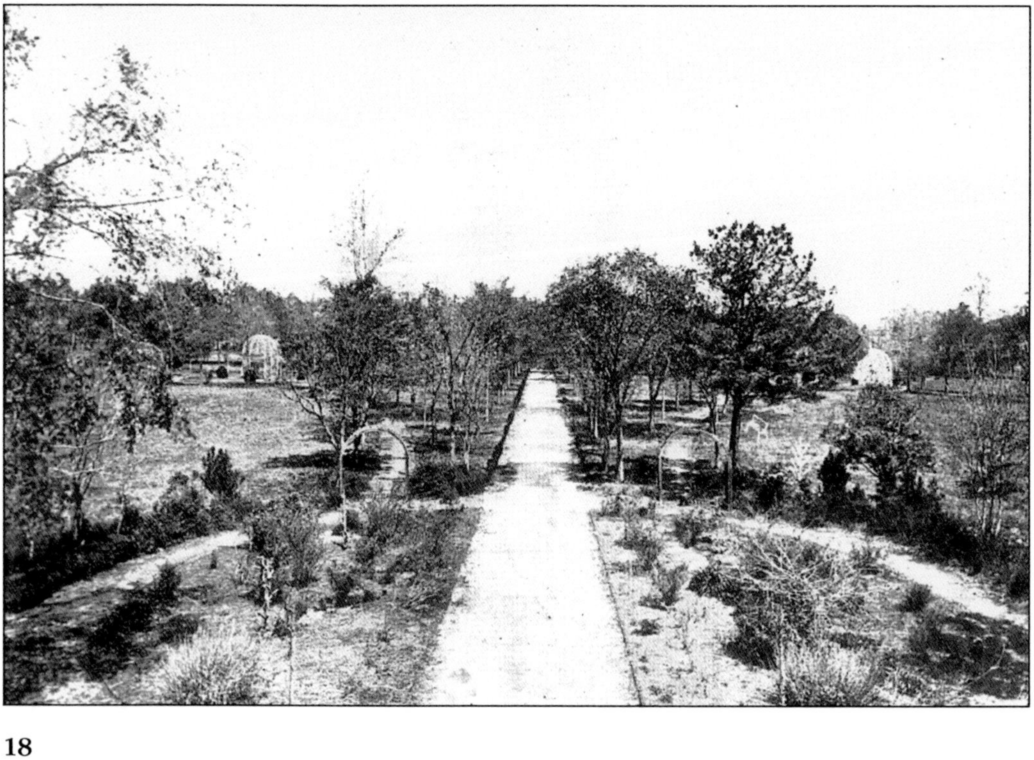

This is Mary Owen McDowell, wife of Dr. Archibald McDowell, first president of Chowan College. Dr. McDowell and Mary H. Owen first met at a girl's school where he was a tutor and she was a teacher. They were married in 1847 and, in less than a year, he became president of Chowan College. Mary Owen McDowell was a devoted wife and mother. She also taught English and French at Chowan. (Courtesy of Mr. and Mrs. David A. Day III.)

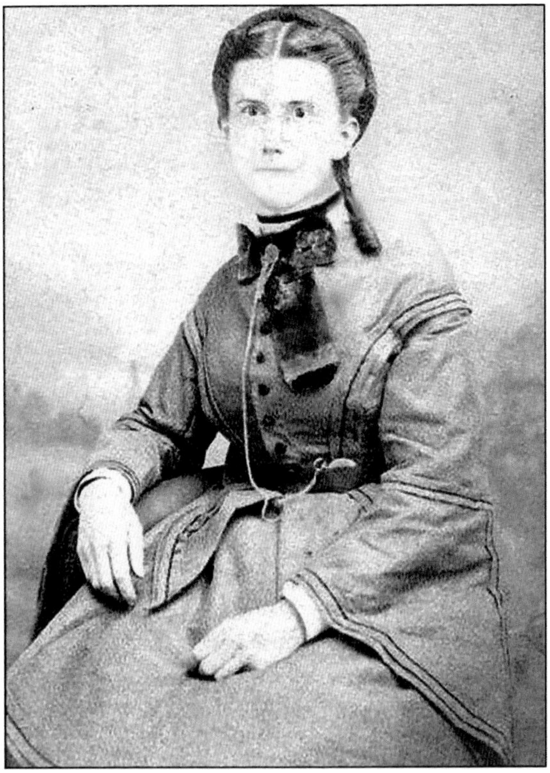

This is an 1860 diploma for Chowan Female Collegiate Institute. It is signed by Dr. William Hooper, third president of the college. Dr. Hooper's educational background and experience were extensive and included two years as president of Wake Forest College. His grandfather, William Hooper, signed the United States Declaration of Independence.

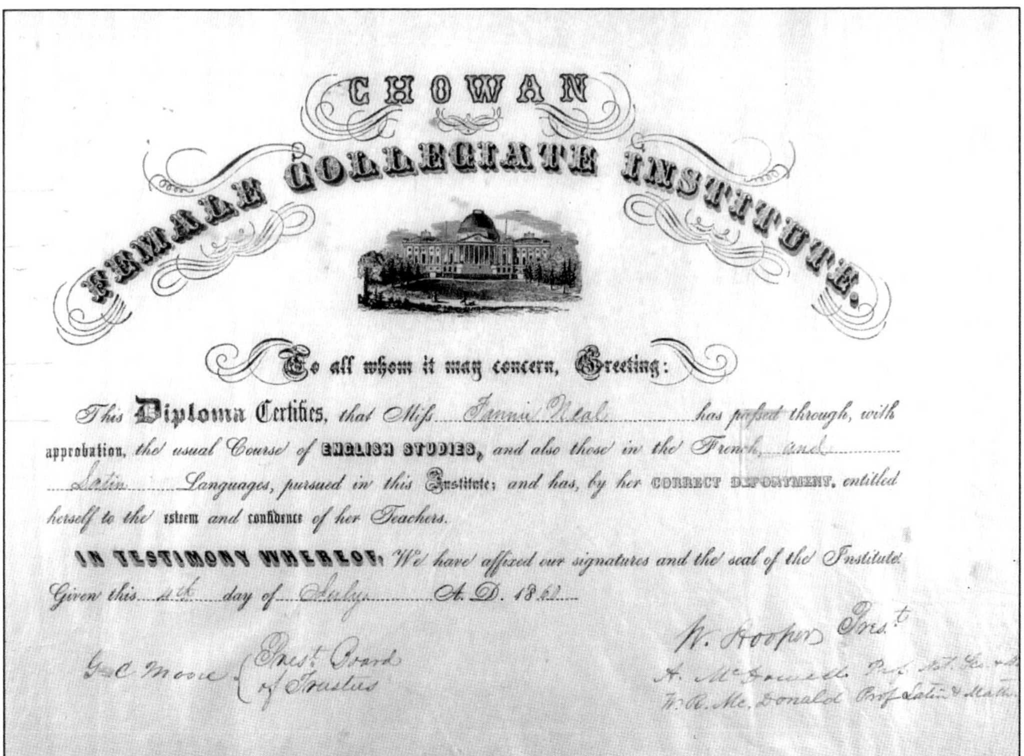

CHOWAN

FEMALE COLLEGIATE INSTITUTE.

To all whom it may concern, Greeting:

This Diploma Certifies, that Miss Fannie Neal has passed through, with approbation, the usual Course of ENGLISH STUDIES, and also those in the French and Latin Languages, pursued in this Institute; and has, by her CORRECT DEPORTMENT, entitled herself to the esteem and confidence of her Teachers.

IN TESTIMONY WHEREOF, We have affixed our signatures and the seal of the Institute.

Given this 4th day of July A. D. 18 60.

W. Hooper Prest.

G. C. Moore { Prest. Board of Trustees

A. McDowell

W. R. McDonald Prof. Latin & Math.

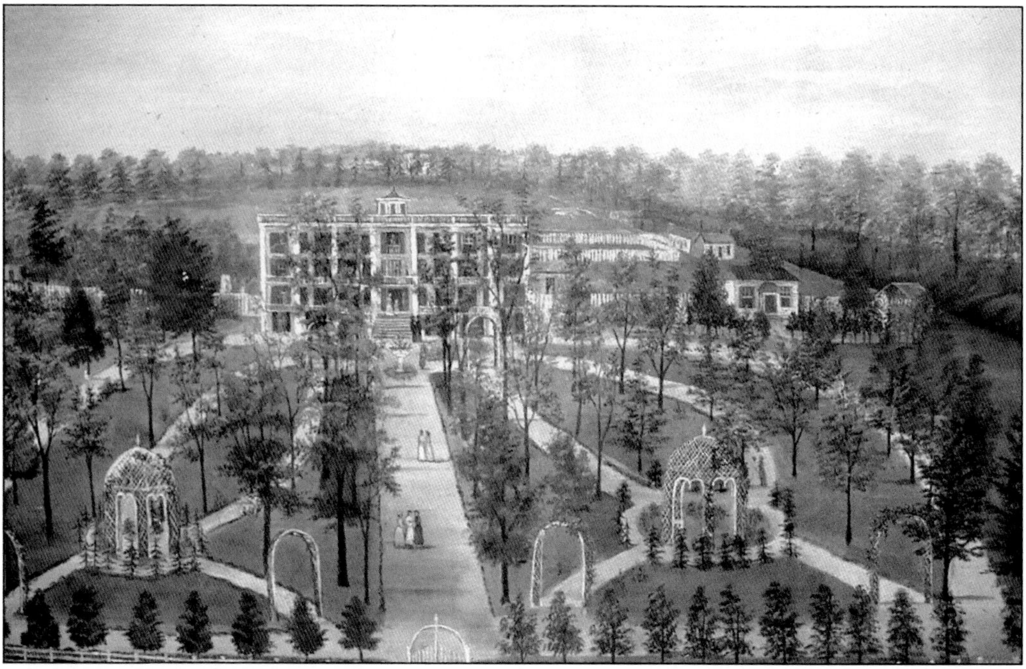

This is an undated painting of the Chowan College campus by an unknown Chowan student. A careful study suggests the painting was done in the late 1860s or early 1870s, based on the size of the trees. The master landscape plan was implemented in 1856–1859.

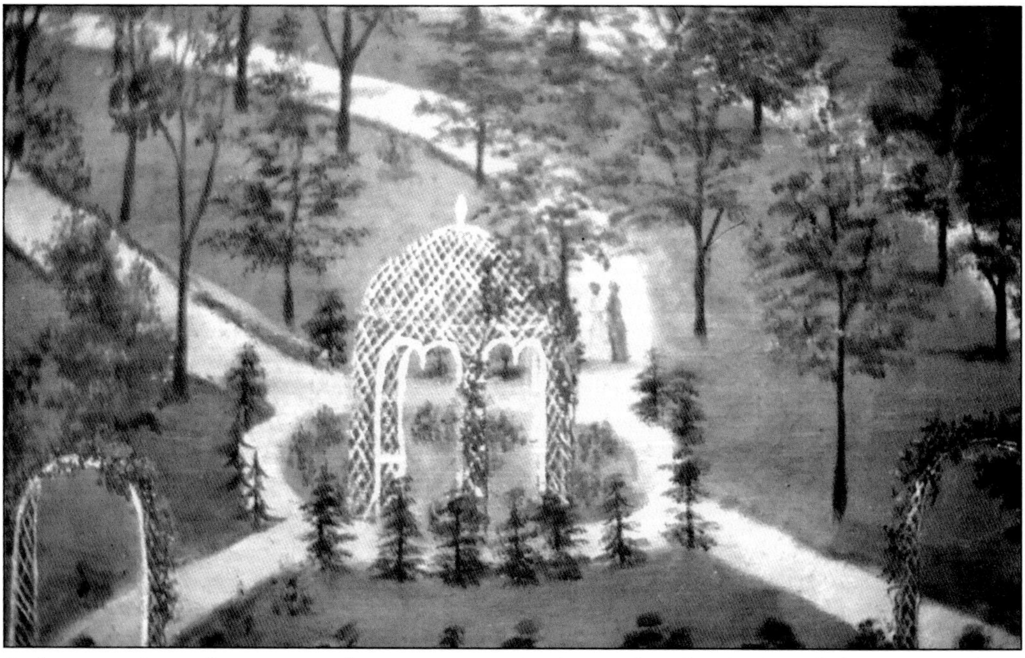

A close-up view of a summer house appears in the undated painting of the campus by a former student. The painting was probably created in the late 1860s or early 1870s. The design for the summer houses was inspired by similar summer houses in one of the New York Expositions.

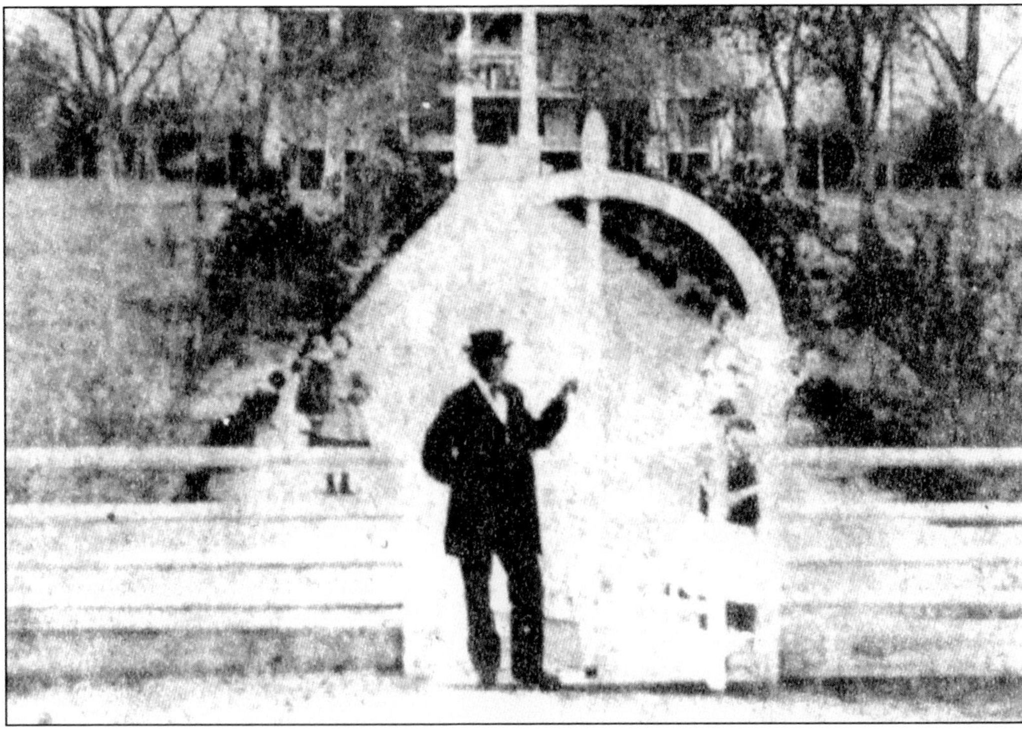

This is an 1870s view of the Columns Building and the front entrance gate and fence. The grounds in front of the Columns Building were fenced off for a number of years, primarily to prevent wild animals, particularly hogs, from eating the plants and rooting up the property.

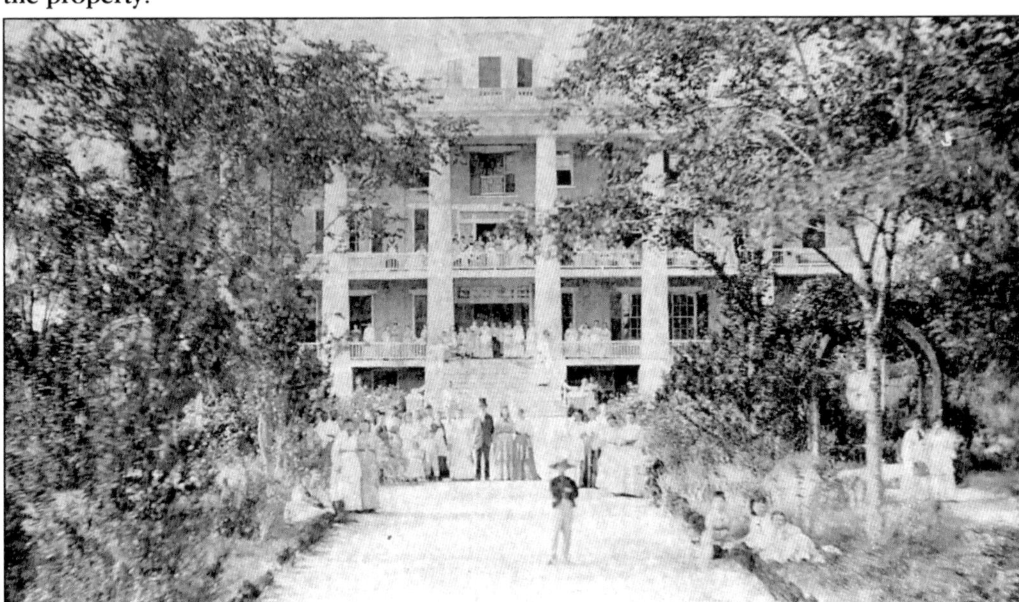

This is another 1870s view of the Columns Building. The gentleman wearing the stove pipe hat and standing in the center is believed to be President Archibald McDowell. The lone male figure standing out front is not identified.

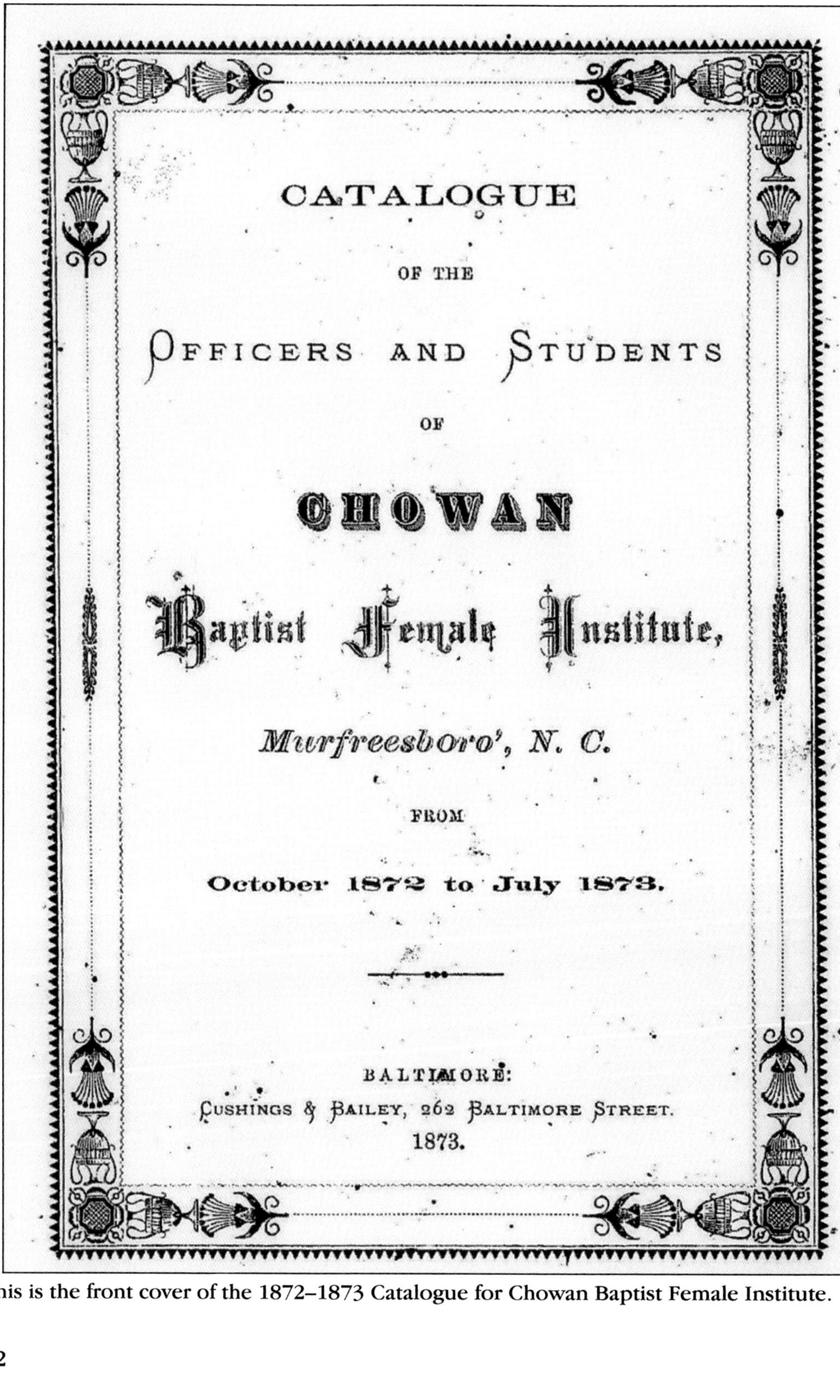

CATALOGUE

OF THE

OFFICERS AND STUDENTS

OF

CHOWAN

Baptist Female Institute,

Murfreesboro', N. C.

FROM

October 1872 to July 1873.

BALTIMORE:
CUSHINGS & BAILEY, 262 BALTIMORE STREET.
1873.

This is the front cover of the 1872–1873 Catalogue for Chowan Baptist Female Institute.

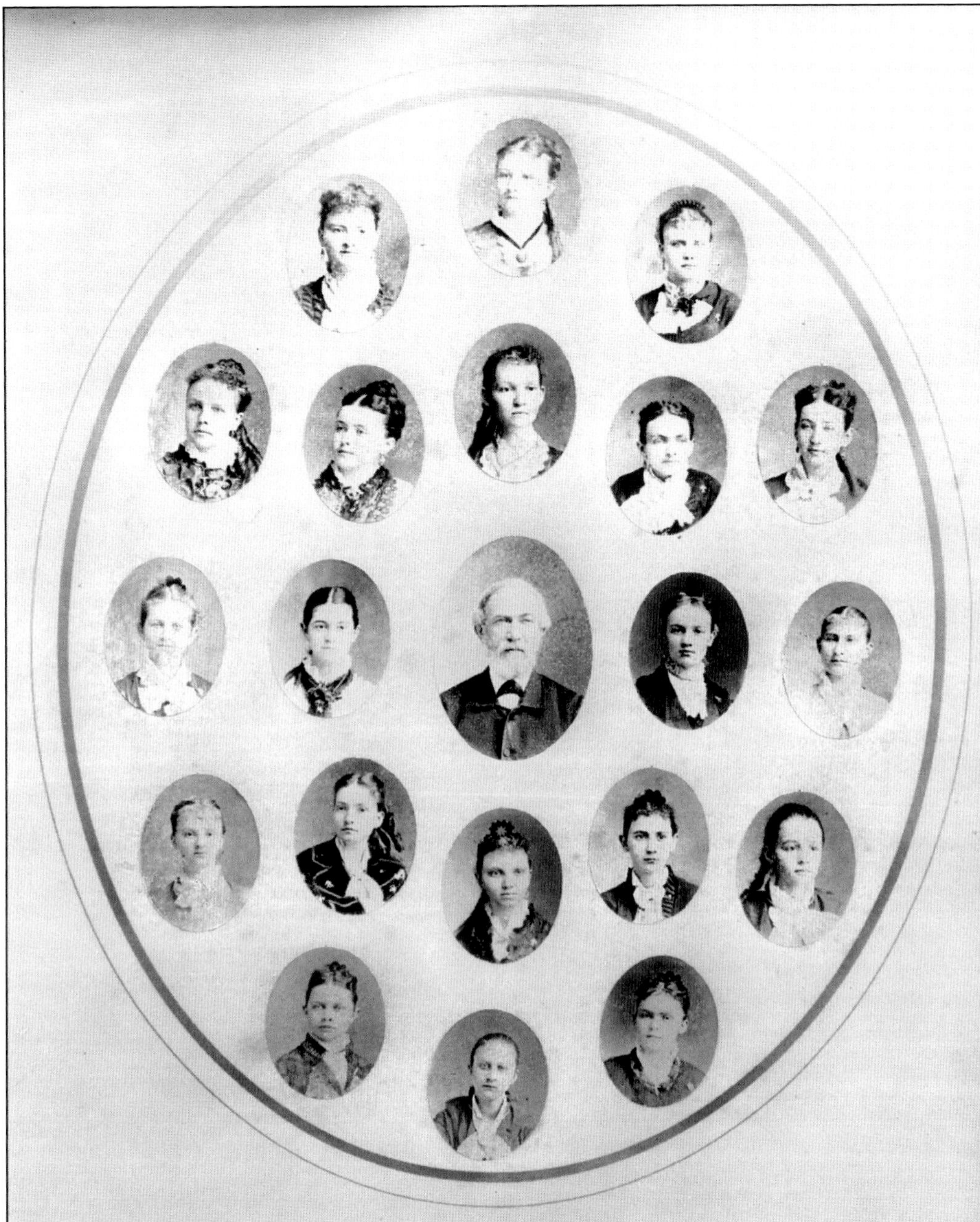

This is the graduating Class of 1876 with Pres. Archibald McDowell. The members included Lizzie M. Brett, Alice F. Burt, Annie M. Dunaway, Nannie A. Field, Ellie M. Gibbs, Alice L. Griffith, Maria A. Gwathney, Theodosia R. Hoggard, Lucy B. Hoskins, Florence R. Land, Linnie F. Larkin, Zoa McCumber, Eunice McDowell, Mary Green Mitchell, Lelia J. Norfleet, Mary E. Riddick, Venie S. Speight, Katie R. Whitehead, Ella M. Winborne, and Mary F. Wright. Mary Green Mitchell, the fourth person in the third row from top, left top right, was the mother of Mr. W.A. Thomas, Miss Ruth Thomas, and Miss Mary Thomas, all strong, generous supporters of Chowan College.

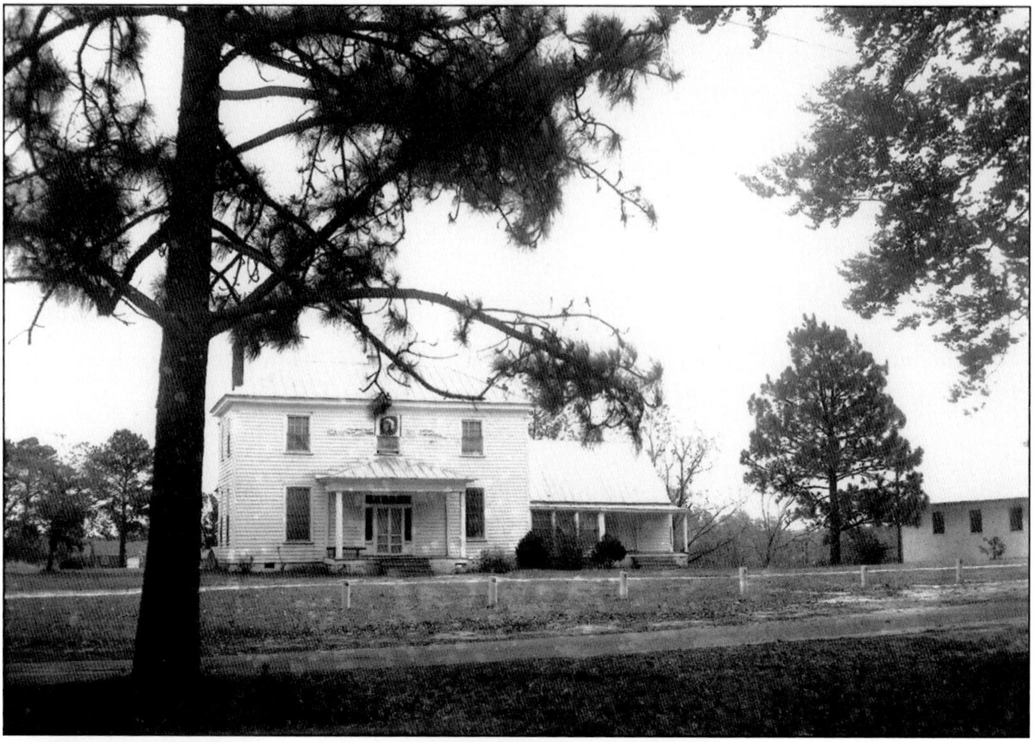

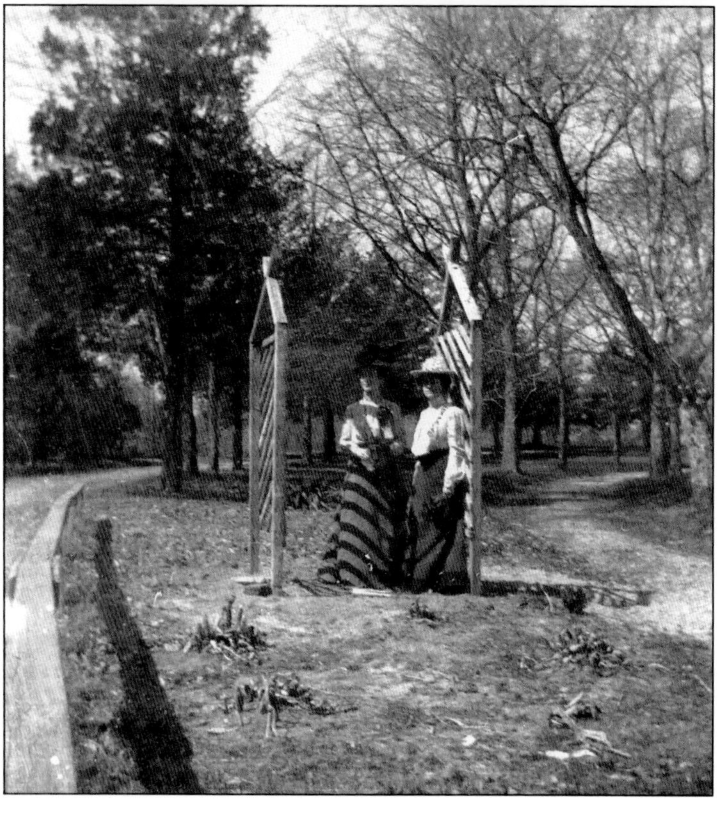

This is the old president's home, which was constructed prior to the Civil War and torn down in 1963. The site is now occupied by Robert Marks Hall, a three-story classroom building. The building to the immediate right is the original graphics building, built in 1953.

In the late 1850s, when the landscape work on the front lawn was done, there were a number of gazebo houses and other lawn structures built. This is an 1890s photograph of one such structure.

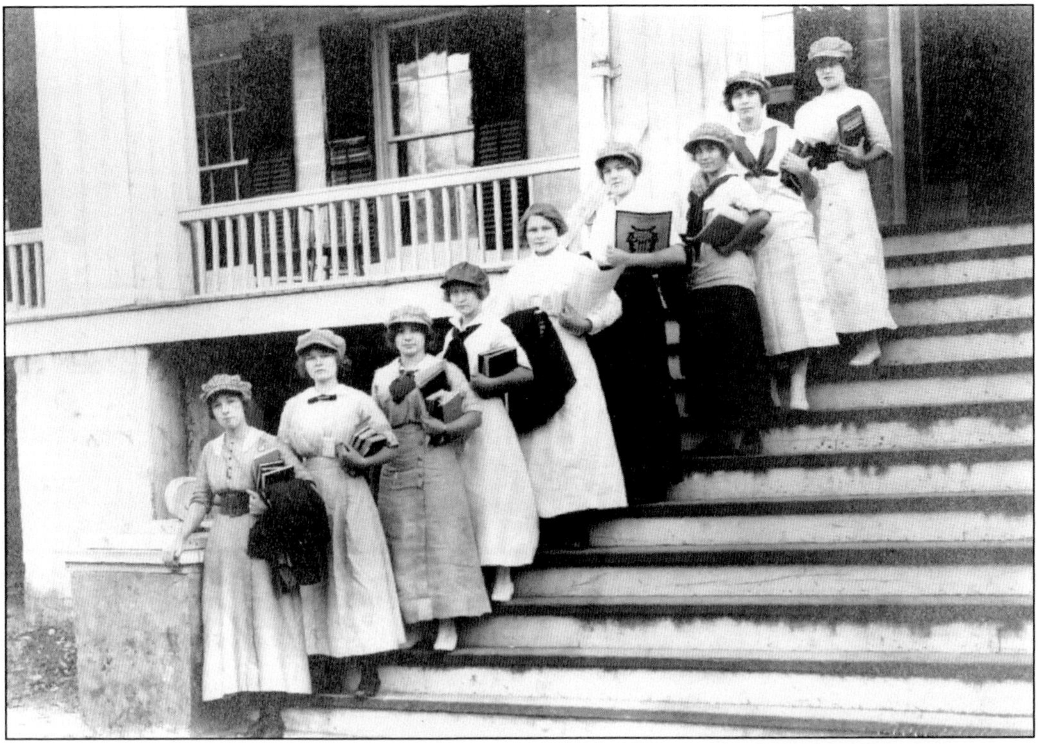

An 1870s photograph shows Chowan students standing on the front steps to the Columns Building.

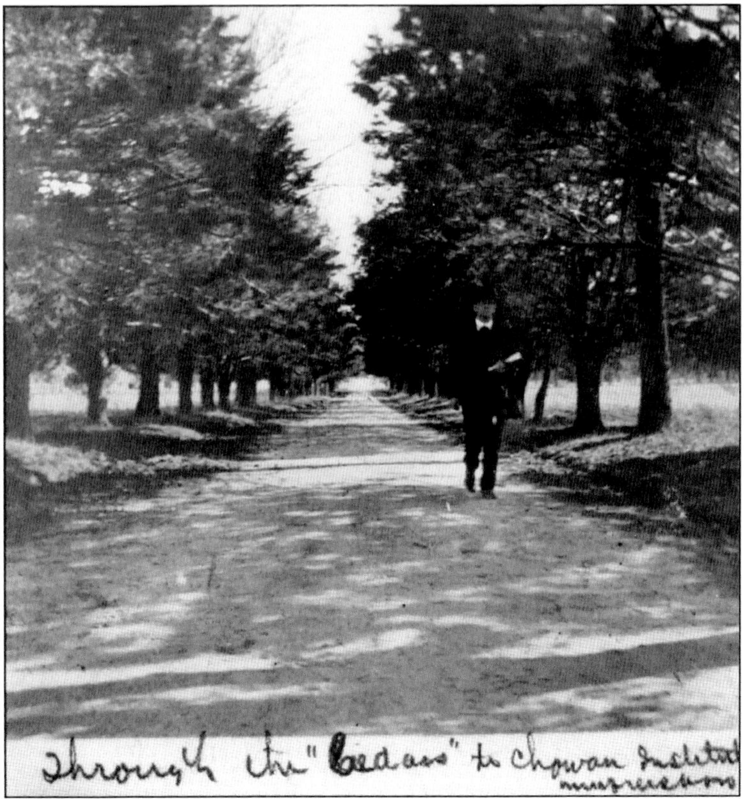

The center walk at Chowan College was always a favorite for both college members and town residents. This is a late 1880s photograph from the Uriah Vaughan photograph album.

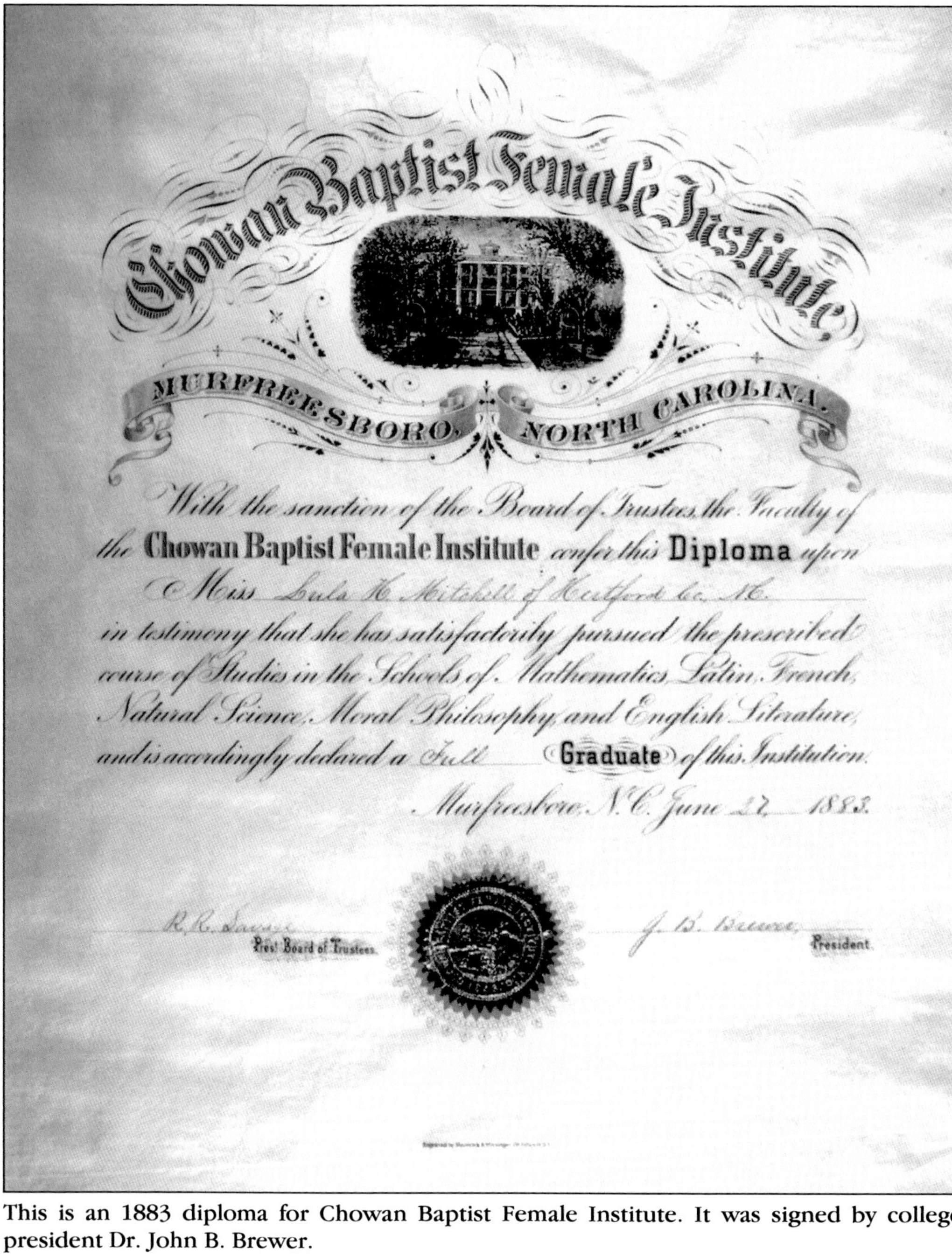

Chowan Baptist Female Institute

MURFREESBORO, NORTH CAROLINA.

With the sanction of the Board of Trustees, the Faculty of the Chowan Baptist Female Institute confer this Diploma upon Miss Lula H. Mitchell of Hertford Co. N.C. in testimony that she has satisfactorily pursued the prescribed course of Studies in the Schools of Mathematics, Latin, French, Natural Science, Moral Philosophy, and English Literature, and is accordingly declared a Full Graduate of this Institution.

Murfreesboro, N.C. June 27 1883.

Prest. Board of Trustees.

J. B. Brewer, President.

This is an 1883 diploma for Chowan Baptist Female Institute. It was signed by college president Dr. John B. Brewer.

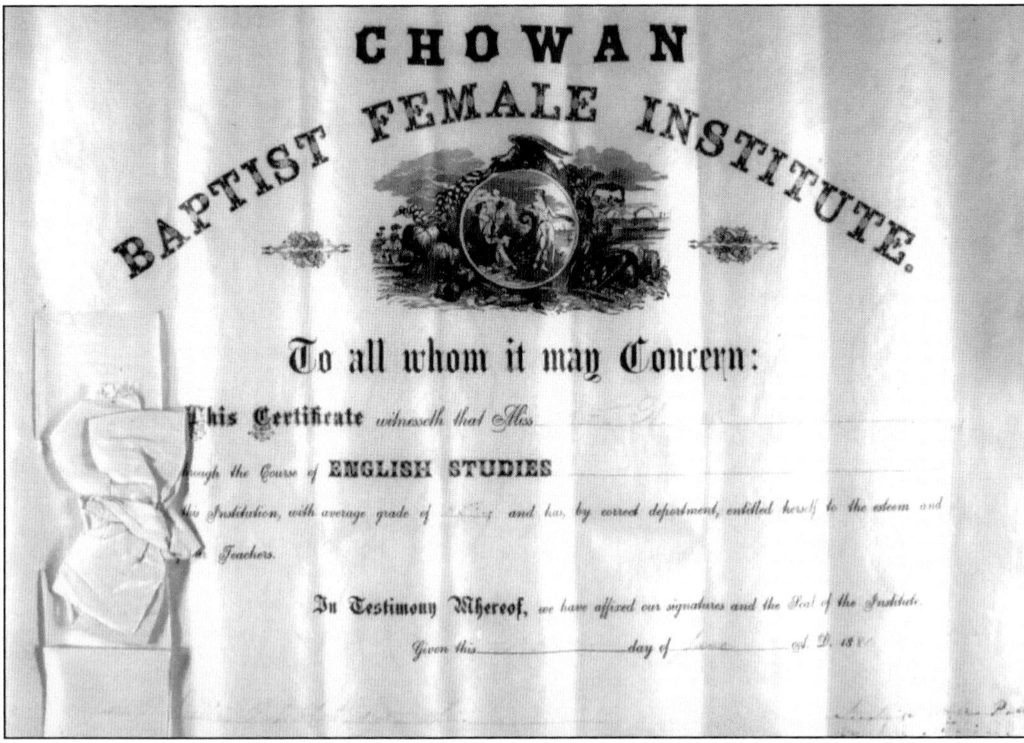

CHOWAN
BAPTIST FEMALE INSTITUTE.

To all whom it may Concern:

This Certificate witnesseth that Miss

ugh the Course of ENGLISH STUDIES

this Institution, with average grade of and has, by correct deportment, entitled herself to the esteem and

Teachers.

In Testimony Whereof, we have affixed our signatures and the Seal of the Institute.

Given this day of A. D. 188

This is an 1881 certificate for the successful completion of English studies at Chowan Baptist Female Institute.

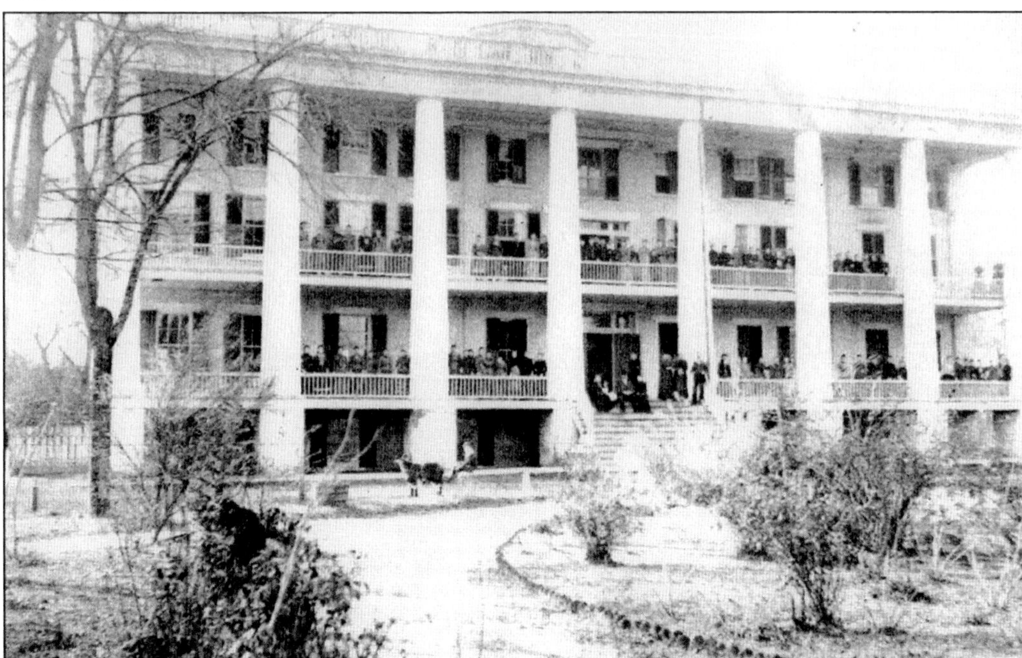

In the early 1870s, the students and faculty of Chowan College gathered on the front porches of the Columns Building for this photograph.

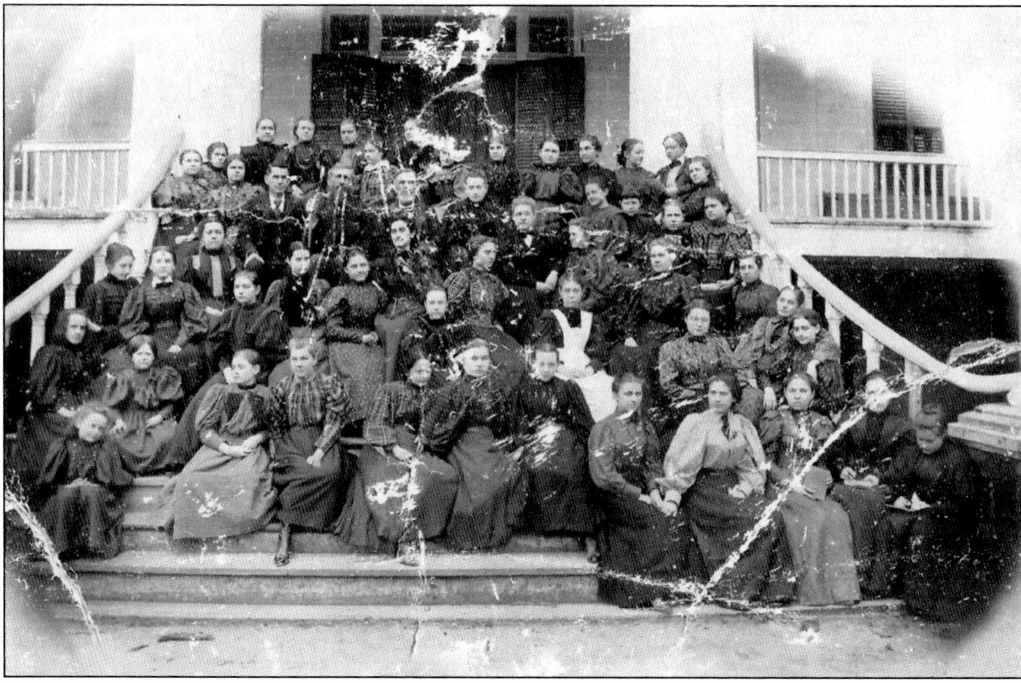

This is an 1898 photograph of Chowan College students and Pres. John C. Scarborough sitting on the steps of the Columns Building. Dr. Scarborough served as president of Chowan College from 1897 to 1909. He had served as superintendent of Public Instruction in North Carolina in 1887–1885 and 1893–1897.

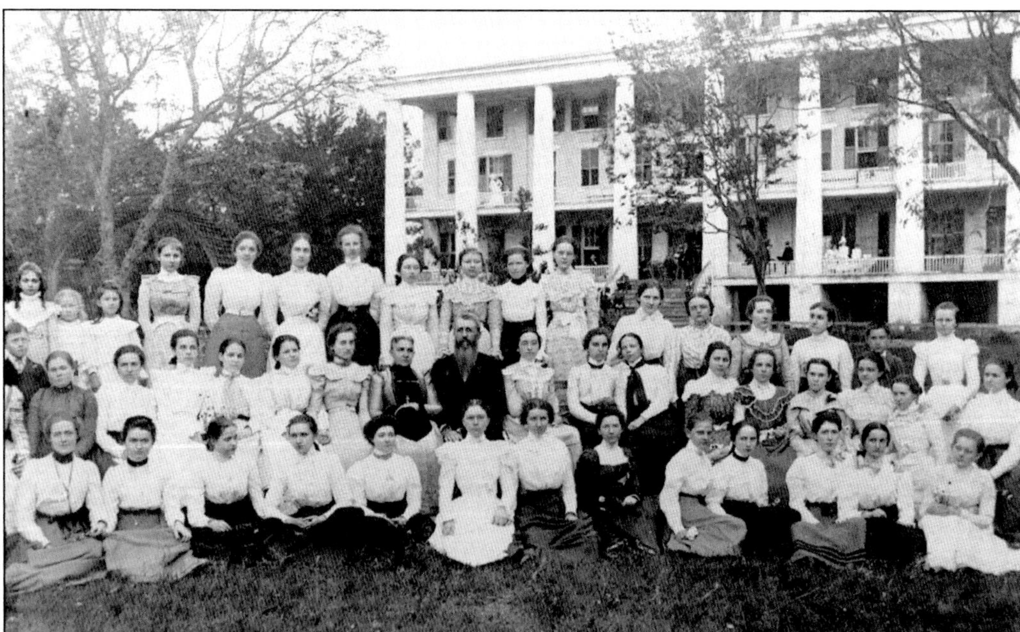

An 1898 photograph depicts Chowan College president John C. Scarborough and a group of students in front of the Columns Building, which remains in use today as the college's administration building.

Two

MATURITY AND TRAGEDY 1900–1943

Chowan College began the new century with a solid foundation for educating young women. The future looked bright as the college grew and the need for new facilities increased. In 1906, the East Wing—which housed a new dining room, chapel, kitchen, library, and rooms for 25 girls—opened. In 1923, a contract was signed for the construction of a building at the back of the Columns Building that would contain a swimming pool, auditorium, and dormitory rooms. Later in 1923, the college celebrated its 75th anniversary. One of the highlights of this celebration was the publication of 3,600 copies of a 75th anniversary edition of the college newspaper, The Chowanian. *In 1923, things were optimistic, and there were no thoughts of tough times ahead for the college. In 20 years, however, with World War II on the horizon, Murfreesboro's academic success would be threatened with the closing of Chowan College in May of 1943, an even more tragic loss considering Wesleyan Female College, founded in 1853, had burned for the second time in 1893 and never reopened.*

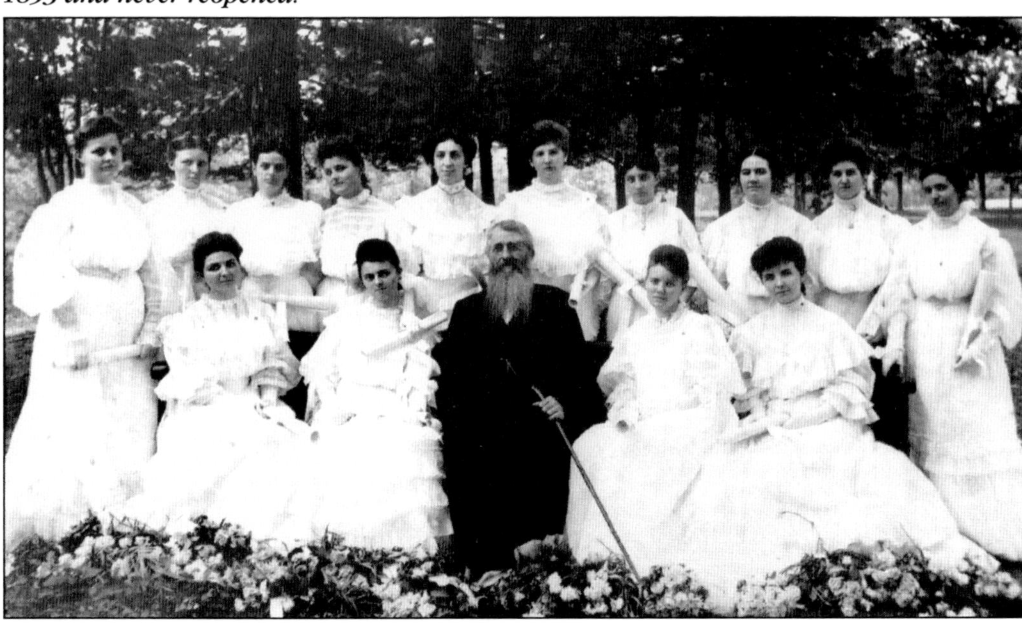

Dr. John C. Scarborough, president of Chowan College, posed with the 1905 graduating class. The graduates, listed in alphabetical order, are Mamie E. Baum, Daisy B. Bowers, Fanny A. Gary, Ella W. Harrell, Lizzie D. Hoggard, Denie M. Horton, Sallie M. Litchfield, Mary Maddrey, Eva M. Martin, Francis A. Sears, Pearl O. Sears, Mary E. Stephenson, Mattie E. Sykes, and Harriet L. Vann.

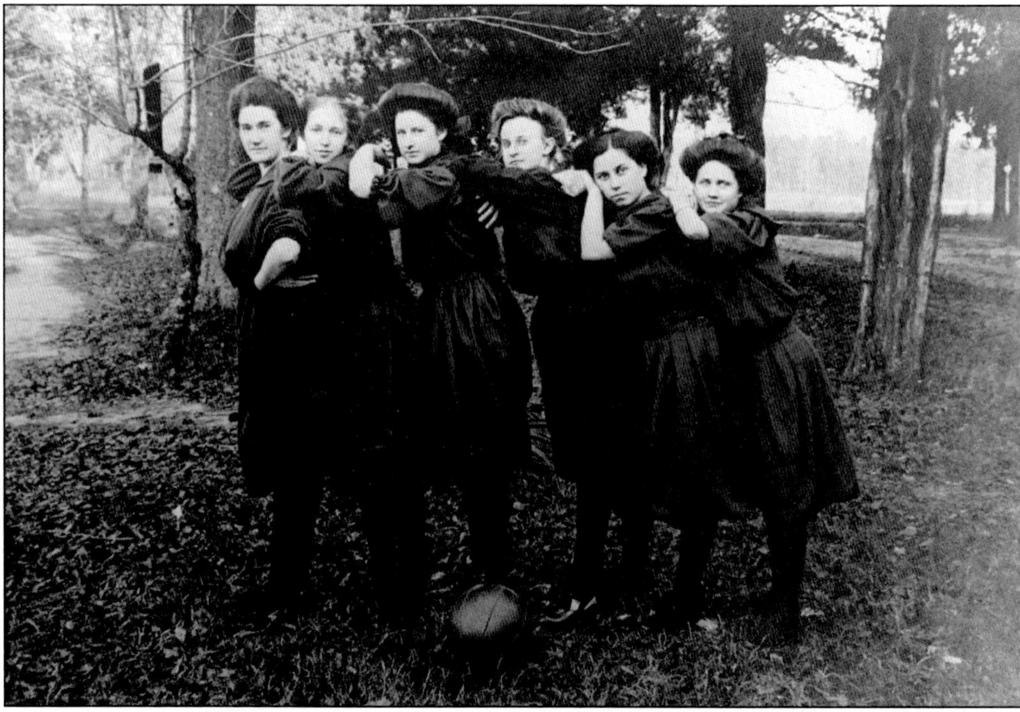

Members of the Chowan College 1910 basketball team, from left to right, are Mary Parker, Ruth Boyette, Mary Josephine Peele, Linnie Mizelle, Bernice Howell, and Zenova Etheridge.

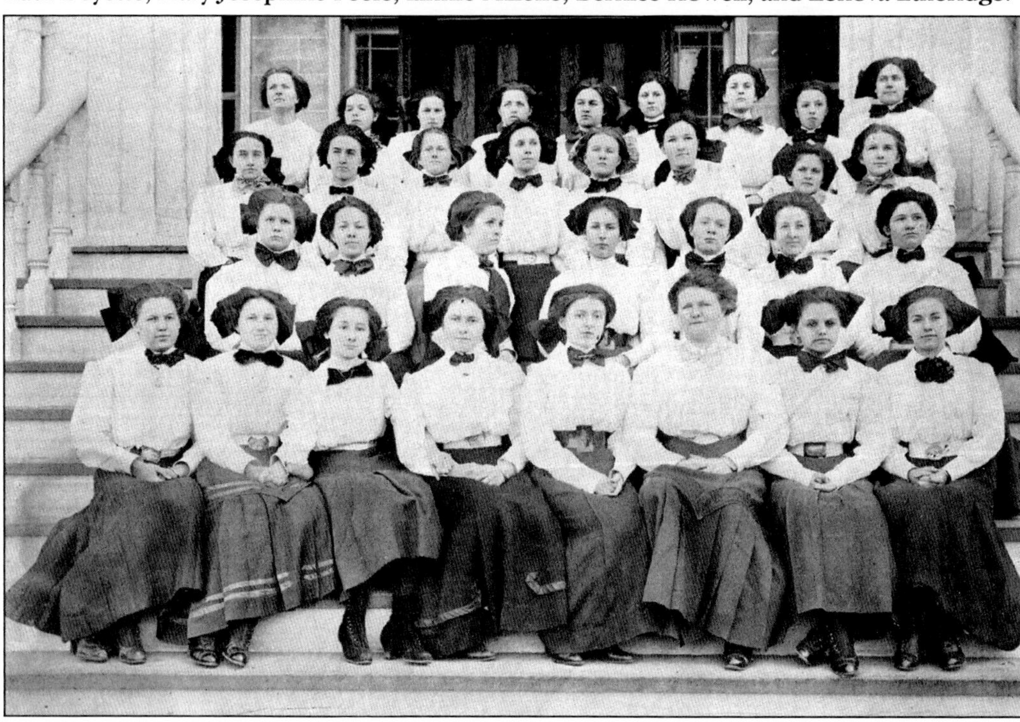

This photograph of the freshman class of 1911 was taken on the front steps of the Columns Building.

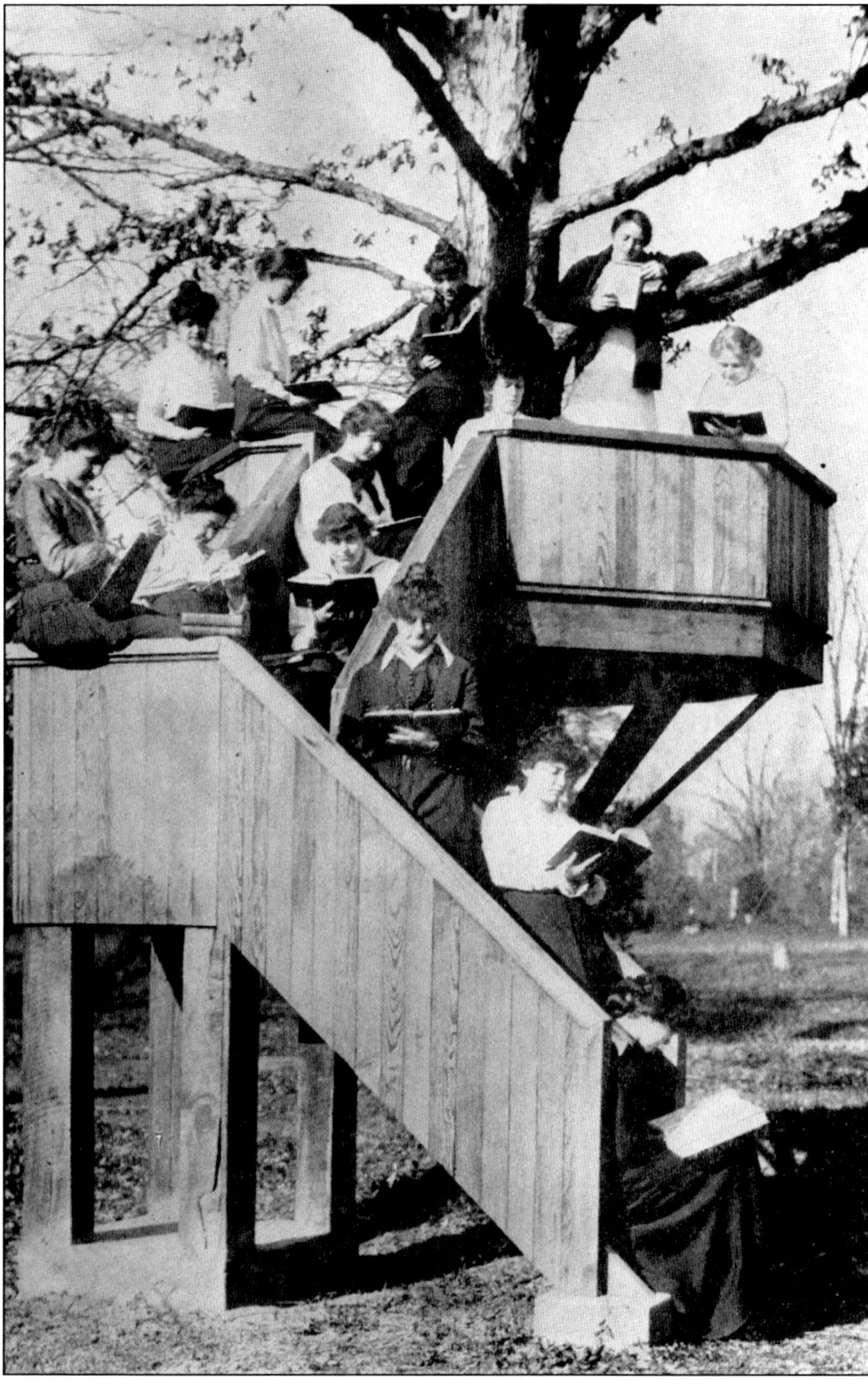

Here is the 1916 senior class in the Crow's Nest, given to the class members by one of their own, Miss Rose Nowell (Mrs. S.M. Crisp). The Crow's Nest was located on the front campus between the front center walk and the site of Mixon Dorm. It was exclusively maintained by the seniors of Chowan College for a number of years until it fell into disrepair and was torn down.

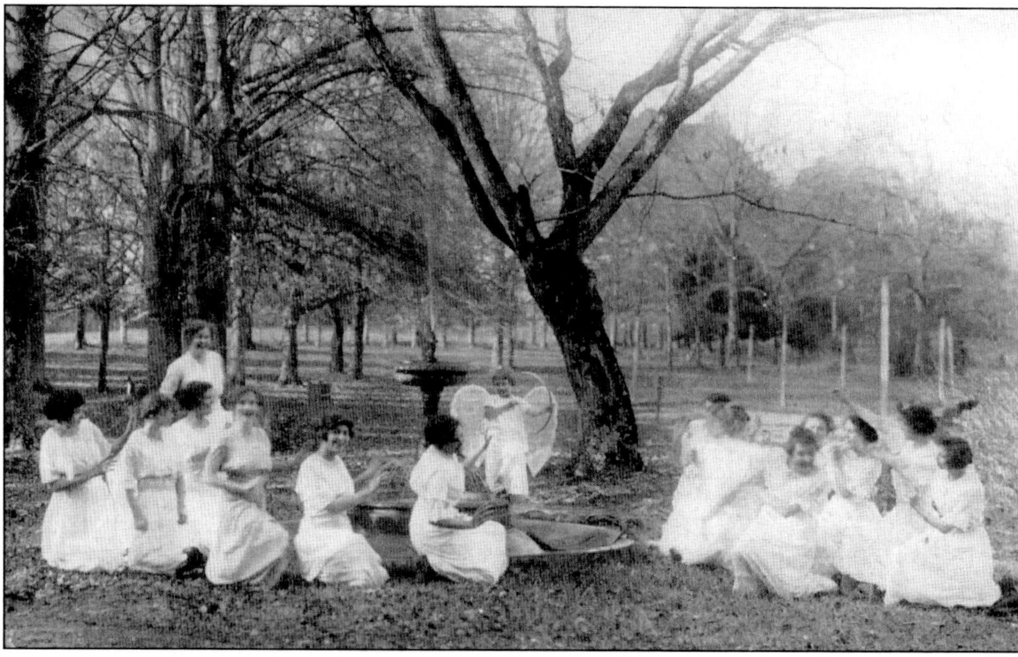

The 1915 dramatic club gathers around the stone fountain that stood in front of the Columns Building. The stone fountain was given to the college by the Class of 1913 in their junior year.

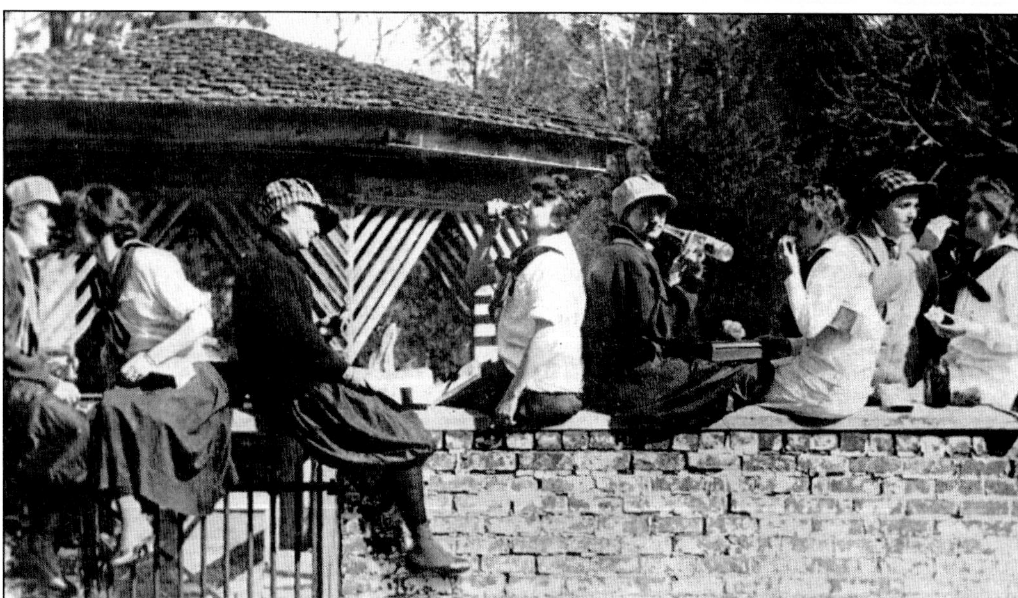

As seen in this 1916 photograph, Wise's old graveyard, located across the west ravine from the front campus, was a favorite gathering spot for students. Numerous ghost stories have been told through the years involving Chowan students, Wise's old graveyard, and the Brown Lady, the story of a student who died at Chowan in 1860. Each year the ghost of this student is supposedly seen walking the top floor of the Columns Building dressed in brown.

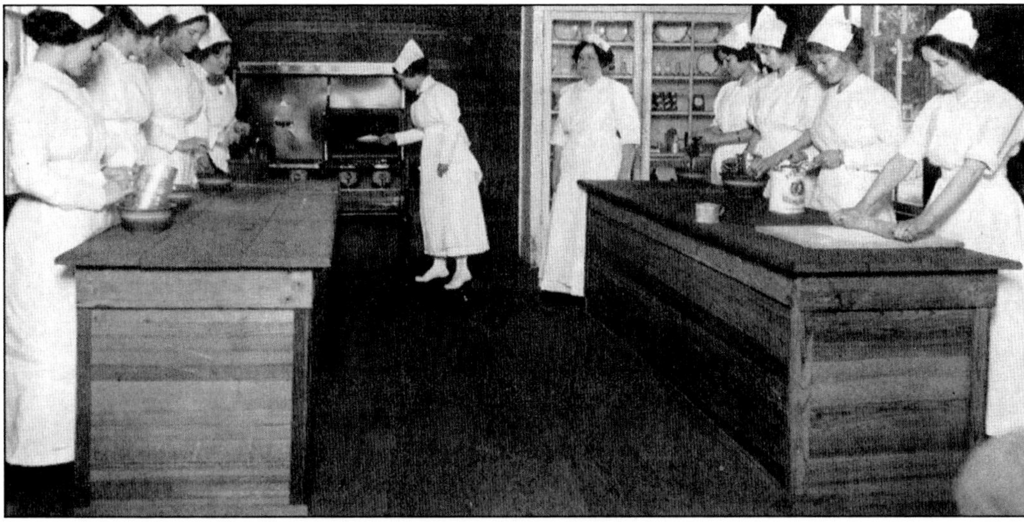

This is a photograph of the 1914 domestic science class.

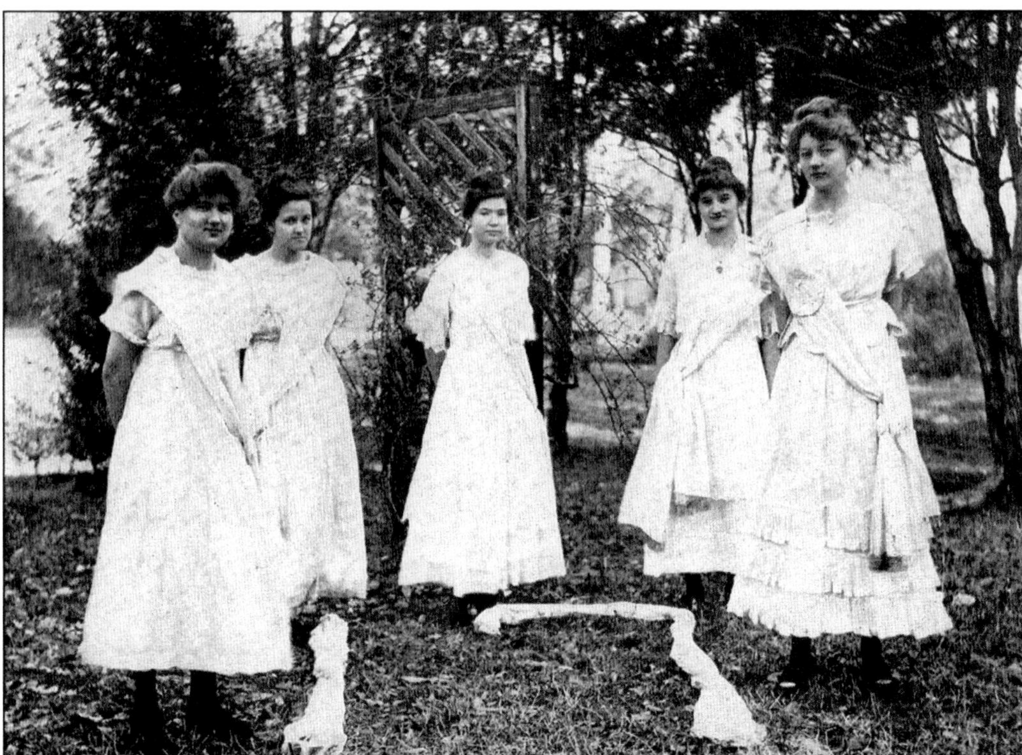

Pictured here are the marshals for 1916.

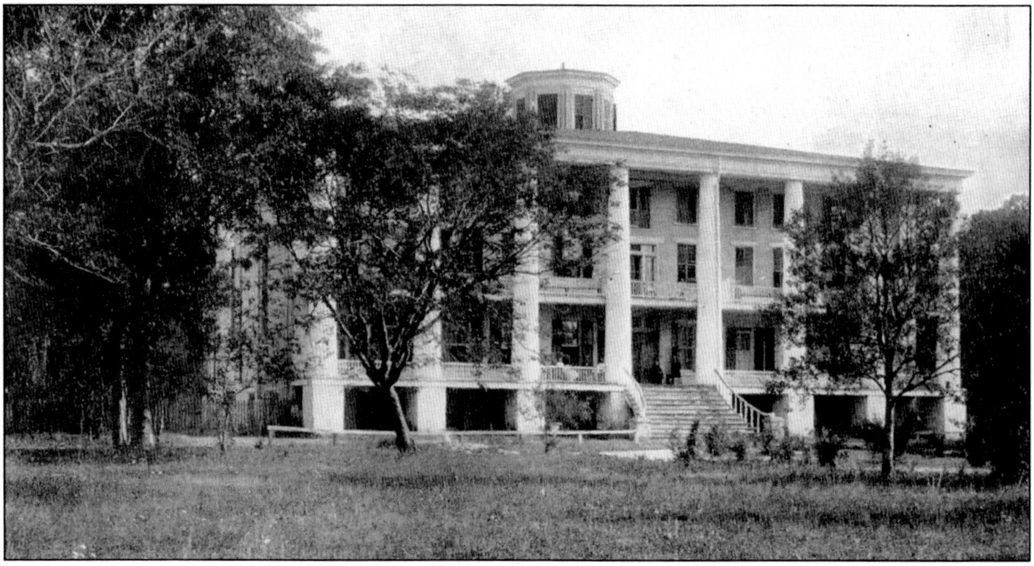

This view of the Columns Building was published in the Catalogue of 1912–1913.

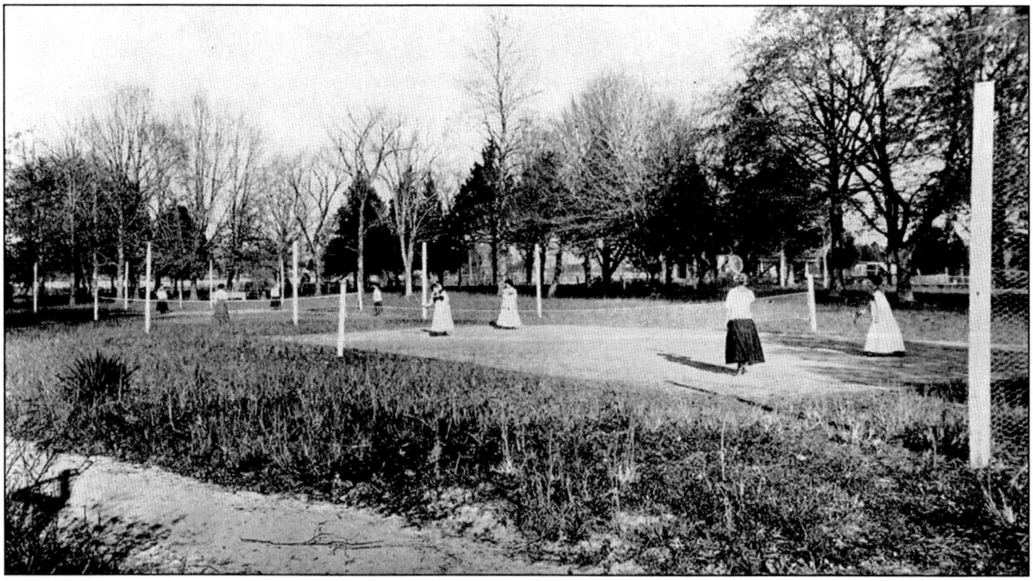

The 1912–1913 Catalogue contained this photograph of the tennis courts that were located on the west side of the center walk at the front campus.

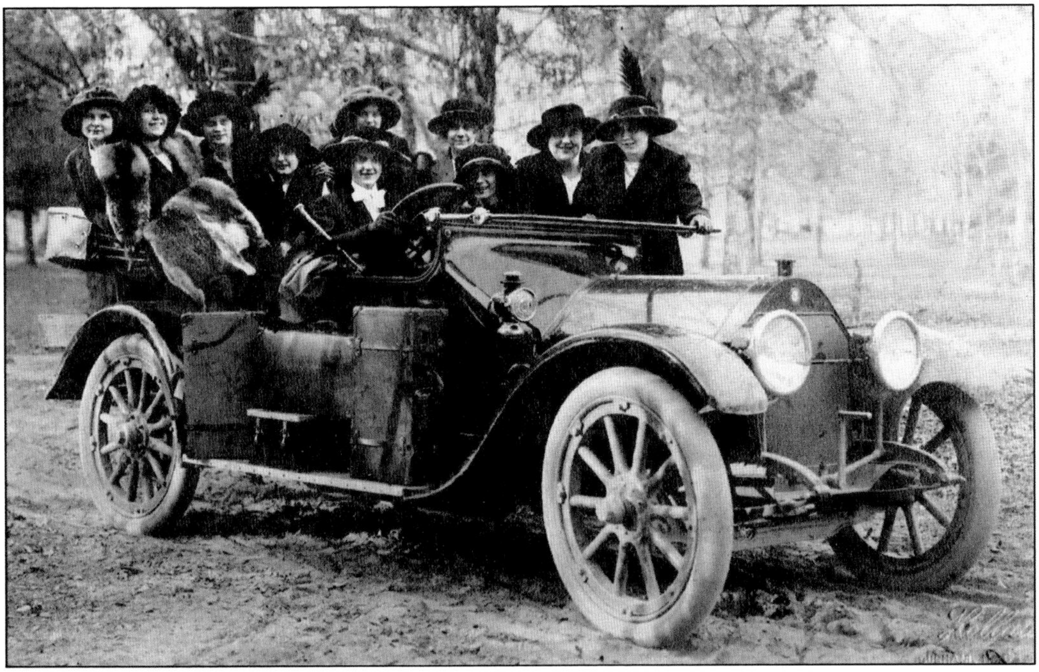

This is the 1913–1914 glee club. Pictured here, left to right, are Eva Boyette, Jessie Garrett, Viola Hayes, Margaret Liverman, Maude Sawyer, Pauline Taylor, Ruth Windsor, Emily Clark, Ruth Godwin (at the steering wheel), and Kate Jenkins (beside the driver.)

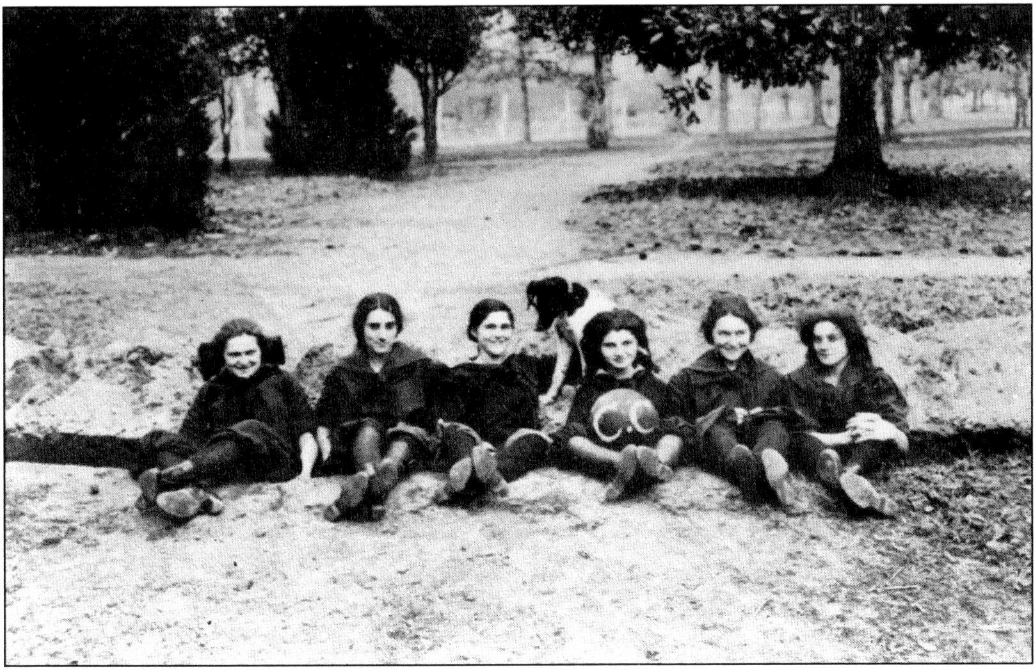

Pictured here is the 1913 basketball team.

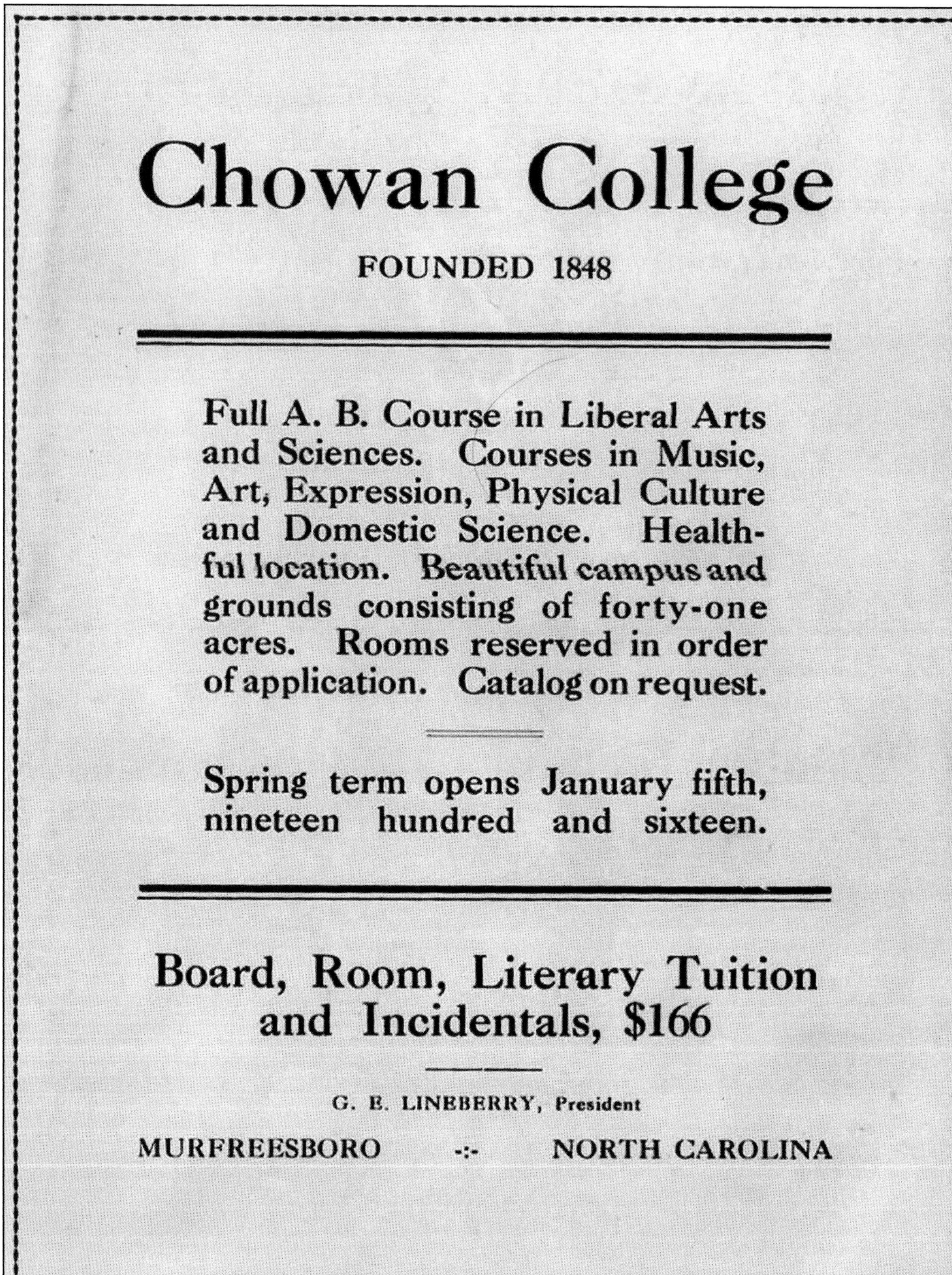

This is an advertisement from the 1916 Chowan College yearbook.

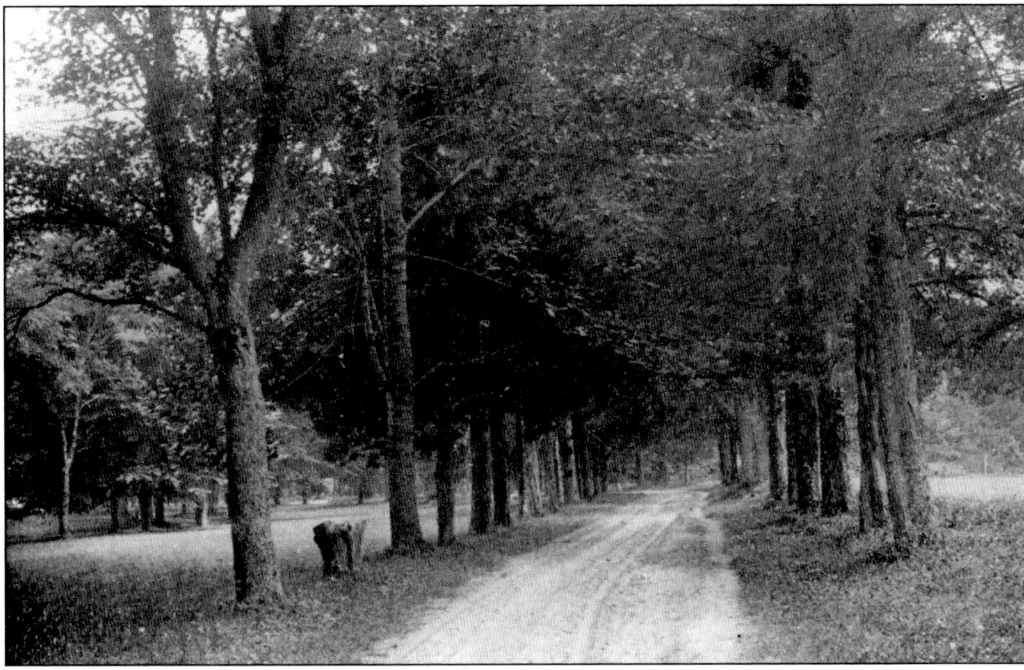

A photograph taken in 1917 depicts the East Carriage Drive. Today, this drive would be in front of McSweeney Hall, Marks Hall, and Belk and Jenkins Halls.

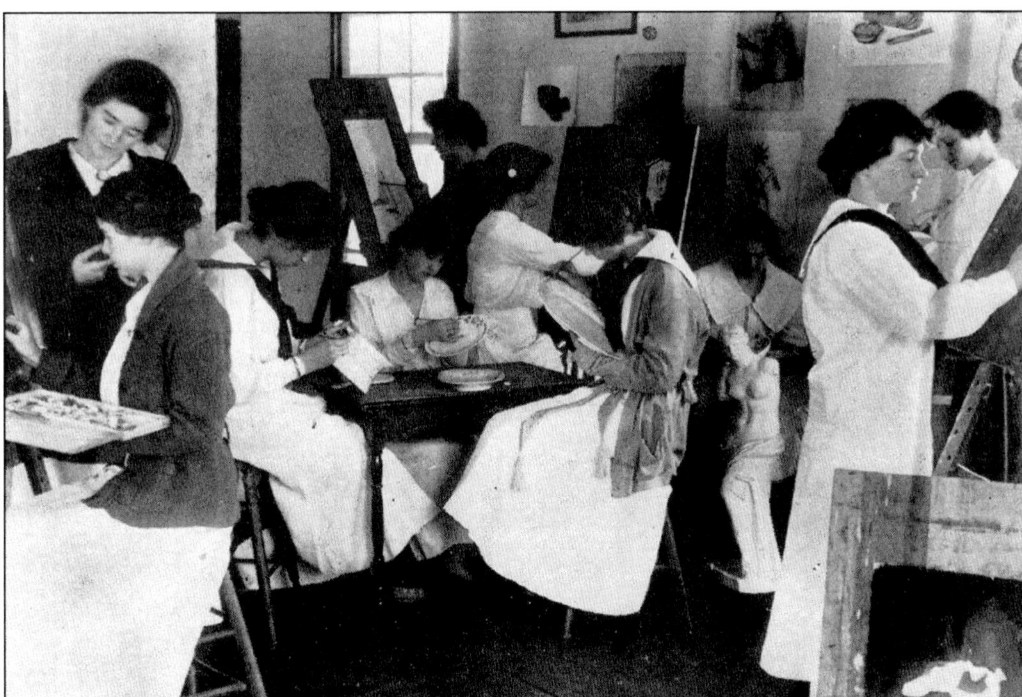

Pictured here is the 1917 art club. The members included Wertie Harrell, Helen Leary, Janie B. Parker, Lida Olive, Inez Benthall, Elsie Benthall, Ruby Dunlap, Fannie Jenkins, Helen Williams, Bertha Mizelle, Lanie Bell Lee, Amber Holloman, Eunice Jones, and Elva Worrell.

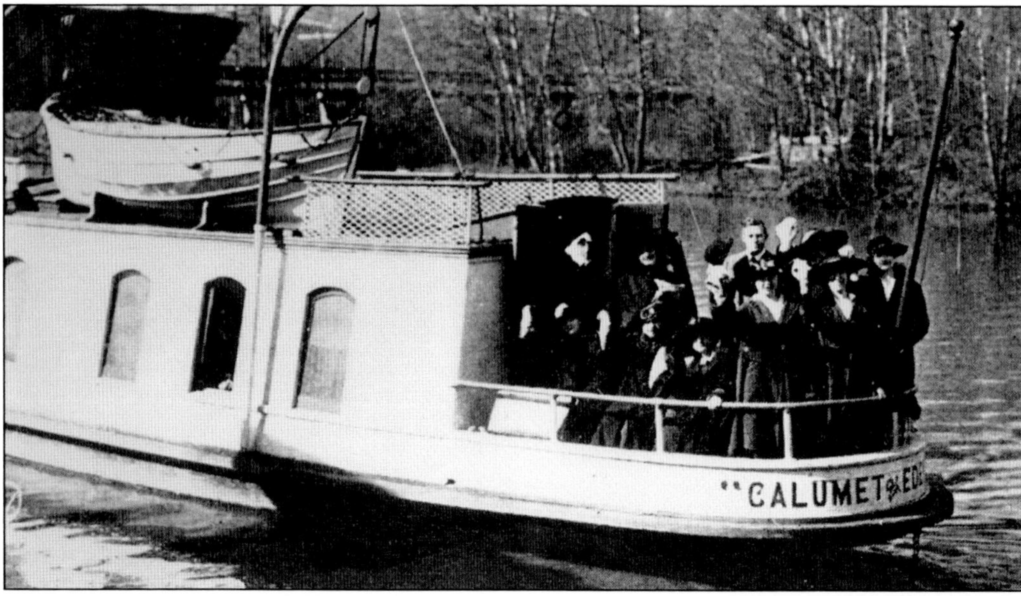

River steamers were one of the early means of transportation available to Chowan students traveling to Murfreesboro and Chowan College. This is a group of students arriving at the Murfreesboro wharf on the Meherrin River in 1918. Other early forms of transportation were carriages and the Murfreesboro Railroad, which operated for about six years in the 1890s and was a part of the Seaboard system.

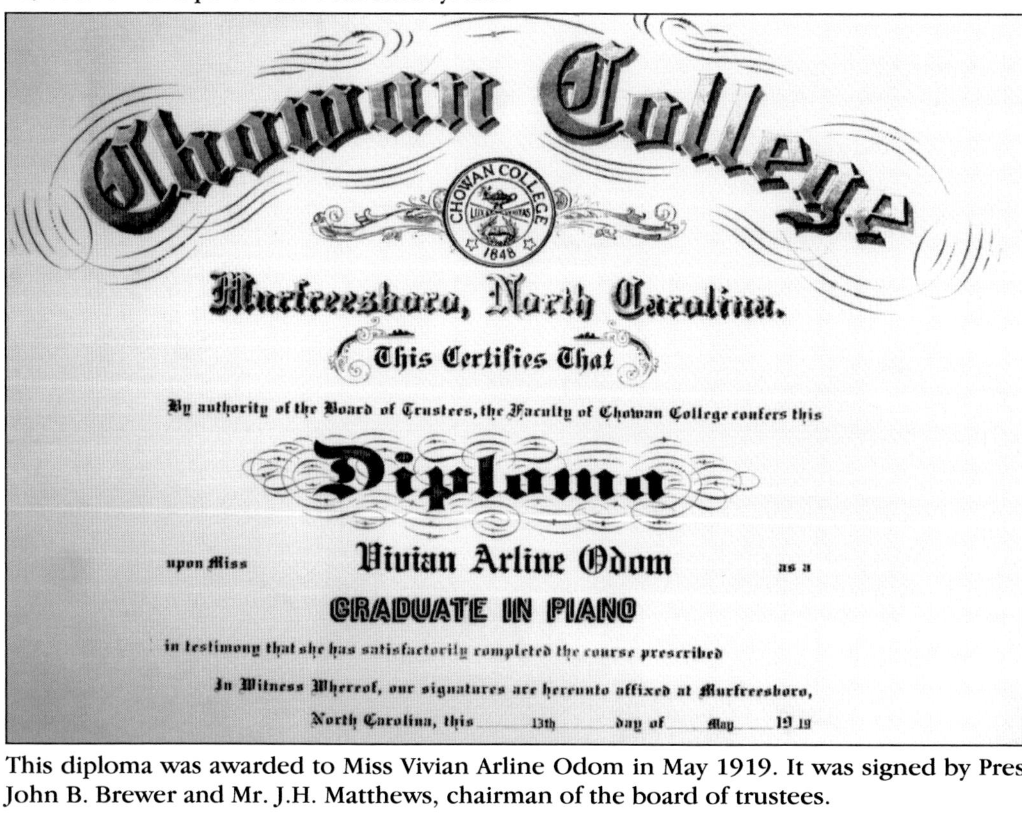

Chowan College

CHOWAN COLLEGE 1848

Murfreesboro, North Carolina.

This Certifies That

By authority of the Board of Trustees, the Faculty of Chowan College confers this

Diploma

upon Miss Vivian Arline Odom as a

GRADUATE IN PIANO

in testimony that she has satisfactorily completed the course prescribed

In Witness Whereof, our signatures are hereunto affixed at Murfreesboro, North Carolina, this 13th day of May 19 19

This diploma was awarded to Miss Vivian Arline Odom in May 1919. It was signed by Pres. John B. Brewer and Mr. J.H. Matthews, chairman of the board of trustees.

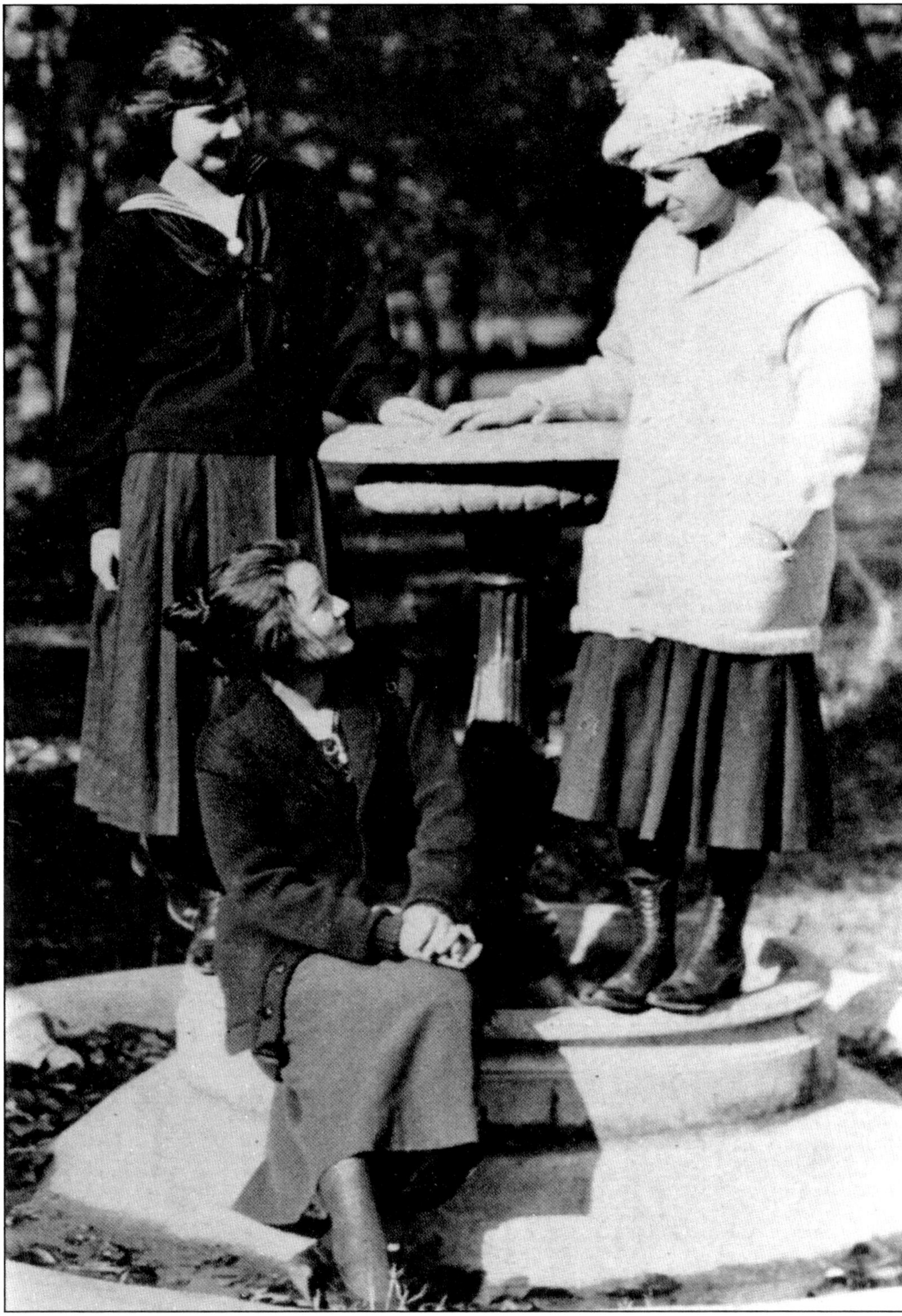

In 1921, the Dell Club had this photograph taken at the stone fountain that stood in front of the Columns Building. The fountain was a gift to the college from the Class of 1913.

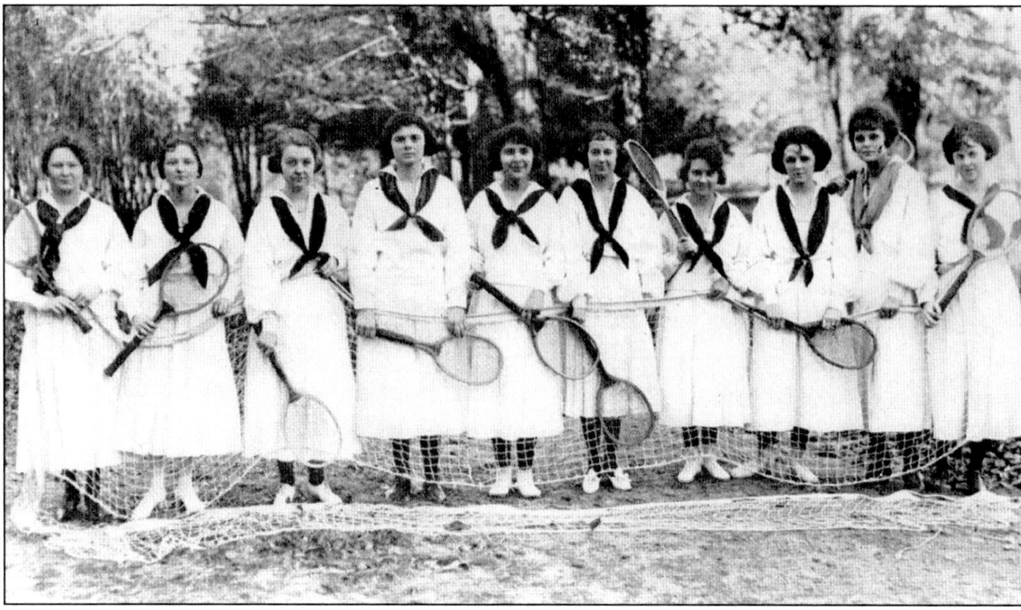

This is a 1921 photograph of the tennis club.

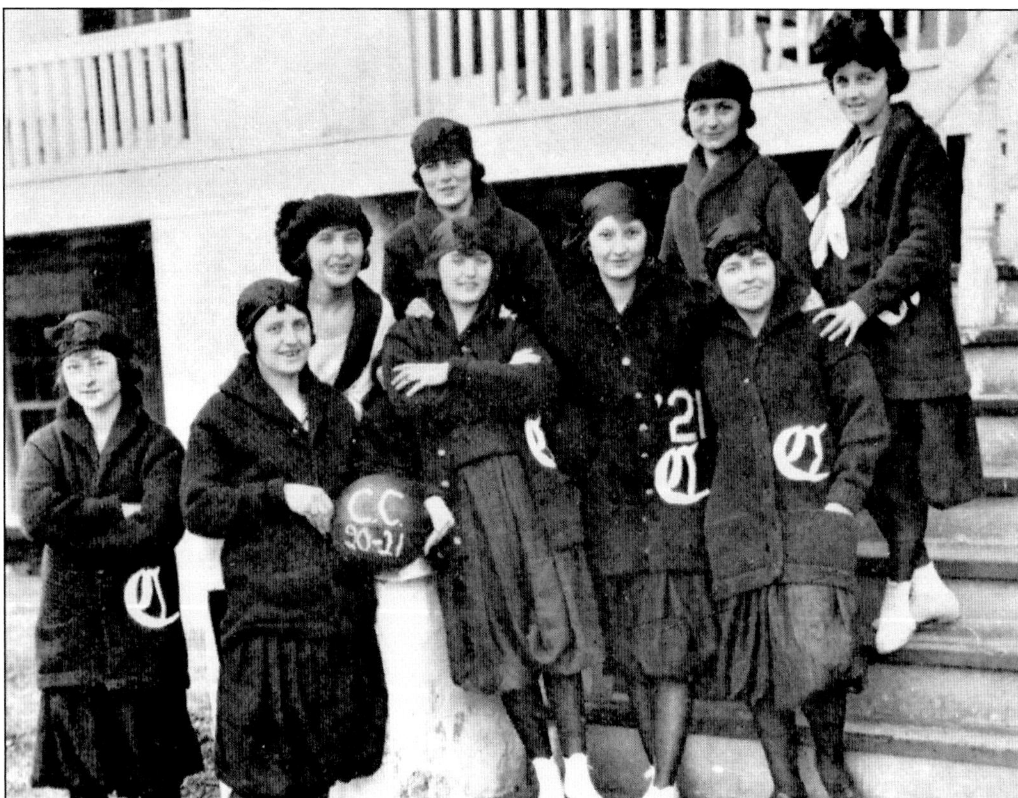

Pictured here is the 1920–1921 basketball team. From left to right are Josie Piland, Josephine Futrell, Genevieve Taylor, Mary Parker, Bernice Matthews, Elizabeth Turnley, Helen Craig, Annie Lee McDaniel, and Bessie Jordan.

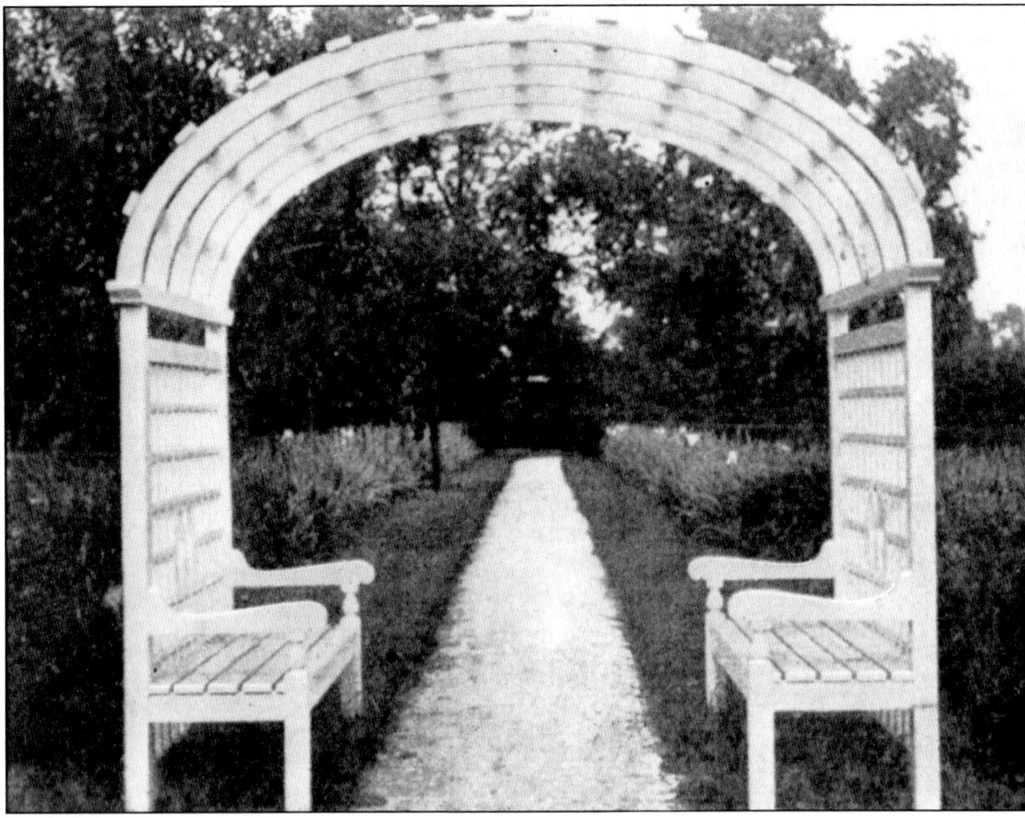

The Senior Class of 1922 had two of these rose arbors erected on the front campus. They remained in use until the late 1950s.

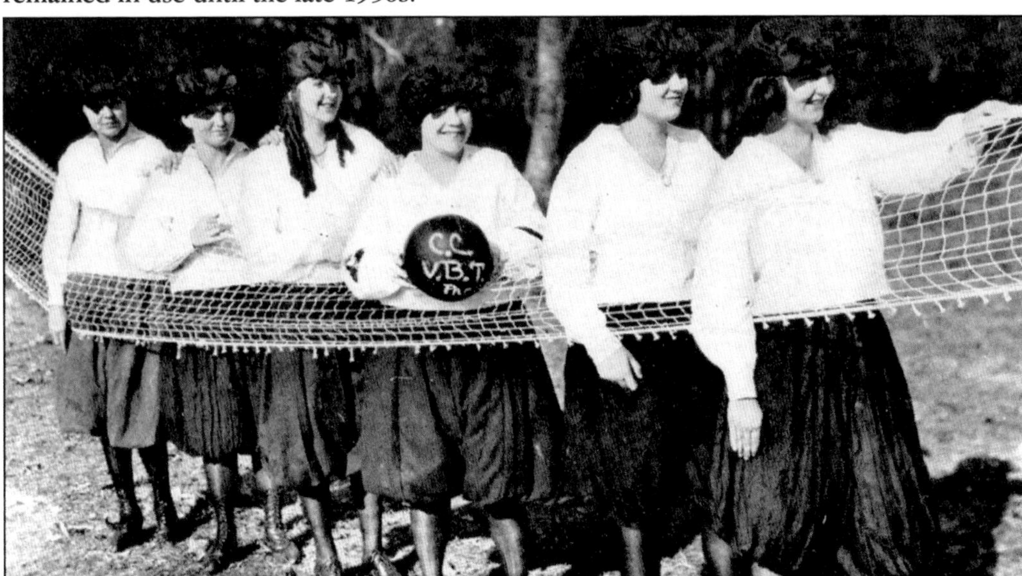

Here is the volleyball team of 1921. The team played such colleges as Meredith, Longwood, and the Women's College of North Carolina.

CHOWANOKA TWENTY-FIVE

1848 1925

CHOWAN COLLEGE

77 YEARS OLD

77 YEARS STRONG

77 YEARS THE SERVANT

of

NORTH CAROLINA BAPTISTS

INVITES YOU TO SEND
HER YOUR DAUGHTERS

In Order That They May Be Trained for the
Larger Christian Life

WRITE FOR CATALOGUE

CHAS. P. WEAVER, Ph.D., *President*

MURFREESBORO, N. C.

This advertisement appeared in the 1925 yearbook. Dr. Charles Weaver was president of the college from 1923 to 1925.

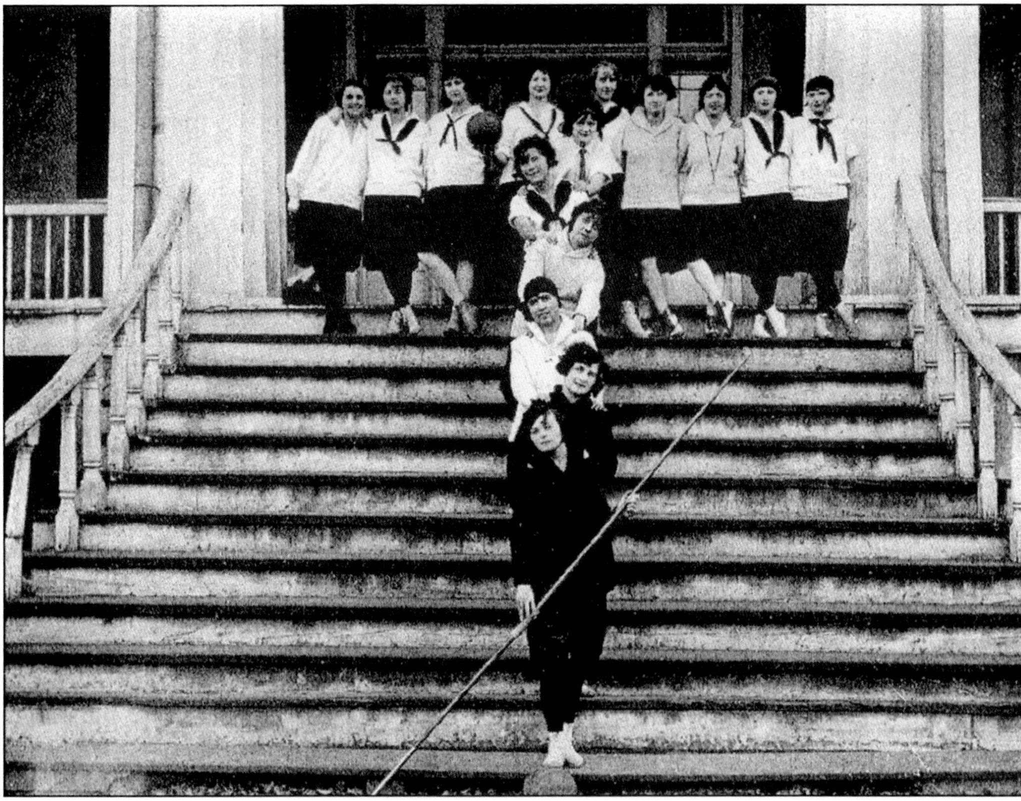

Pictured here is the track team of 1926. The team had a 9-1 record, losing only to Westhampton College.

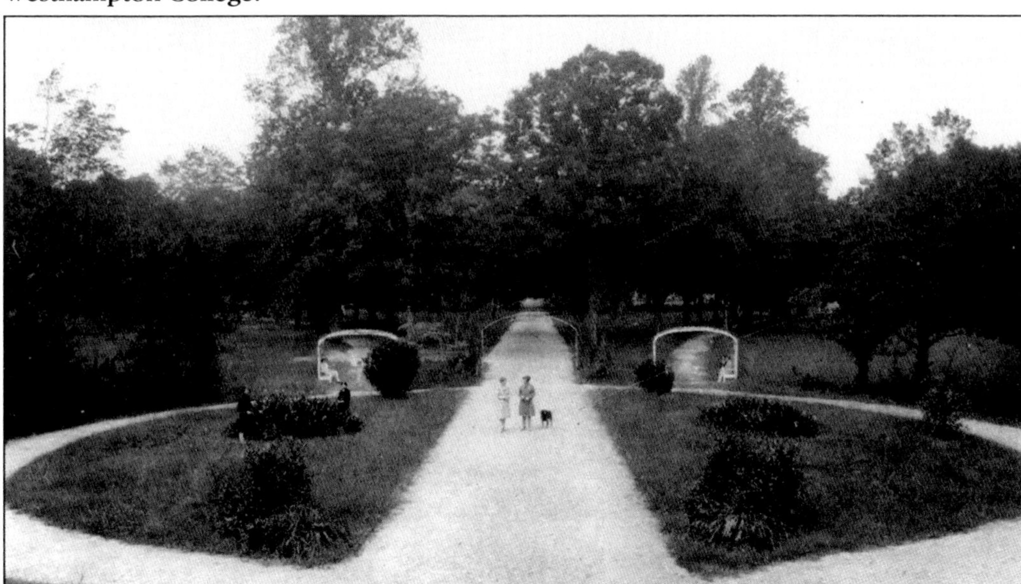

This is a 1927 photograph of the front campus showing the location of two arbors that were donated to the college by the class of 1922. When this photograph was taken, much of the original landscape plan was intact.

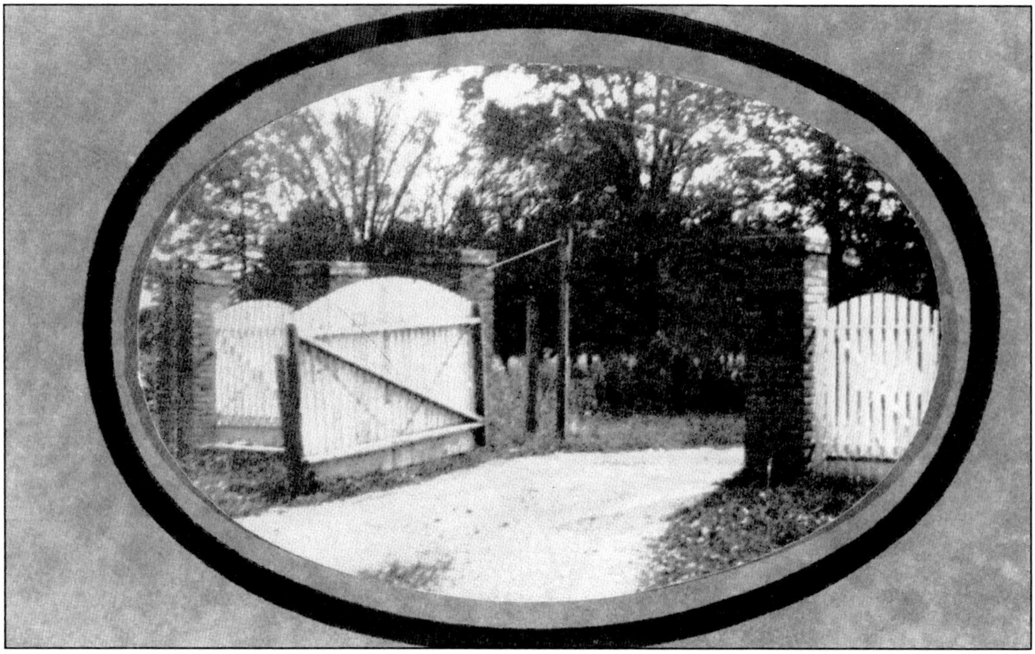

The front gate is seen as it appeared in the 1923 yearbook. The front entrance took on a number of appearances through the years.

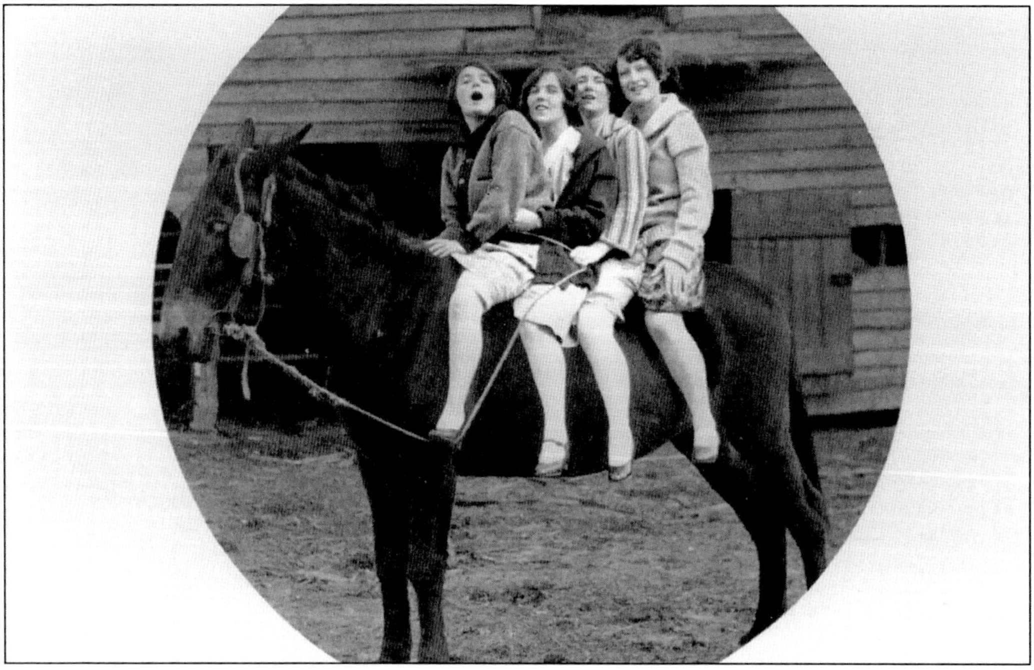

Members of the Barnyard Quartette of 1927 are found sitting atop a mule, looking a little uncomfortable—since there was not a saddle large enough to seat four.

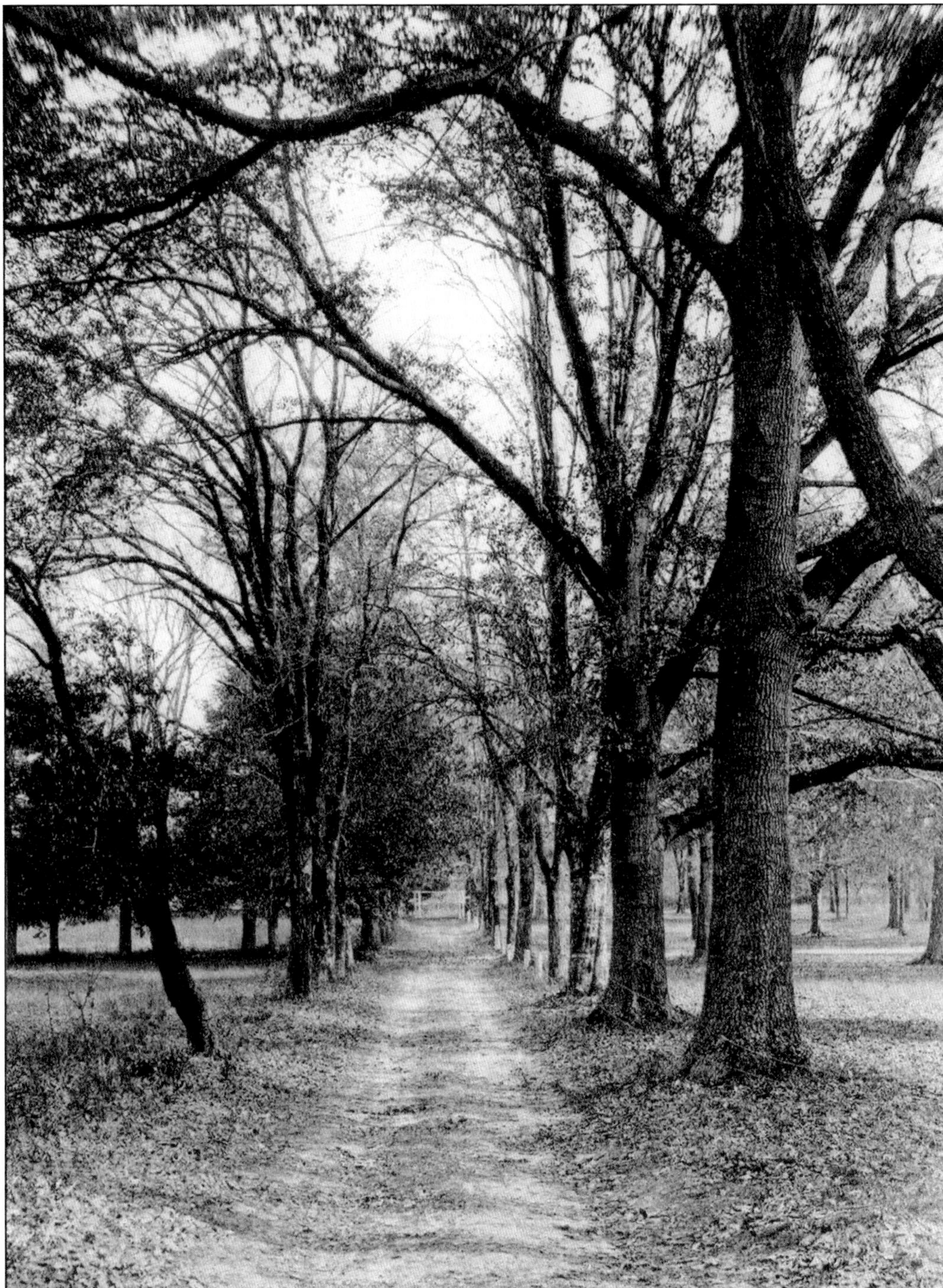

This is the center walk/drive as it appeared in 1926. The center walk was always a favorite with students through the years.

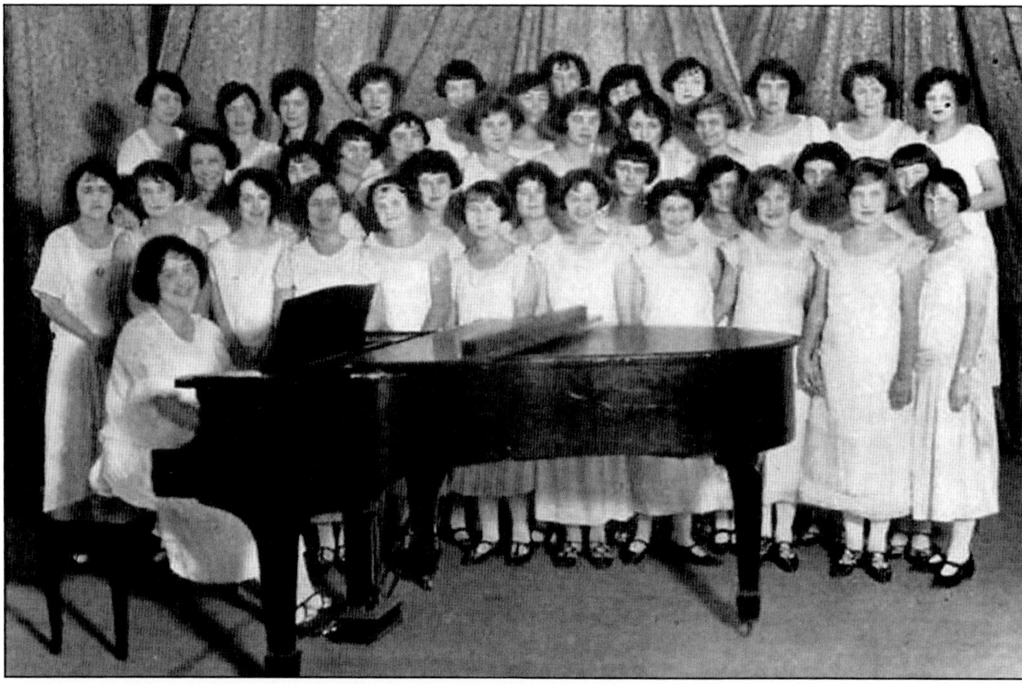

The glee club of 1925 was a fairly large group. These students performed at area churches and schools.

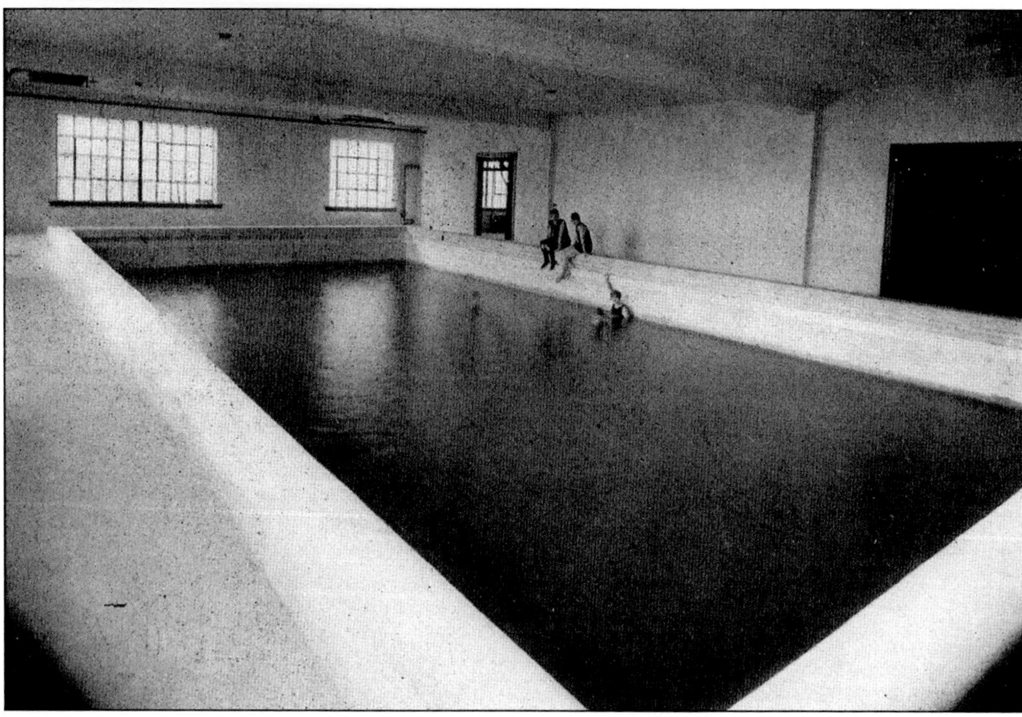

A 1925 image depicts the college's newly constructed swimming pool. When the Helms Physical Education Center was constructed in 1980, it contained a new pool and the 1920s pool was closed. The college's bookstore is now where the old pool used to be.

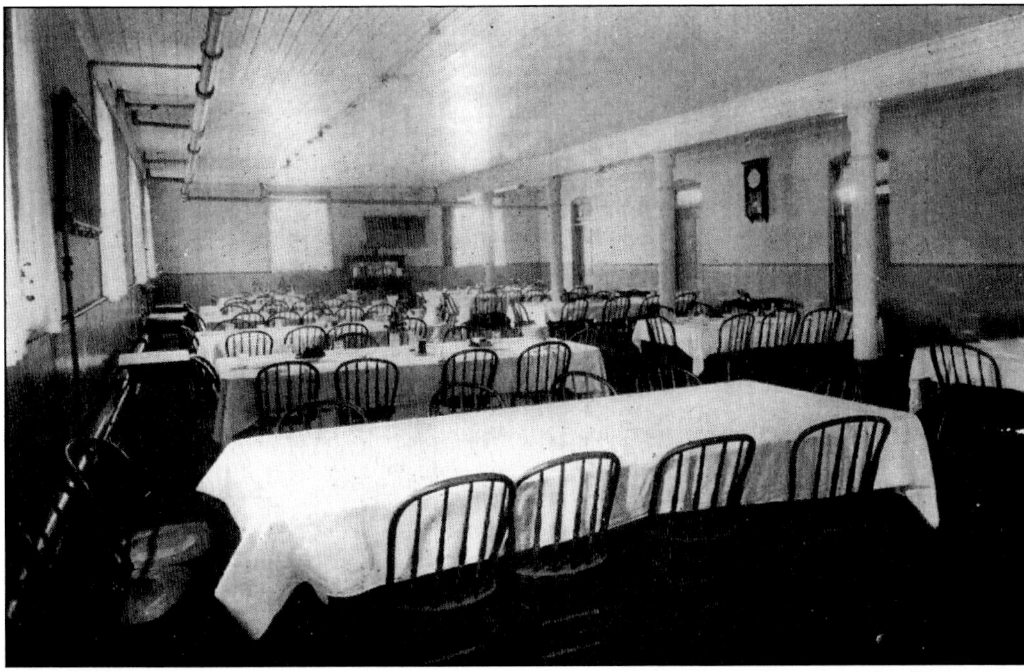

The college dining hall was located on the ground floor of the East Building when this photograph was taken in 1928. This building was constructed in 1906 and torn down in the late 1960s.

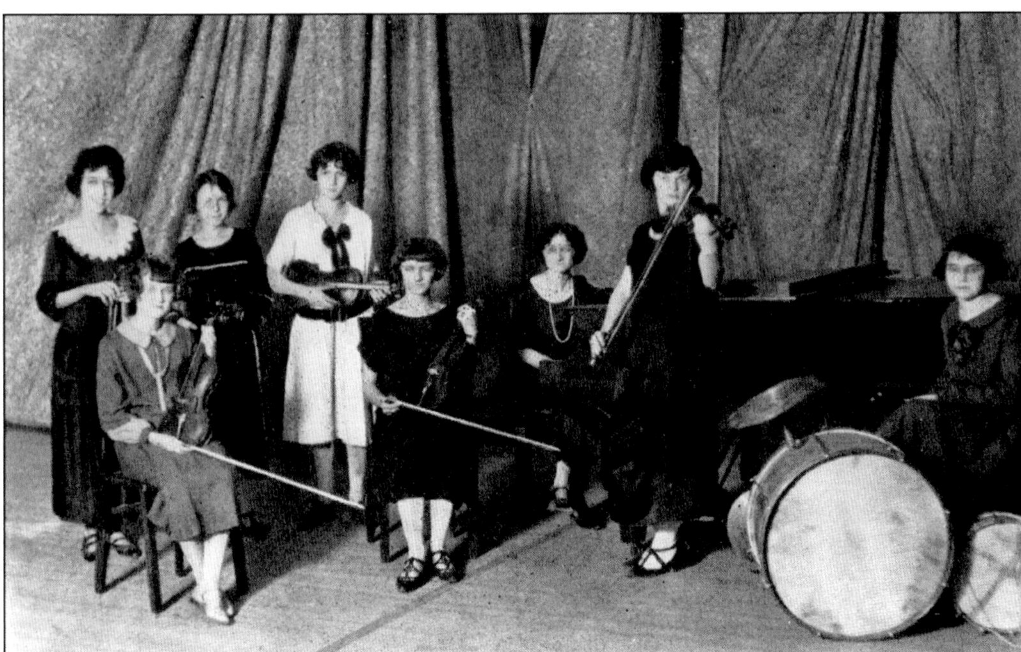

Here is the 1925 Chowan College orchestra. Members are Nela Knowles, Camilla Manson, Matilda Weaver, Hazel Griffin, Edna Lassiter, Mrs. E.N. Nicholson, Mildred Pipkin, Ada Harrell, Mary Whitley, Doris Chitty, Ella Mae Parker, and Inez Matthews.

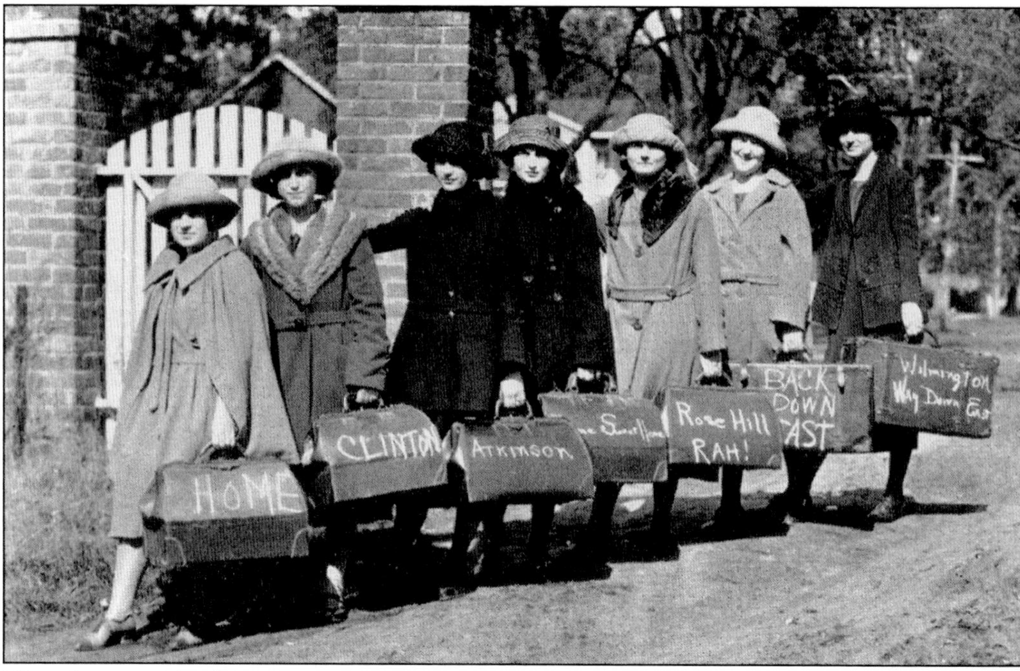

This photograph of the Down East Club appeared in the 1923 yearbook. The club was made up of students who hailed from Eastern North Carolina.

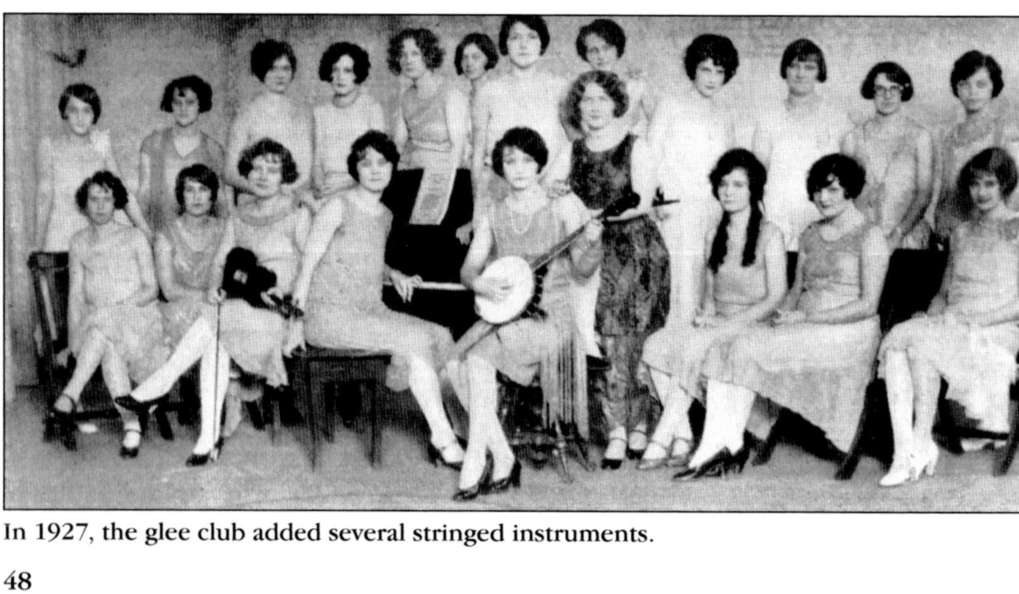
In 1927, the glee club added several stringed instruments.

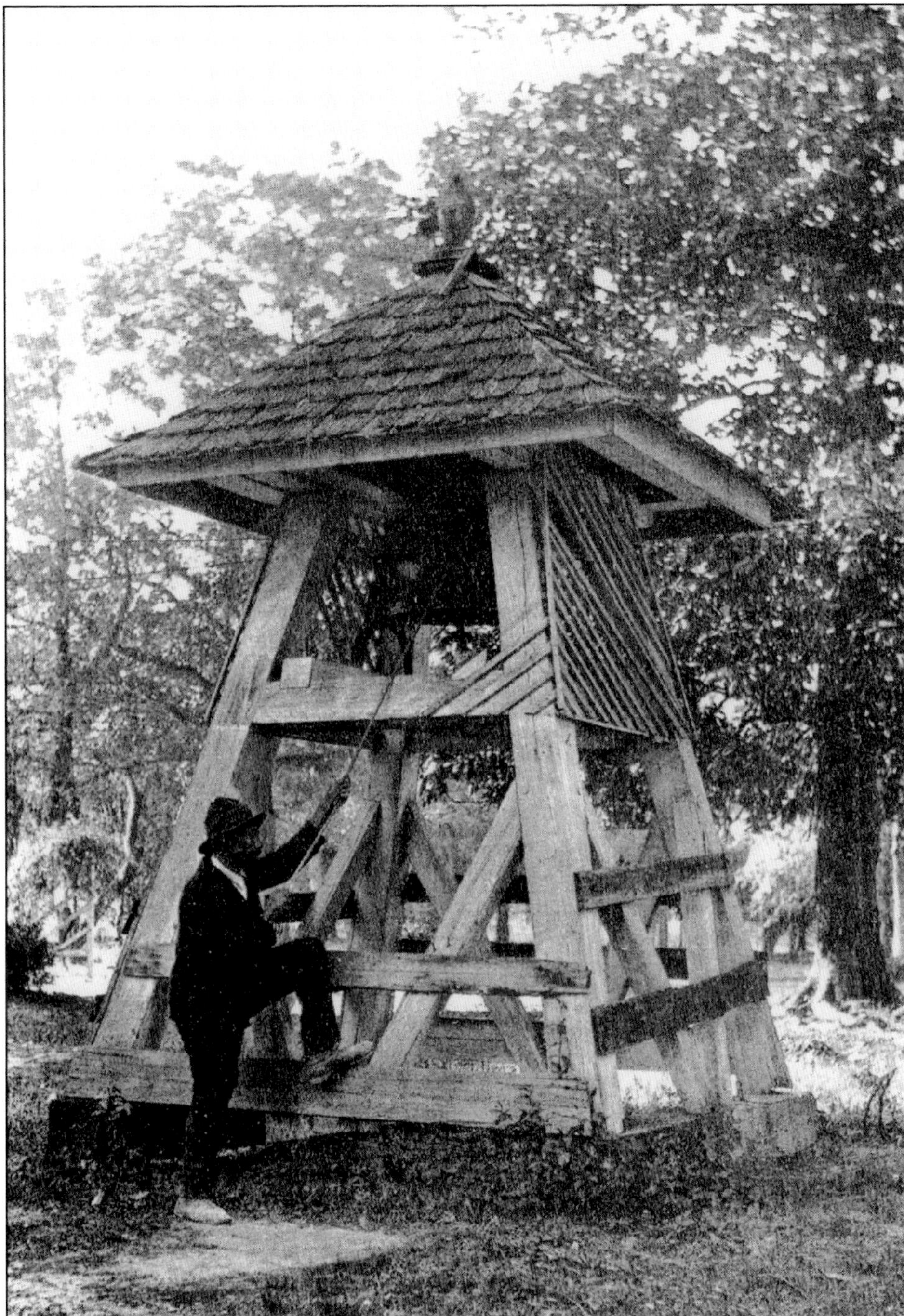

This photograph of the college bell appeared in the 1928 yearbook. Moses Porter, one of the longtime stewards at the college, is seen ringing the bell. The bell swung from two stone pillars until 1880, when it was placed in the Bell Tower, a favorite meeting place for students. The bell was used to change classes, call students to chapel, and celebrate athletic victories.

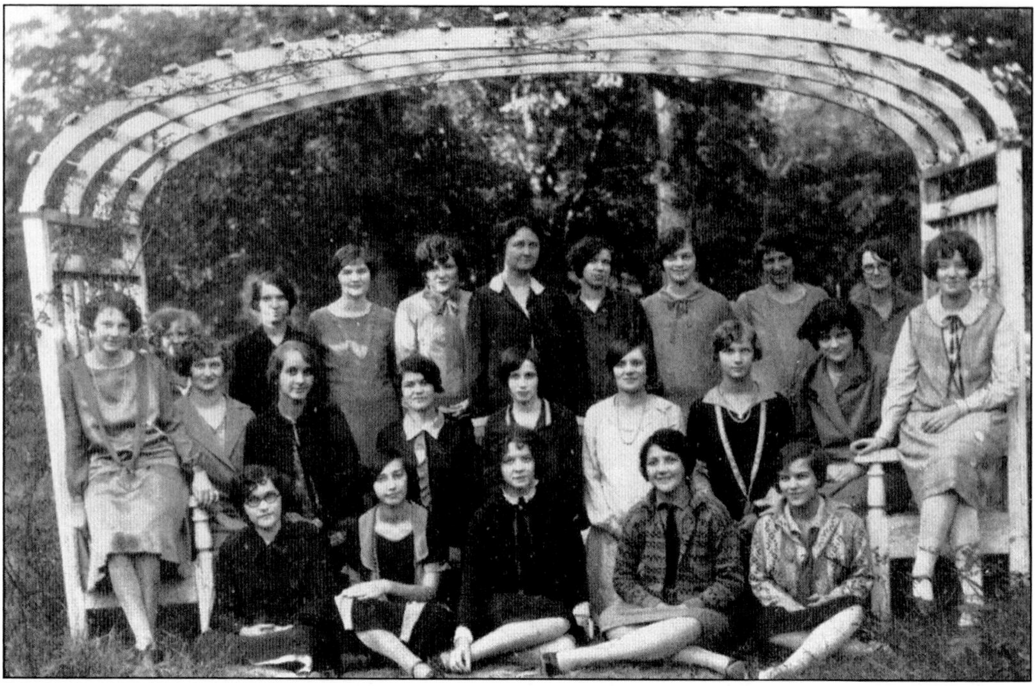

Members of the 1927 math club pose under one of the rose arbors donated by the Senior Class of 1922.

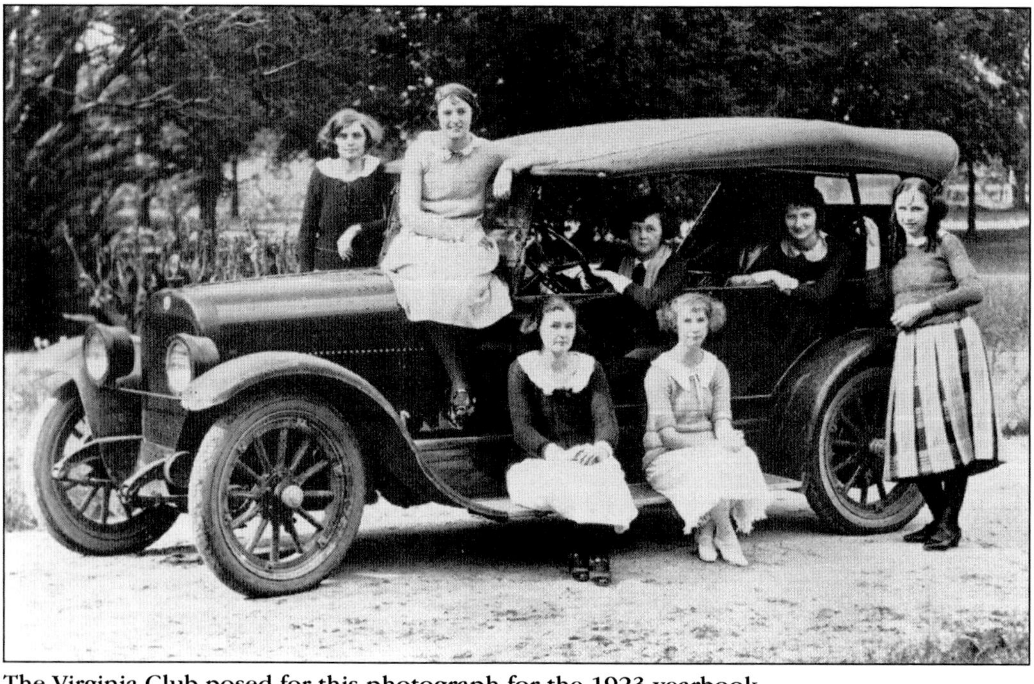

The Virginia Club posed for this photograph for the 1923 yearbook.

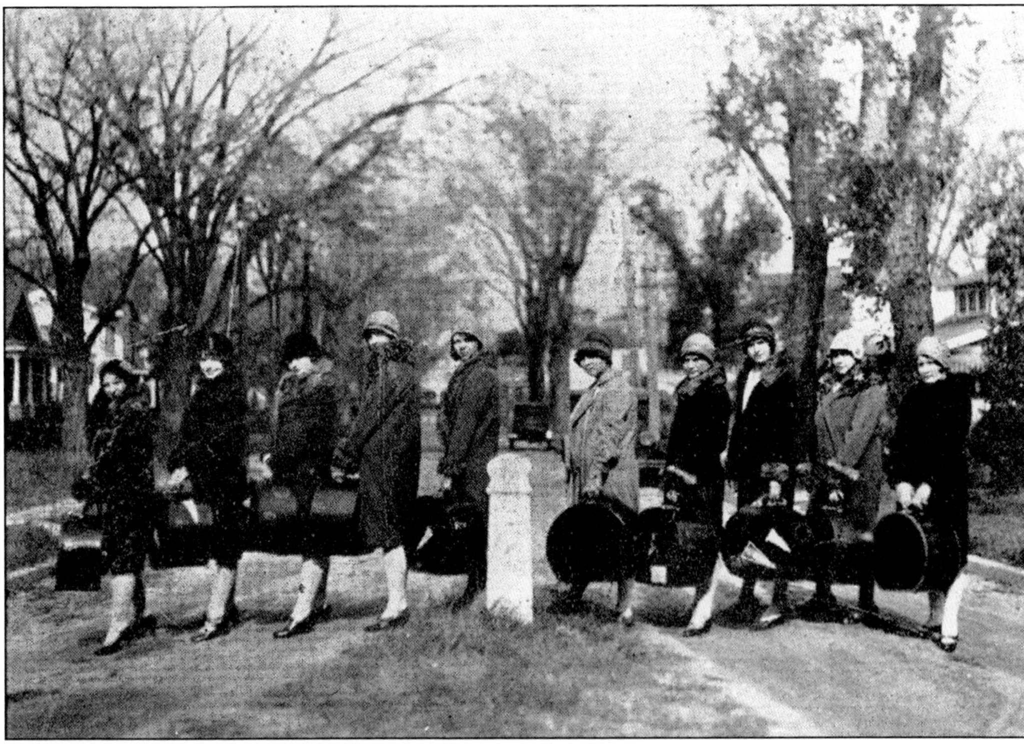

The Roaring Twenties were alive and well on the Chowan College, as shown by this photograph shot at the split main entrance to campus. The street in the background is College Street, formerly known as Seminary Avenue.

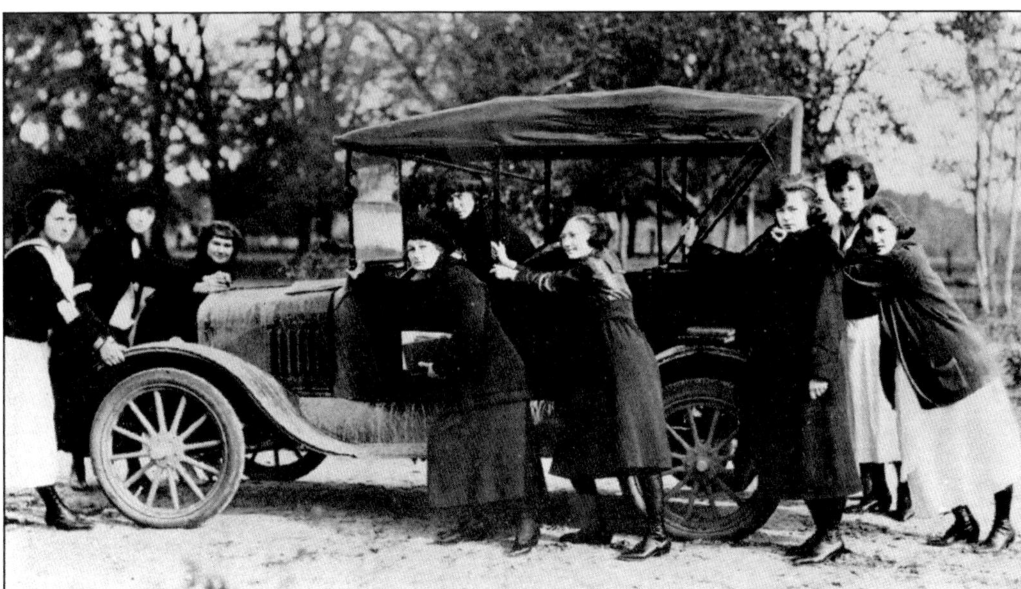

This is a 1922 photograph of the Downtown Club. The members of the club were students who lived in Murfreesboro.

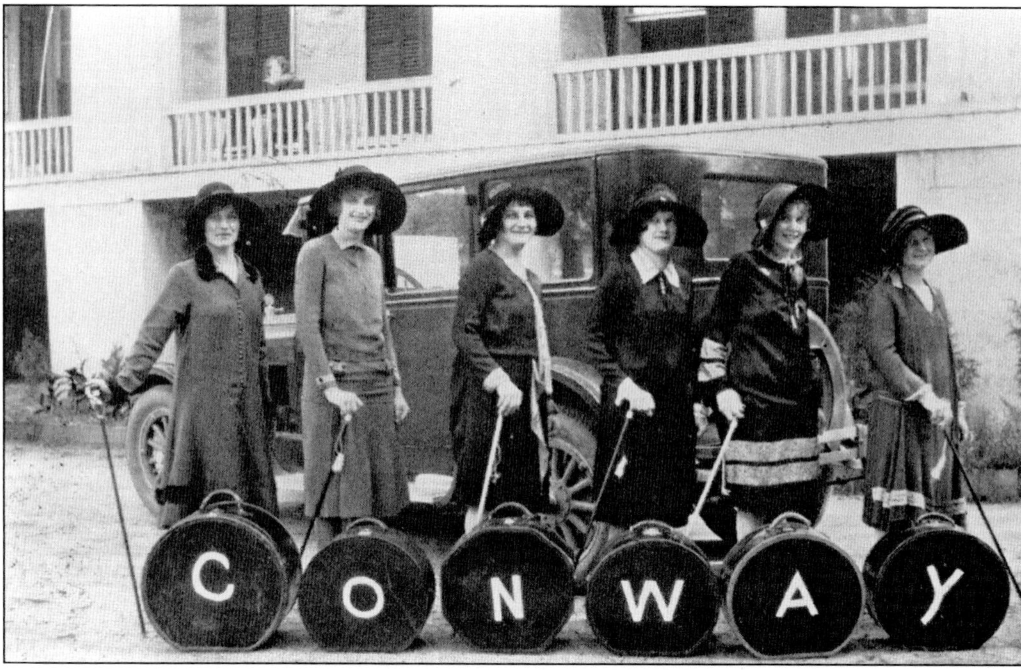

In 1927, members of the Conway Club posed for this photograph in front of the Columns Building. Membership was made up of students from Conway, North Carolina.

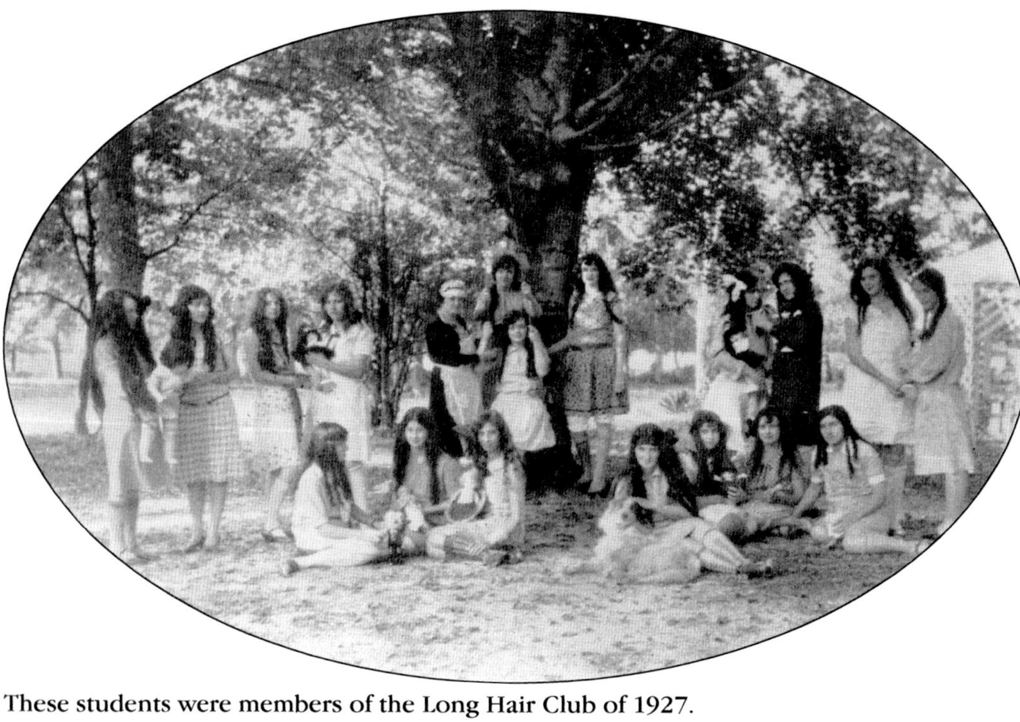

These students were members of the Long Hair Club of 1927.

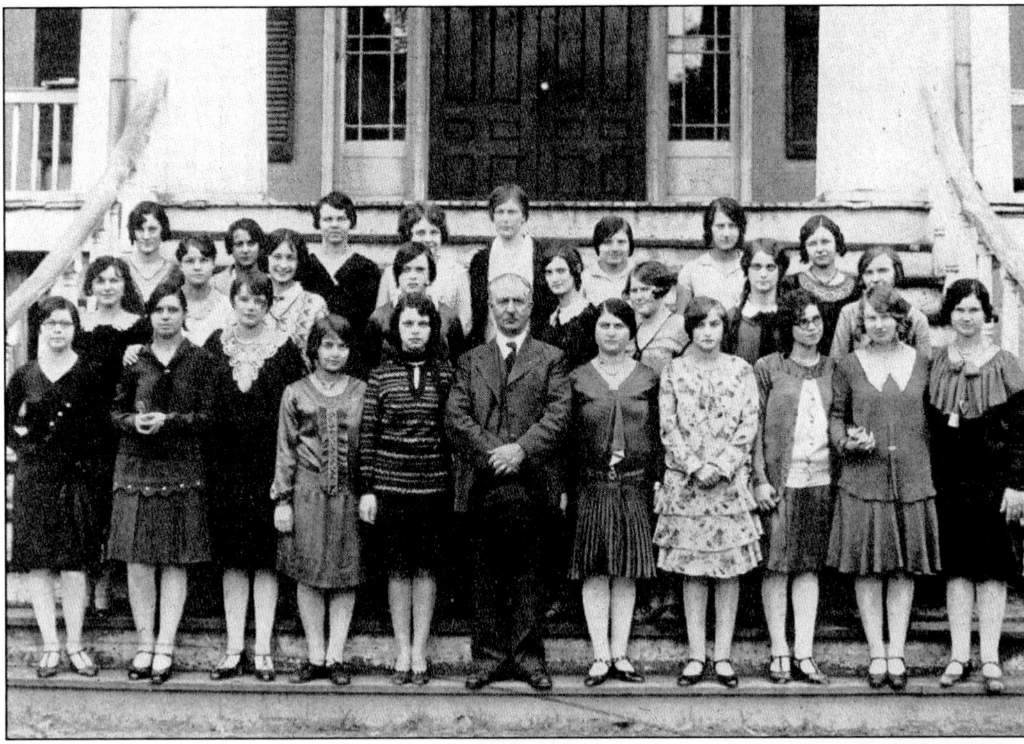

In 1930, these students were members of the Bible class. Included in the photograph are Rhodes Holder, Reba Mills, Dorothy Askew, Elizabeth Forbes, Margaret Kidd, Reba Taylor, Carrie Askew, Mary Mills, Addie Mae Cooke, Alice Miller, Christine Brett, Josie Mae Barkley, Myrtle Huff, Edna Earle Harrell, Martha Williams, Fannie Brown Harrell, Anna Spiers, Lyda Jane Brooks, Vivian Jenkins, Myra Glover, Maywood Modlin, Doris Lawrence, Minnie Vinson, Helen Flythe, Airey Barnes, and Marguerite Payne. The man in the middle of the front row is Dr. W.R. Burrell.

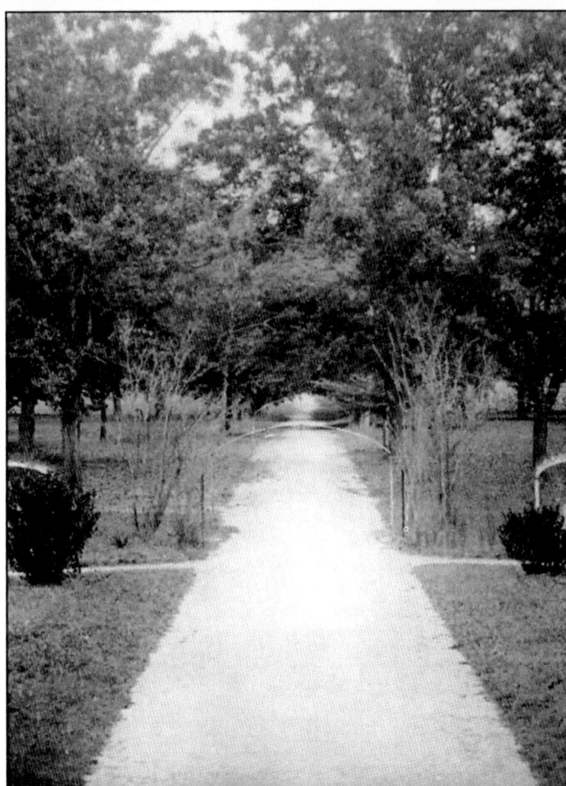

This is the center walk as it appeared in 1930.

1848 1935

CHOWAN COLLEGE

Standard "A" Grade Institution

87 Years Old : 87 Years Strong

87 Years the Servant of North Carolina Baptists

Invites You to Send Her Your Sons and Daughters That They May Be Trained for the Larger Christian Life

SPECIAL FEATURES

1. Small Student Body.
2. Well-Trained Faculty.
3. Personal Individual Attention.
4. Strong Department of Education Practice Teaching.
5. Strong Fine Arts Department: Expression, Piano, Voice, Violin.
6. Moderate Expenses.
7. Christian Influence.

Recognized By State Department of Education

For Catalogue and Other Information, Write to

W. B. EDWARDS, *President*

MURFREESBORO, N. C.

This advertisement appeared in the 1935 yearbook.

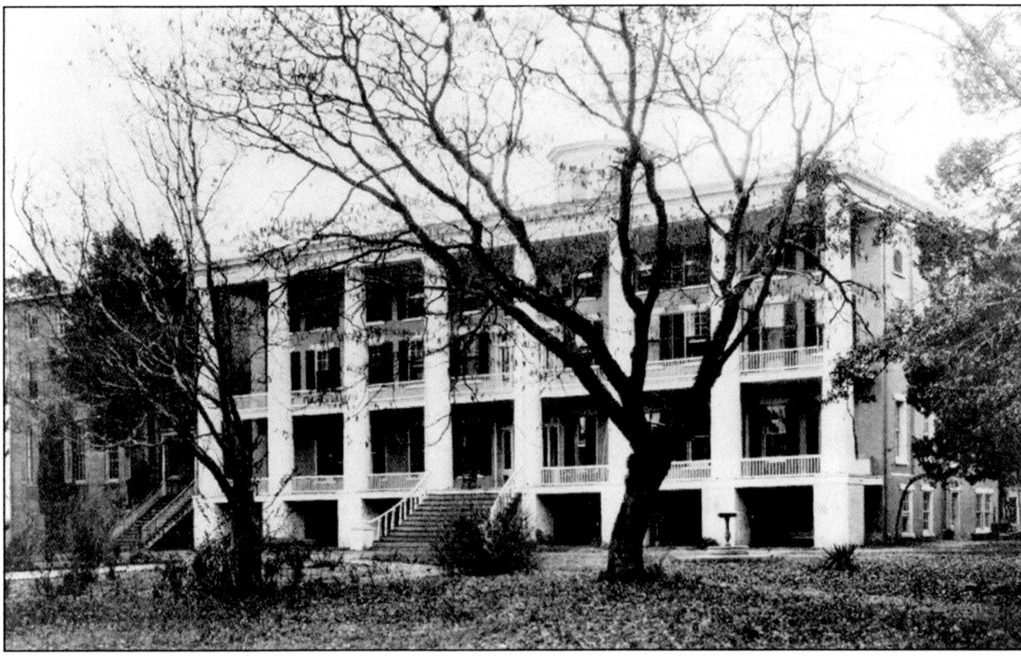
In this 1935 view, the Columns Building appears just as stately as the day it was built.

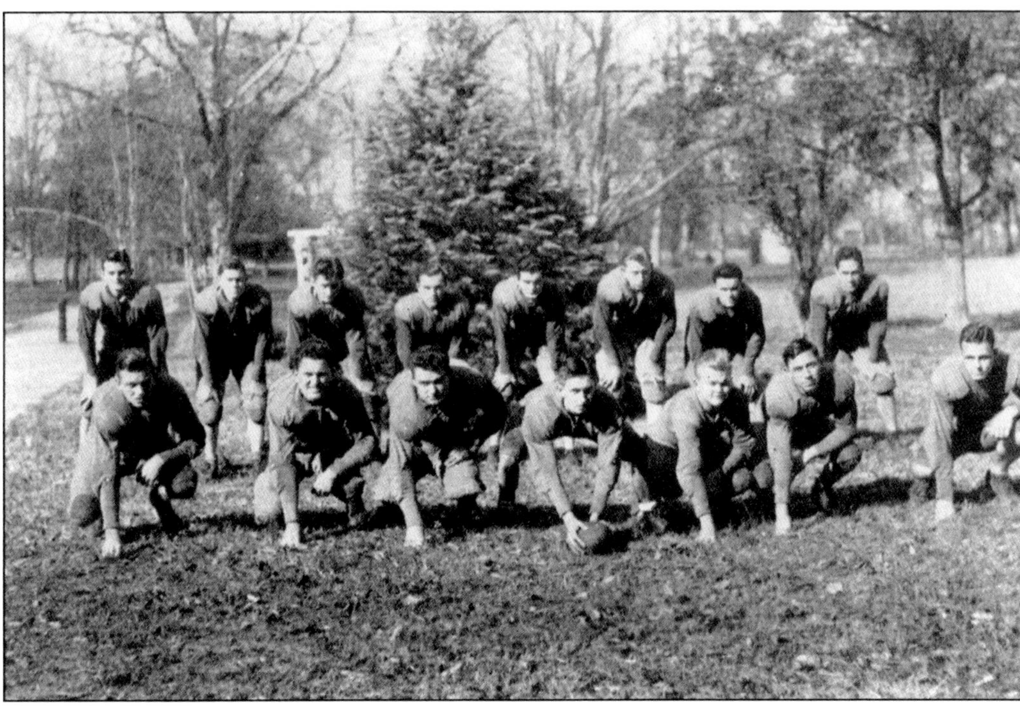
The 1935 football team lined up on the front campus, right of the center walk, for this photograph. The center on this football team was J.M. Jenkins, for whom the fitness and recreational center is named.

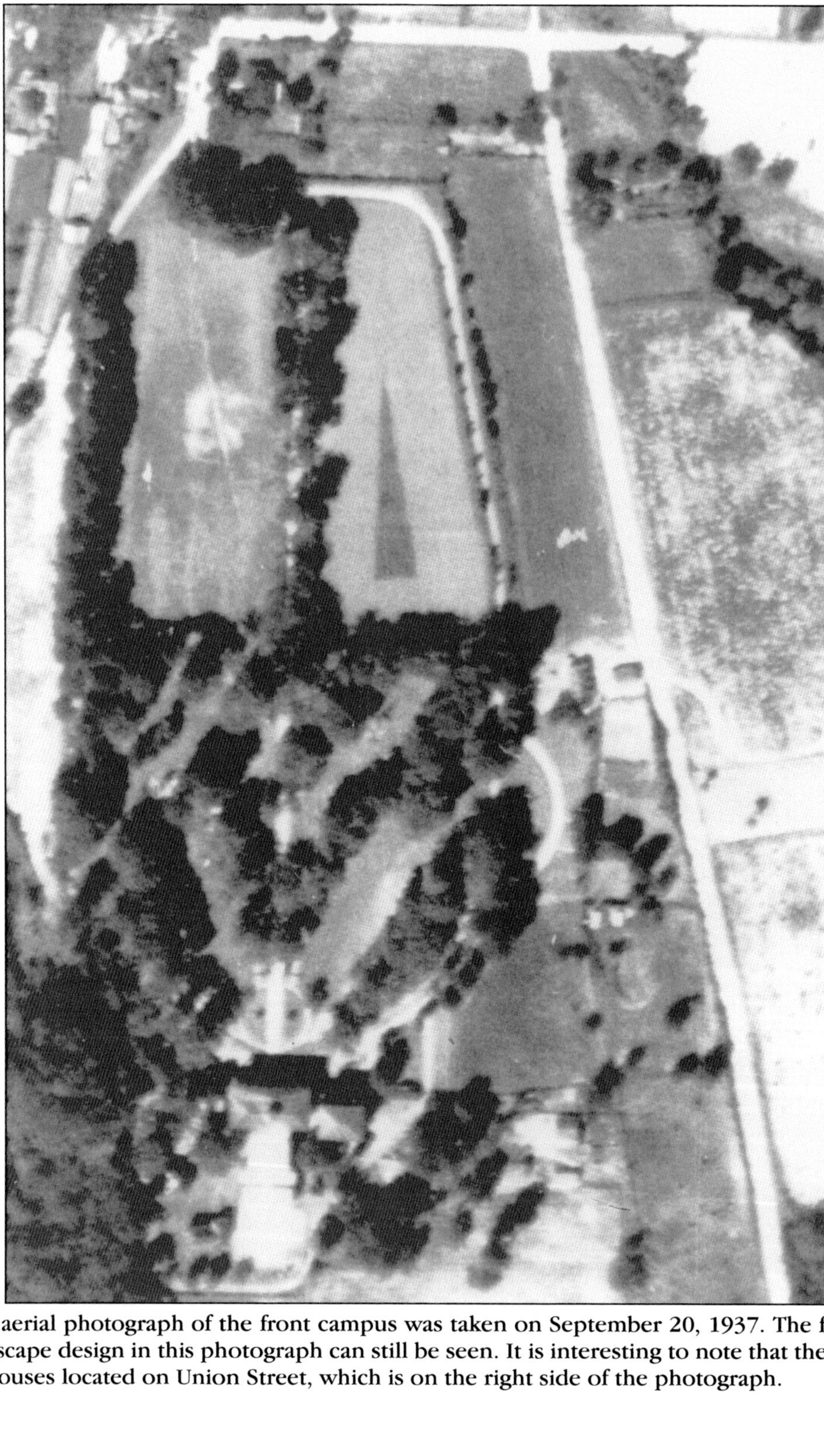

This aerial photograph of the front campus was taken on September 20, 1937. The formal landscape design in this photograph can still be seen. It is interesting to note that there are no houses located on Union Street, which is on the right side of the photograph.

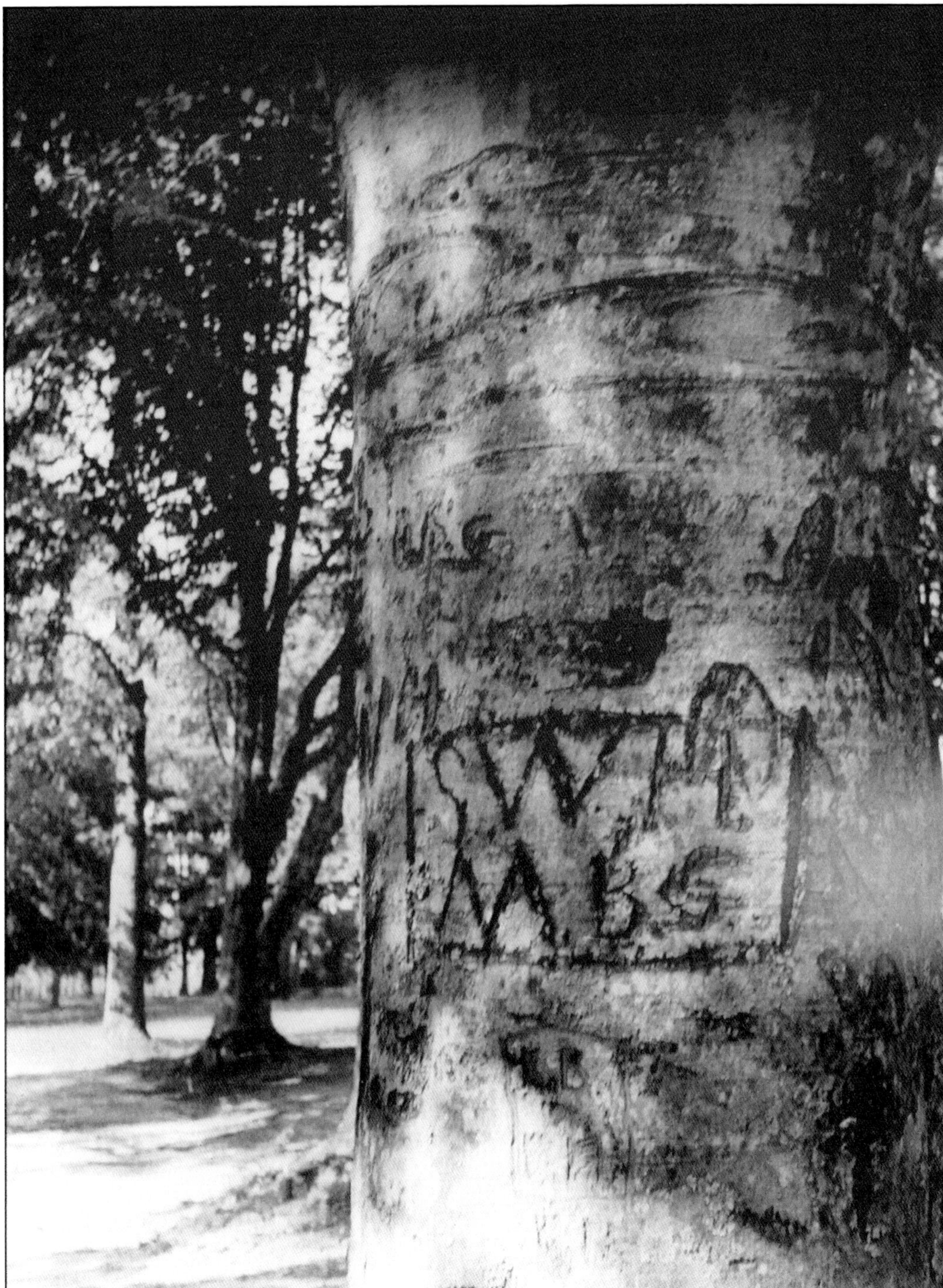

As seen in this 1938 photograph, Chowan students used to carve their initials in campus trees. Over time, as the trees grew, the initials became distorted and unreadable.

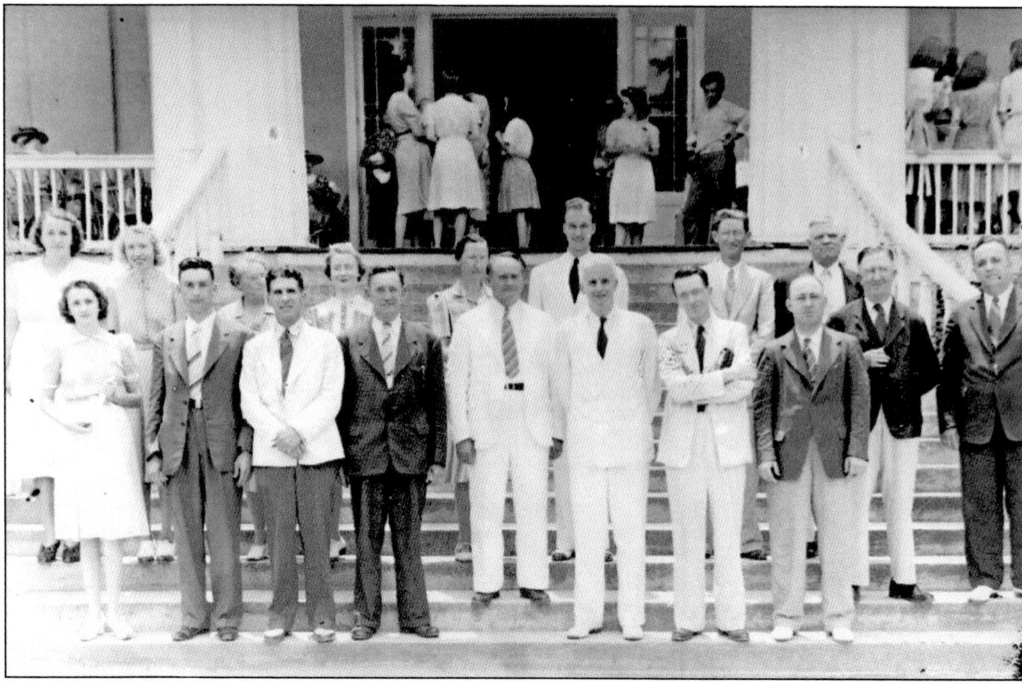

In 1939, Baptists ministers from the area held a meeting at Chowan. Rev. J.M. Duncan is seen standing midway on the second step from the bottom. Reverend Duncan was minister at Meherrin Baptist Church in Murfreesboro for many years.

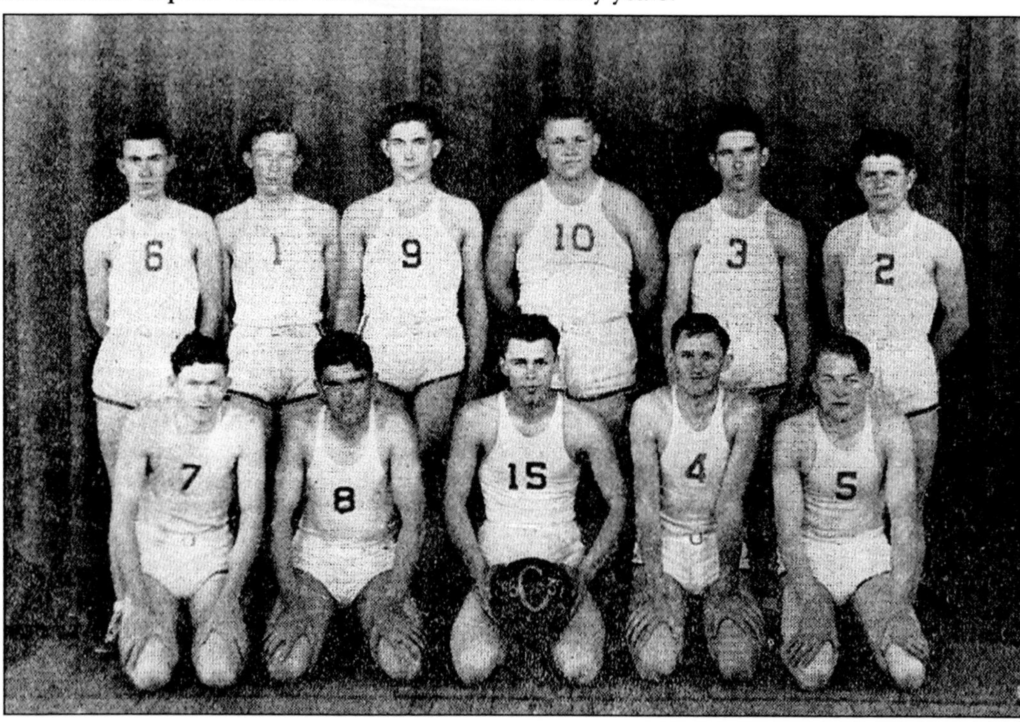

This is a photograph of the 1939–1940 men's basketball team. The player holding the ball in the front is Richard T. Vann, who later served as mayor of Murfreesboro.

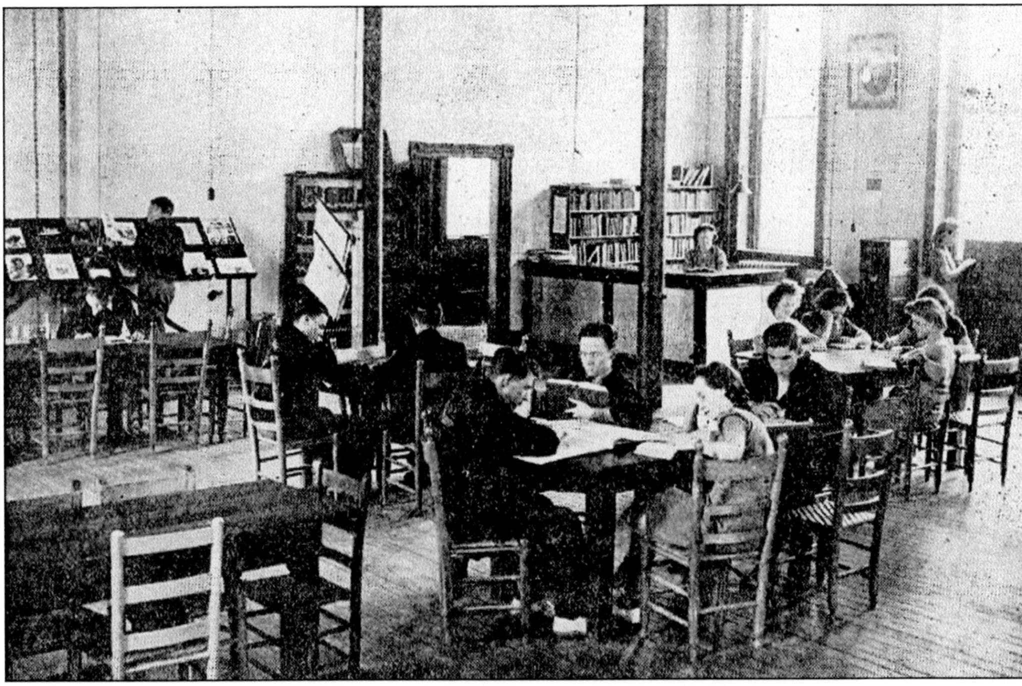

The 1940 Catalogue contained this photograph of the reading room in the library, which was located on the second floor of the 1906 East Building. In 1968 the library moved into the newly completed Whitaker Library.

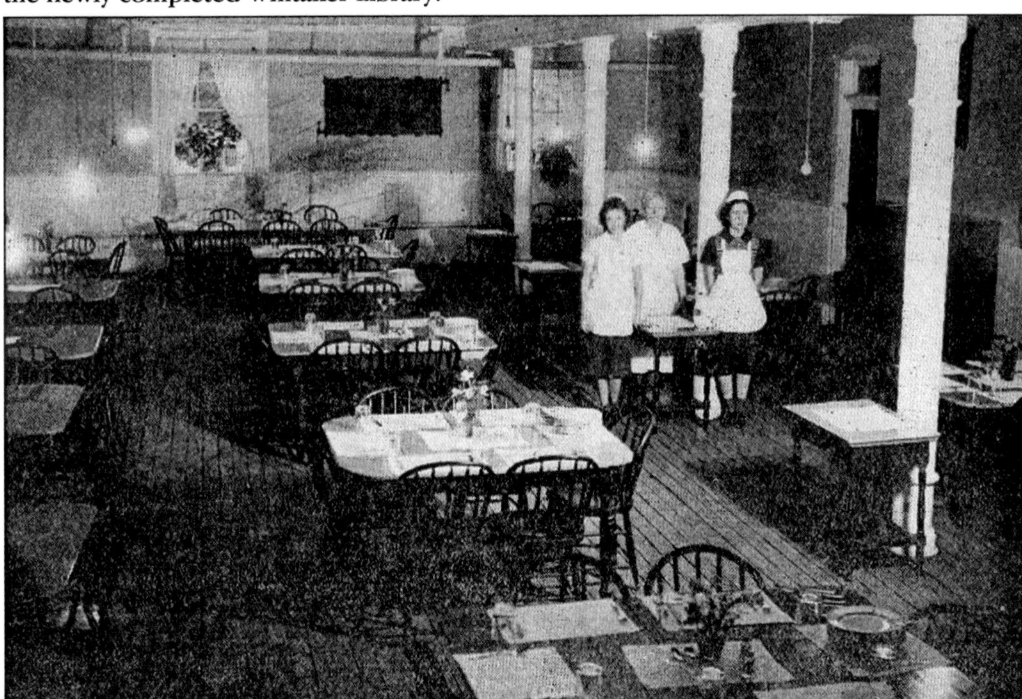

In 1940, the college's dining room was located on the ground floor of the 1906 East Building. This dining room served the college until Thomas Cafeteria was built in 1959.

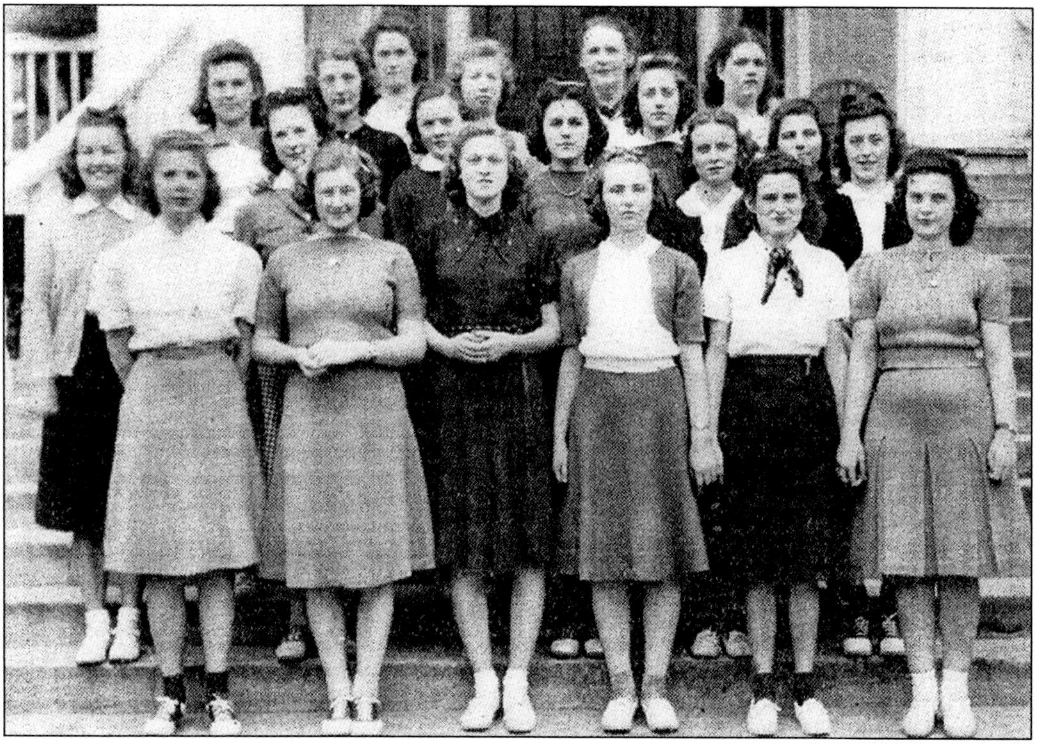

These students were members of the 1940 home economics class. They were photographed on the front steps of the Columns Building.

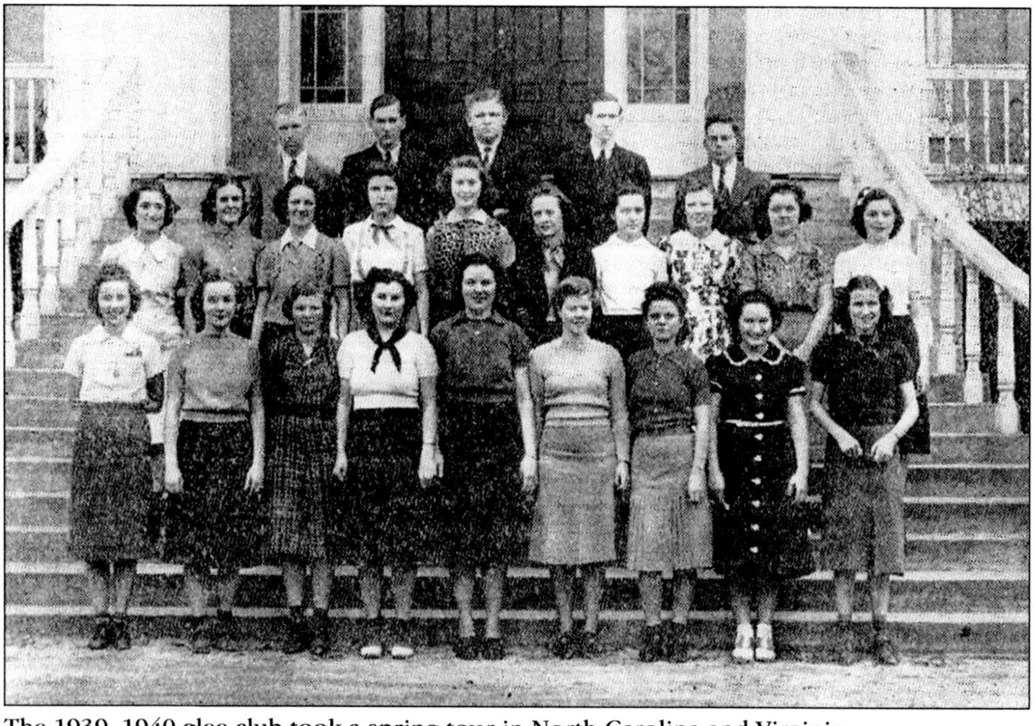

The 1939–1940 glee club took a spring tour in North Carolina and Virginia.

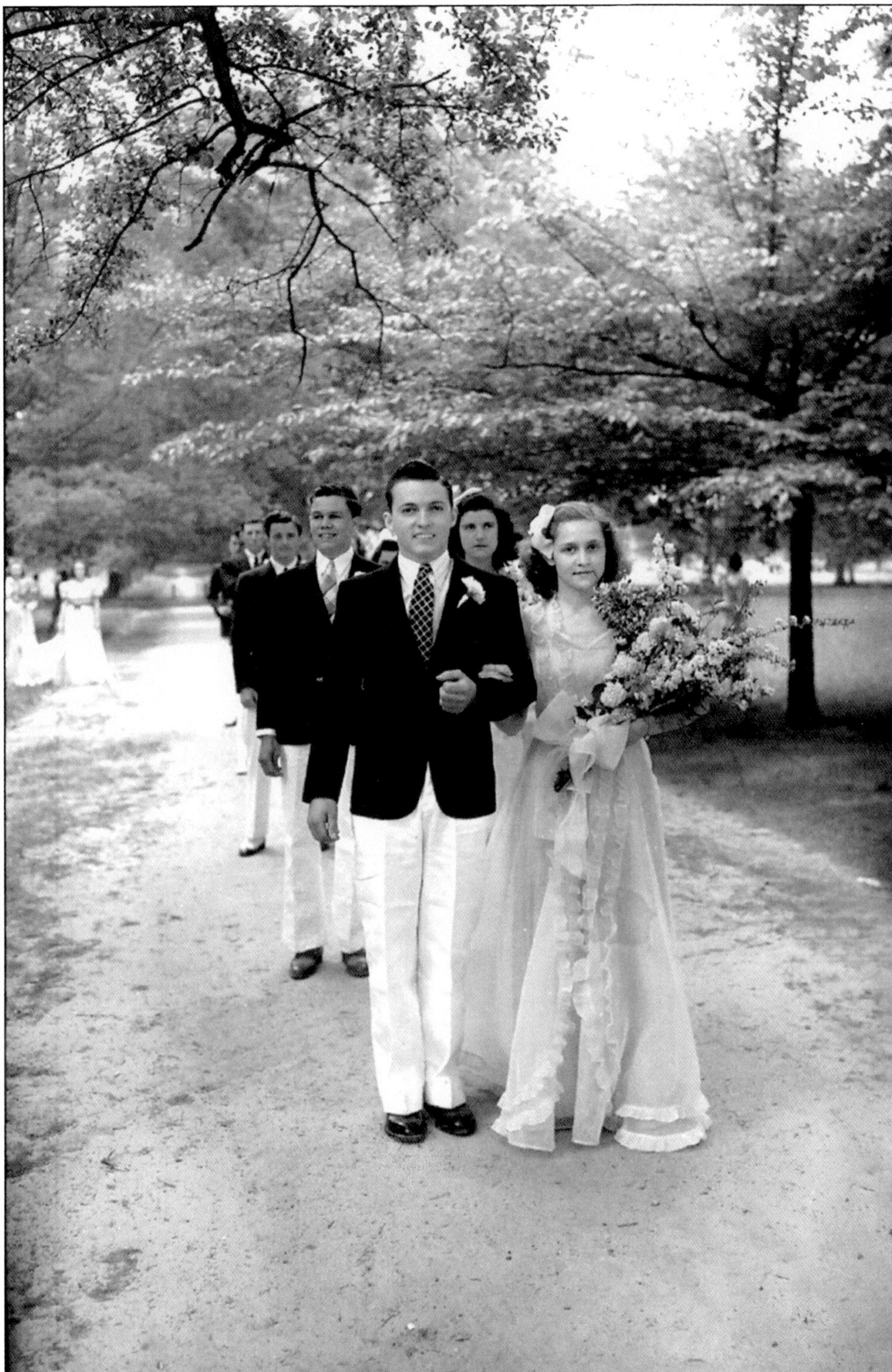

Members of the 1941 May Day Court are seen making their way up the front center walk. May Day celebrations at Chowan College were always a joyous occasion.

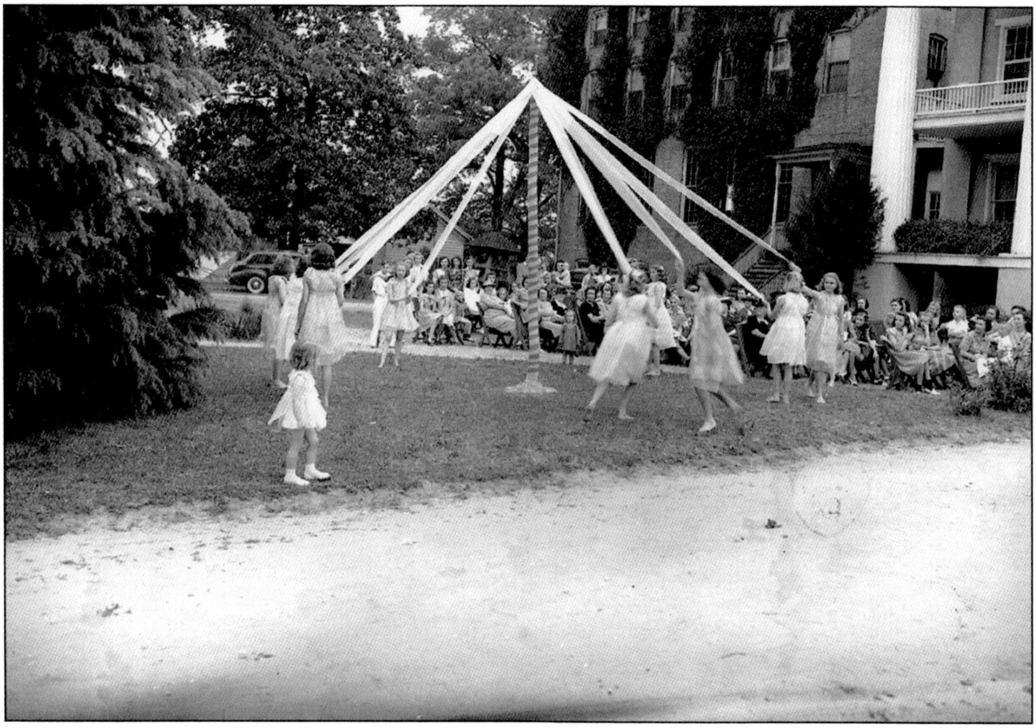

Participants here are winding the May pole in the 1941 May Day celebration.

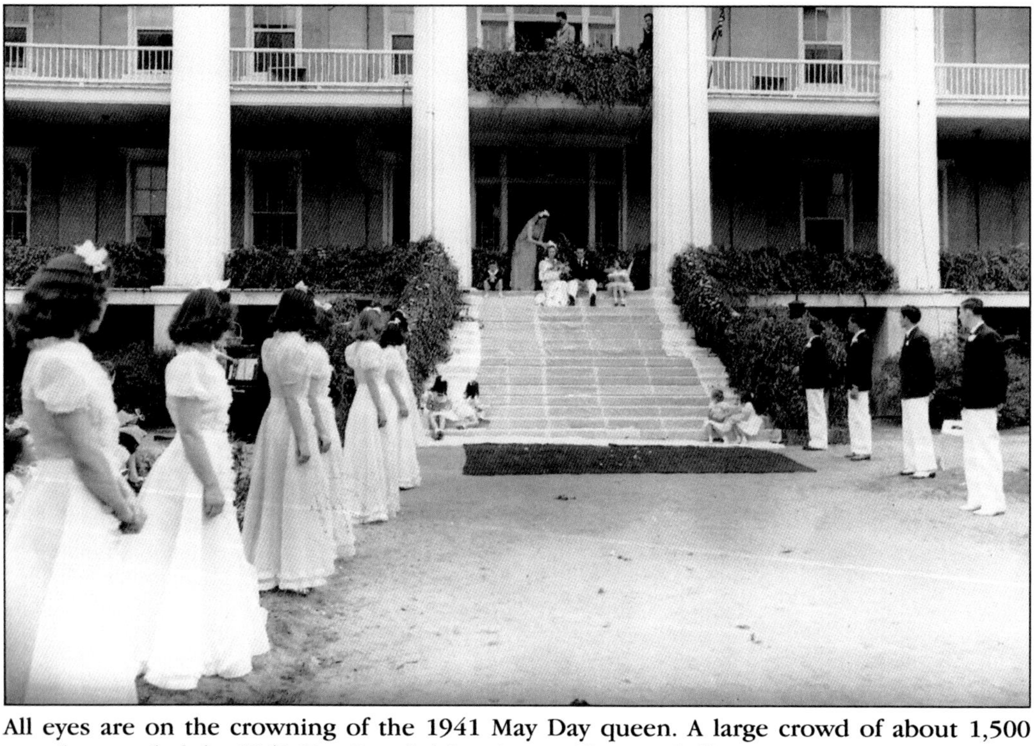

All eyes are on the crowning of the 1941 May Day queen. A large crowd of about 1,500 people attended the 1941 May Day Celebration at Chowan College.

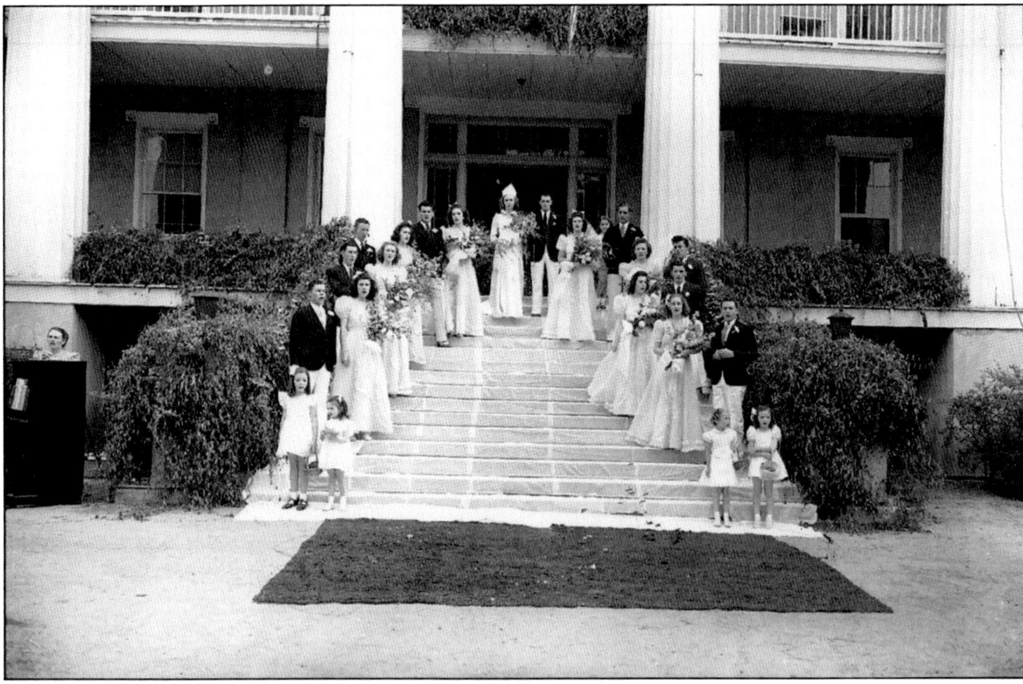

The 1941 May Day queen and her court are pictured here on the front steps of the McDowell Columns Building.

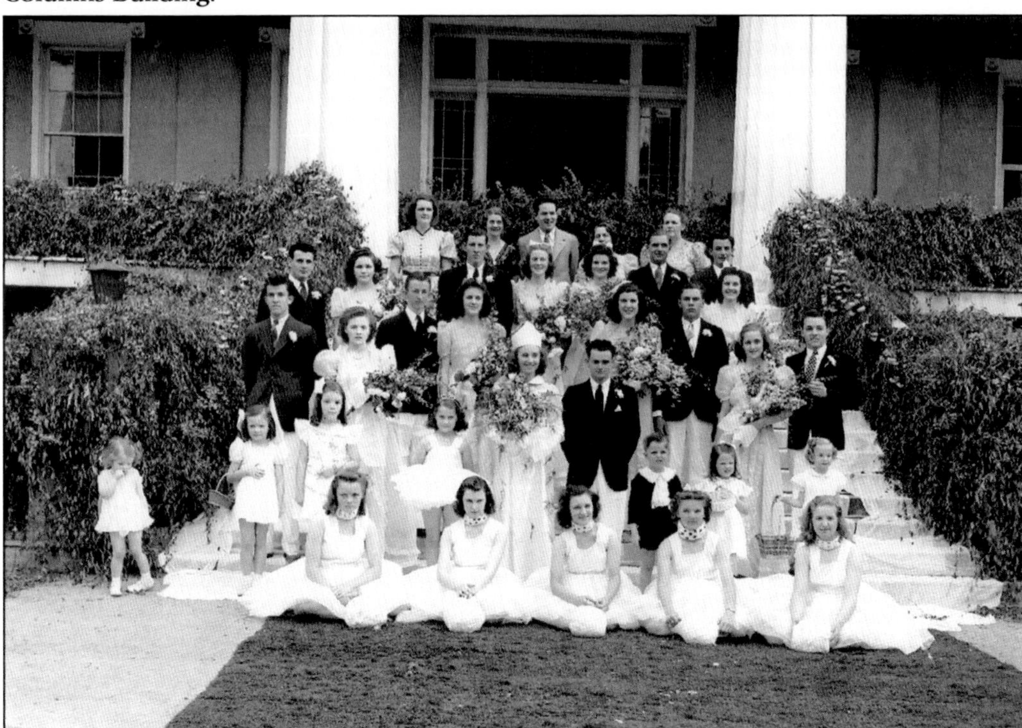

All of the participants in the 1941 May Day celebration are gathered on the front steps of the McDowell Columns Building.

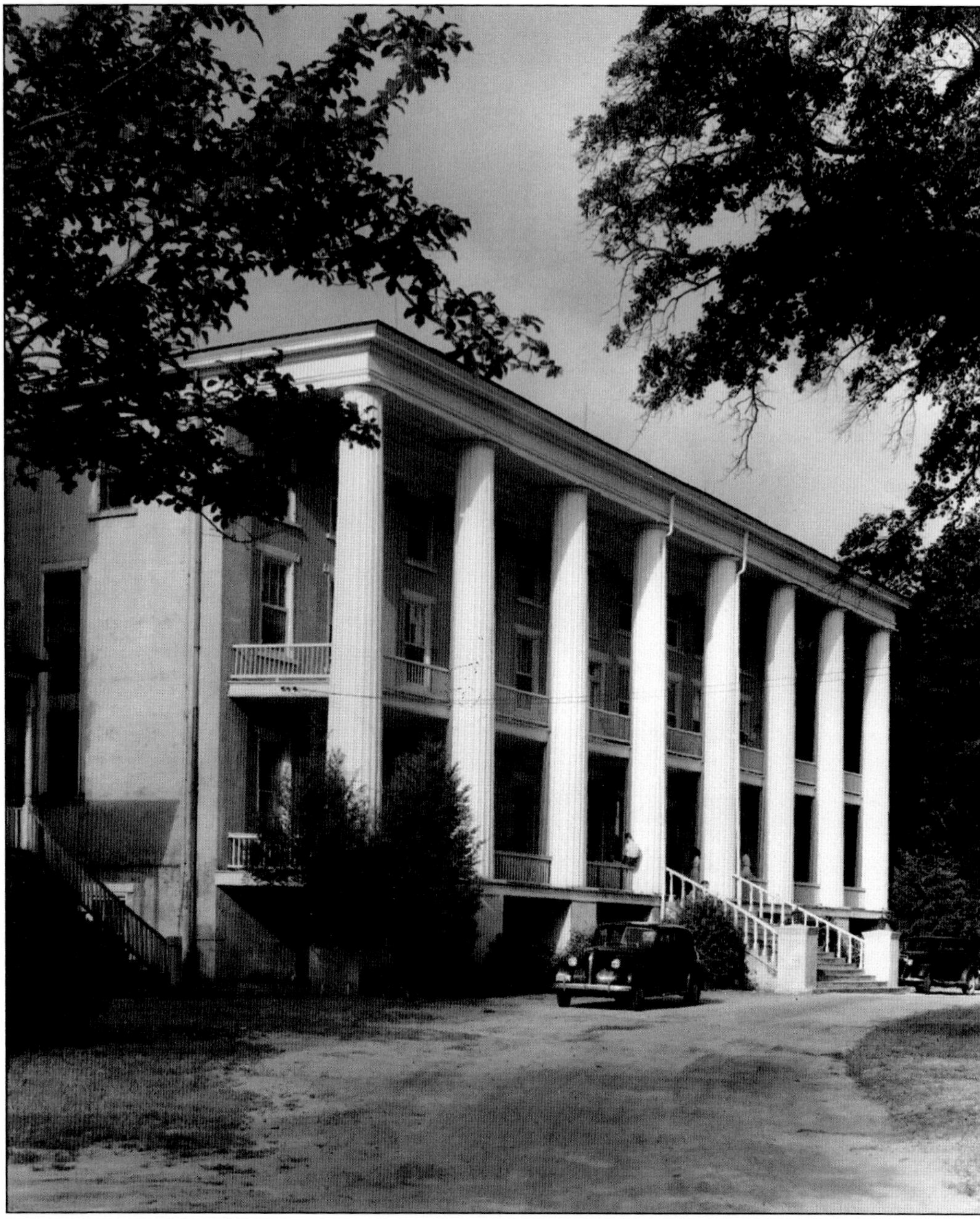

In 1940, Thomas T. Waterman, a well-known photographer, visited the campus and took this photograph of the McDowell Columns Building. In 1970 the McDowell Columns Building was listed on the National Register of Historic Buildings in the United States by the Department of the Interior. (Photograph courtesy of the Library of Congress.)

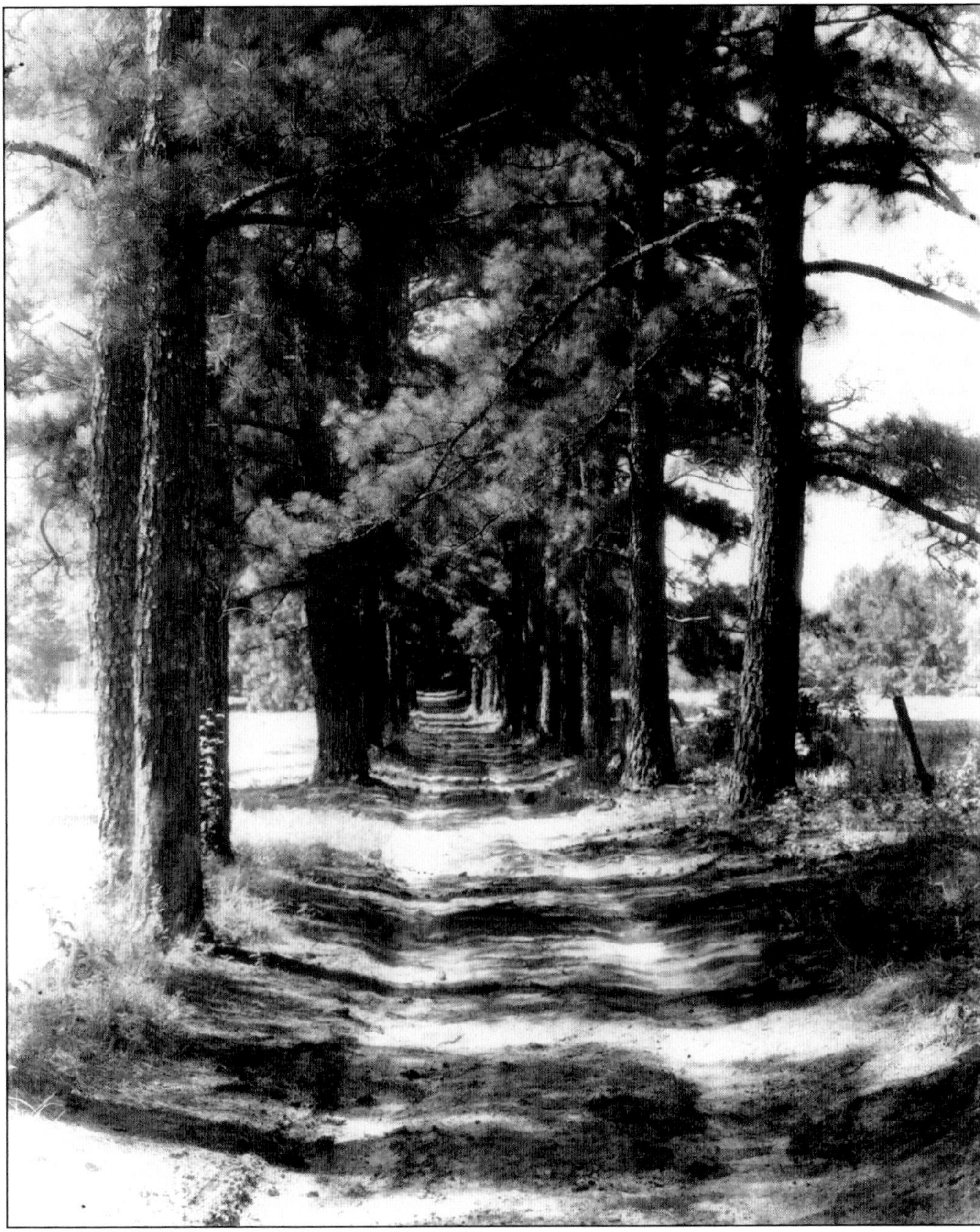

This is a 1942 view of Pine Drive on the right side of campus. In 2004 there are very few of the original pines remaining on Pine Drive as weather-related events have destroyed many of them.

Hertford County Herald, Ahoskie, N. C., Thursday, May 20, 1943

Chowan College Suspends Operation

Resignation of H. Haddon Dudley as president of Chowan college in Murfreesboro has been accepted by the board of trustees and operation of the college will be suspended for the duration of the war, J. Mayon Parker, chairman of the board of trustees, announced this week.

Use of the property has been offered to the government for any war use, but as yet the government has not taken the school's offer. Mr. Parker and G. T. Underwood have been named to negotiate with government representatives, if and when the government shows any interest in taking over the property.

Congressman Herbert Bonner has been acquainted with the action and has presented the matter to both war and navy secretaries.

Although to date the location and plant has not been found suitable for use by the government, the trustees still feel that there is a possibility the plant may be utilized in some way in the war effort.

The following statement was released by J. Mayon Parker:

"Facing realistically the abnormal conditions in all civilian life, and particularly as these affect the plans and lives of young people of the age when they would normally be entering college, that have been brought on by the necessities and upheaval of war, the trustees of Chowan college have decided in the course of practical wisdom to suspend the operation of Chowan college as an educational institution following the close of the present session for the duration of the war.

In the early 1940s, the United States saw its resources and manpower directed toward World War II. This drain of resources and manpower would ultimately lead the Board of Trustees of Chowan College to vote on May 17, 1943, to cease operations at the end of the term. Thus, at the end of the 1943 spring semester, Chowan College closed its doors. The campus and buildings were abandoned. Vital records were moved to Wake Forest College for safekeeping. This article on the closing of Chowan College appeared in the May 20, 1943 issue of the *Hertford County Herald*.

Three

CHOWAN RETURNS 1949

Chowan College reopened in 1949. Many thought the college would never reopen and, if it did, never survive. When the announcement was made in May 1943 that the college was going to close, numerous proposals were discussed regarding the fate of the property. Several people wanted to bury Chowan College forever and sell its property for development. Others attempted to move the college from Murfreesboro and reopen it in another location. Luckily, a loyal group wanted to revive Chowan on its original site. These supporters never gave up. Rev. Lonnie Sasser of Murfreesboro and the Murfreesboro Exchange Club were among many friends of the college who kept the Chowan dream alive. A triumphant reopening parade was held in Murfreesboro on May 13, 1949, and the college experienced unprecedented growth over the next four decades. Today, Chowan College is held in universal respect and admiration as a four-year institution that can truly be called a survivor.

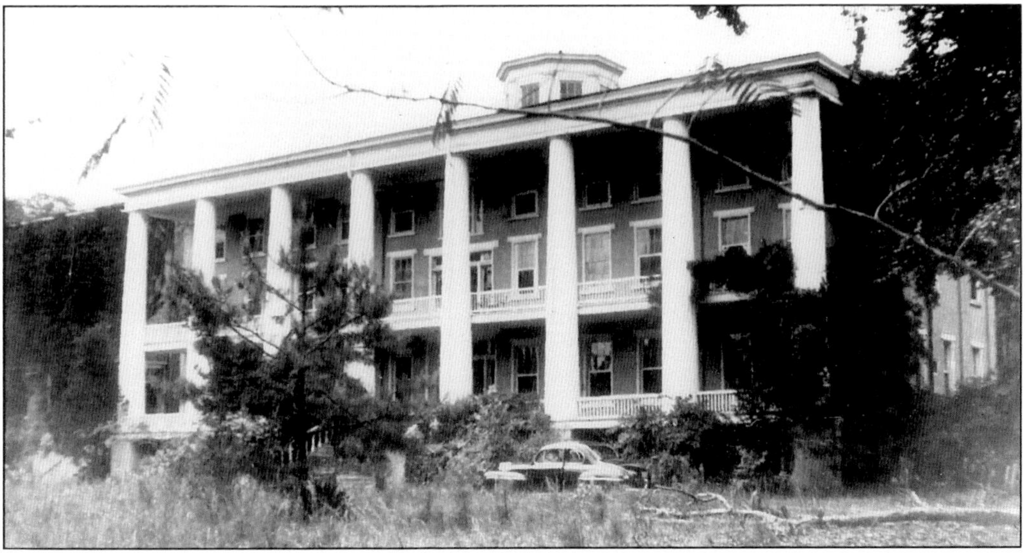

In the fall of 1948, Murfreesboro photographer Joel Holland visited the abandoned Chowan College campus and took this photograph. The college had been closed for over five years, and the campus and the Columns Building were beginning to show signs of serious neglect. The front campus was littered with downed trees and fallen limbs and overgrown with weeds and tall grass. The Columns Building—taken over by vines, snakes, birds, rats, bats, lizards, and dogs—had been heavily vandalized. A number of windows in the Columns Building had been broken out, its roof leaked in places, and much of its furniture was overturned or hauled away.

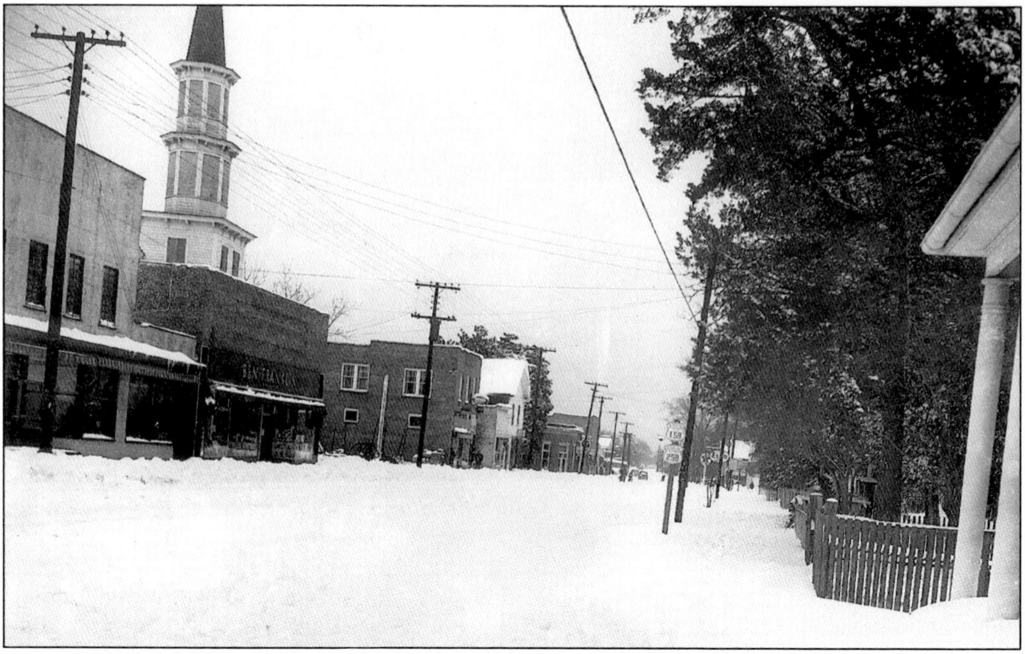

In the winter of 1948–1949 Joel Holland, a Murfreesboro photographer, captured the snow that blanketed the area. For this particular image, Mr. Holland stood on the corner of Main and Wynn Streets, shooting east. This photograph shows the Chowan College reopening fund-raising thermometer, seen as a white line on the left side of Main Street, just past the Methodist Church steeple. The fund-raising thermometer was erected on the side of Murfreesboro Pharmacy by the Murfreesboro Exchange Club, which played a significant role in the reopening of Chowan College.

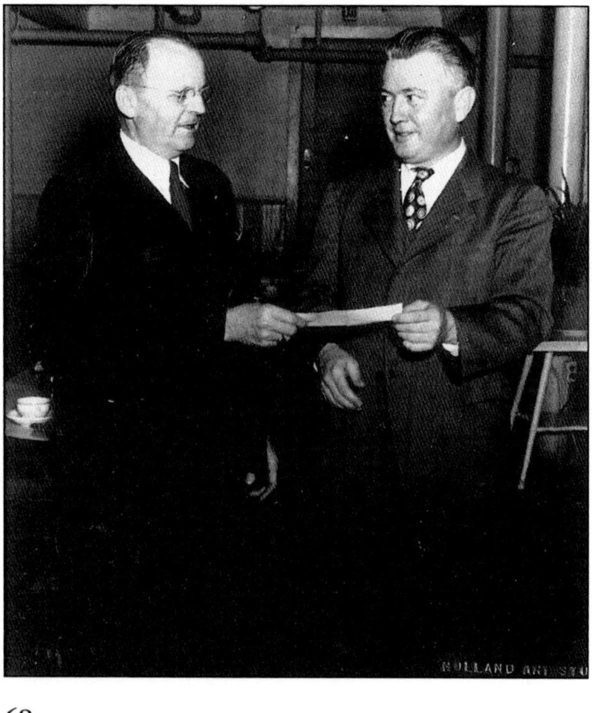

In February 1949, Murfreesboro Rotary Club president Herman Babb (right) presented a check to Chowan College president Dr. B.D. Bunn (left) for reopening the college. The Murfreesboro Rotary Club, like the Murfreesboro Exchange Club, the Murfreesboro Woman's Club, the Murfreesboro Board of Trade, and other civic clubs in the Murfreesboro area, played a major role in the reopening of Chowan College.

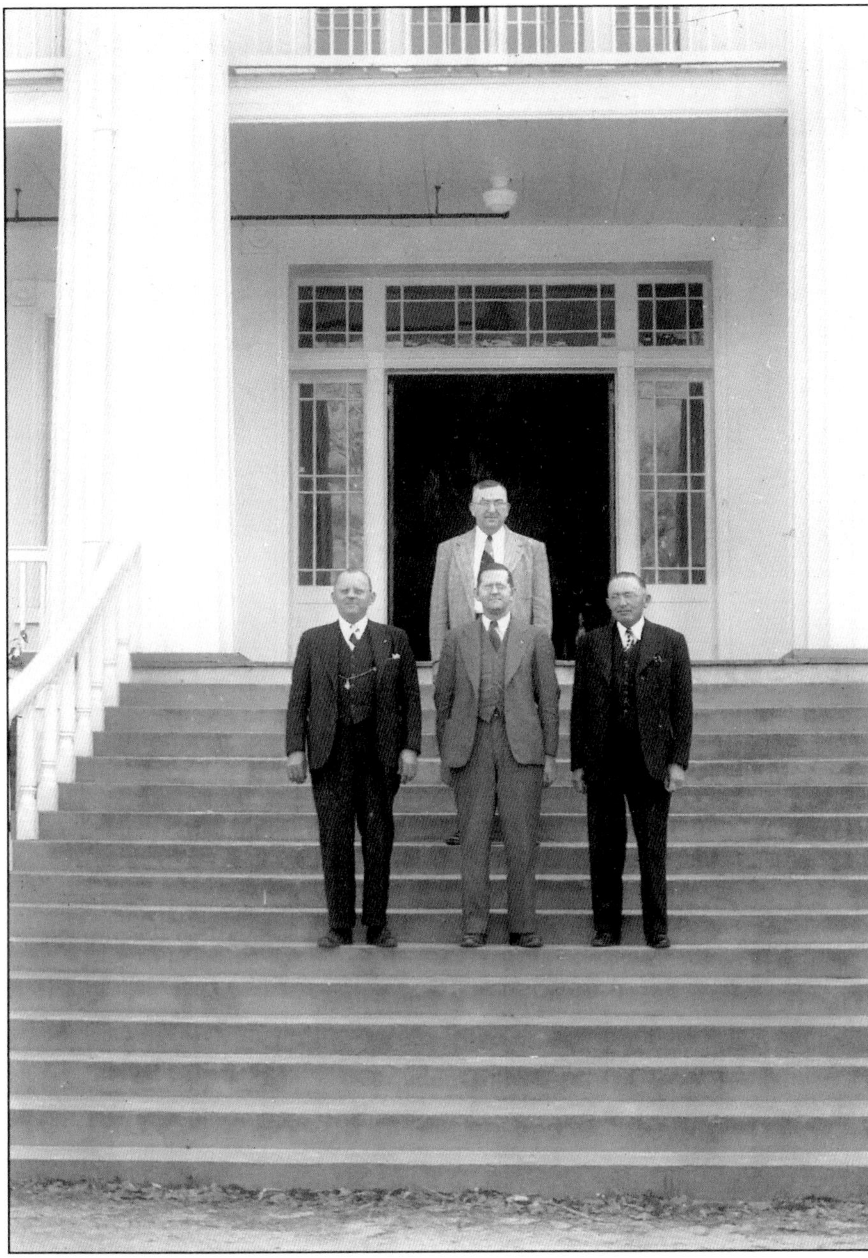

On March 11, 1949, the president and chief executive officers of Chowan College gathered on the steps of the Columns Building for this photograph, taken by Murfreesboro photographer Joel C. Holland. This picture shows, from left to right, Dr. B.D. Bunn, president of the college; Mr. Leon P. Spencer, business manager of the college; and Mr. E.W. Parker, chairman of the college's executive committee. Dr. Raleigh Parker, chairman of the college's board of trustees, stands in the back. Dr. Bunn served as president of the college from 1949 to 1951. Parker Hall, a nine-story residence hall, was constructed in 1970 and named in honor of Mr. Parker. Mr. Spencer was appointed business manager of the college on April 28, 1948, and served until 1951. The 1950 Chowan yearbook was dedicated to Mr. Spencer for his tireless work in getting the college ready for reopening.

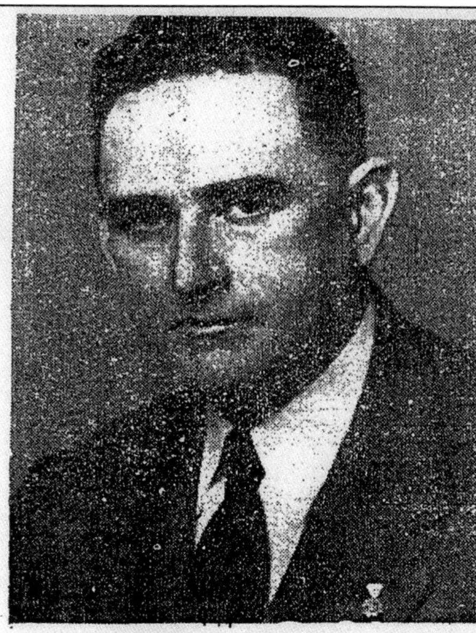

with Pride We Welcome You to Murfreesboro

Friday, May 13th, for the

Chowan College Centennial

—Hear Governor Kerr Scott

—See the Big Parade

—Hear Outstanding Political and Educational Figures

—Stroll the Lovely Campus of Historic Chowan

After many long months of hard work, it was announced that a reopening celebration for the college would be held on May 13, 1949, with North Carolina governor Kerr Scott heading the list of dignitaries. This advertisement for the reopening celebration appeared in the May 12, 1949 issue of *The Hertford County Herald*. One of the highlights of the reopening celebration was a mile-long parade down Murfreesboro's Main Street.

CHOWAN COLLEGE CENTENNIAL CELEBRATION

Friday, May 13, 1949

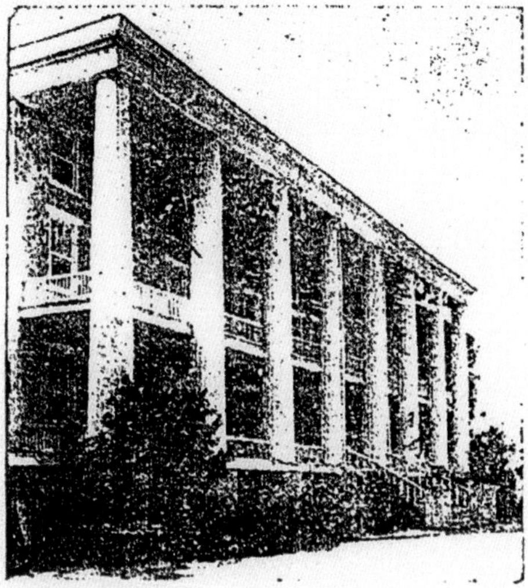

Theme: 'Chowan College—Yesterday, Today, Tomorrow'

+ PROGRAM +

10.30 A. M.—Mammoth Parade—Main Street of Murfreesboro. Scores of flags and banners—Lots of bands—Huge floats—Dignataries riding in 30 swanky new convertibles—Zany clowns—Pretty girls.

11.30 A. M.—Chowan College Auditorium. Hear Gov. Kerr Scott, Gov. William Tuck, Secretary of State Thad Eure, and many other distinguished guests.

1 P. M.—Lunch hour and Band Concert. Delicious box lunches will be sold in the new College Cafeteria for the minimum charge of 65c.

2 P. M.—Auditorium. Greetings from outstanding educational leaders, including Dr. Thurman Kitchin, Dr. S. M. Holton, Mr. Leslie Campbell, and Dr. J. Henry Highsmith. History of Chowan given by Dr. George W. Paschal. Recognition of alumni by classes.

The Daily News of Murfreesboro ran this advertisement for the reopening celebration in its May 11, 1949 issue. *The Daily News* publisher and editor, F. Roy Johnson, had run a number of articles concerning the reopening of Chowan College in earlier issues.

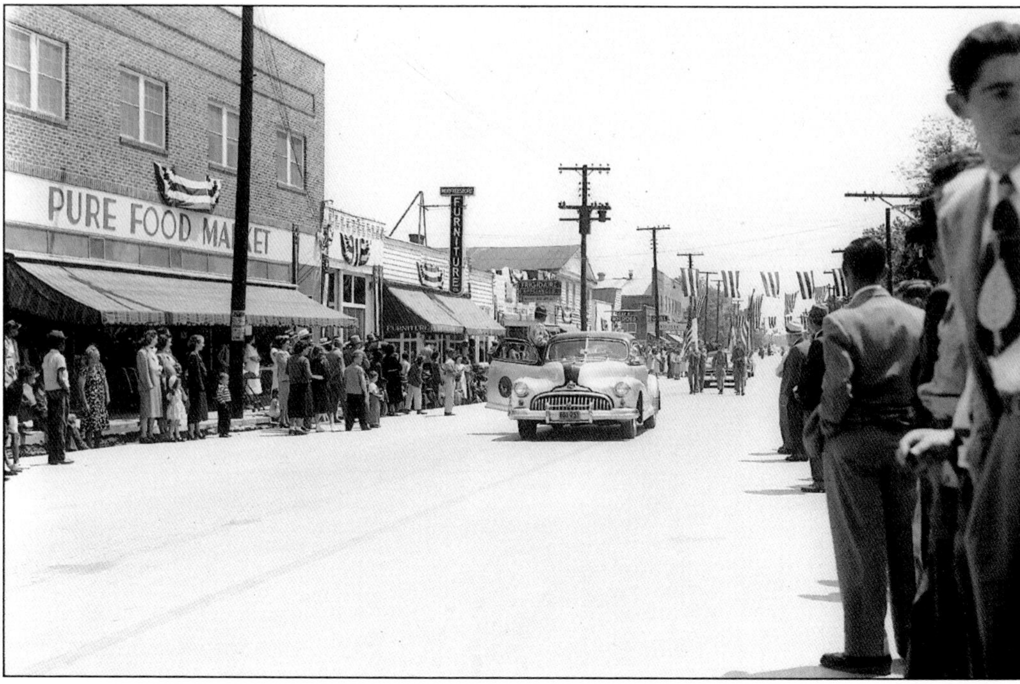

At 10:30 a.m. on the morning of May 13, 1949, a huge parade celebrating the reopening of Chowan College began in front of the Red Apple restaurant on East Main Street. The parade moved west onto Main Street and turned onto Liberty Street, then proceeded to the college campus. In this photograph, North Carolina Highway Patrol Sgt. A.W. Welch of Ahoskie heads the parade. (Courtesy of Conway Photo and Print Shop.)

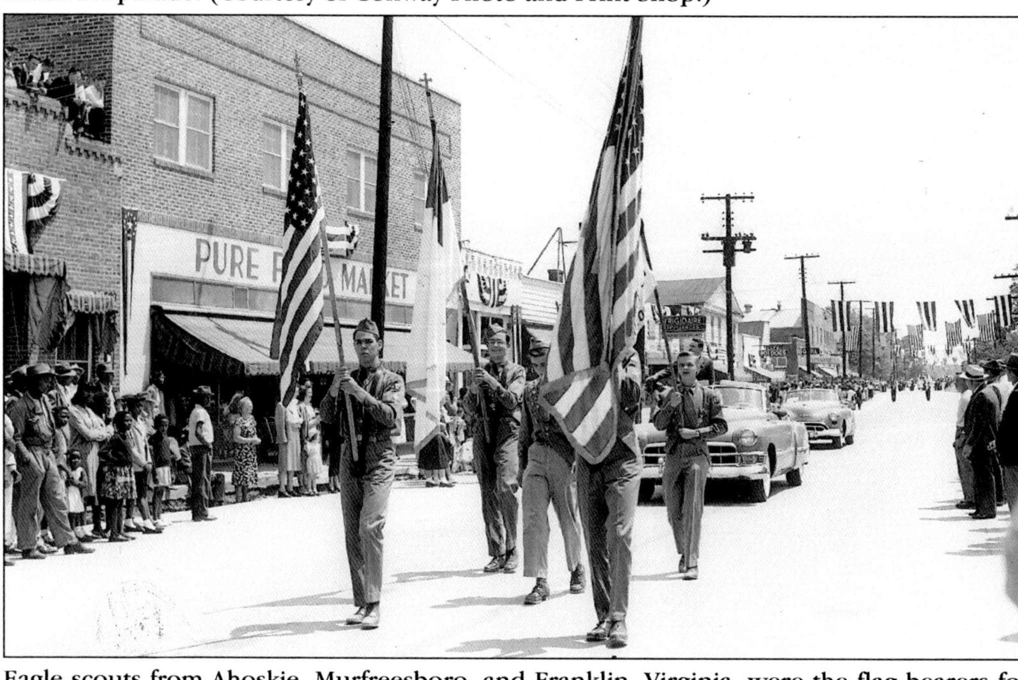

Eagle scouts from Ahoskie, Murfreesboro, and Franklin, Virginia, were the flag bearers for the parade. (Courtesy of Conway Photo and Print Shop.)

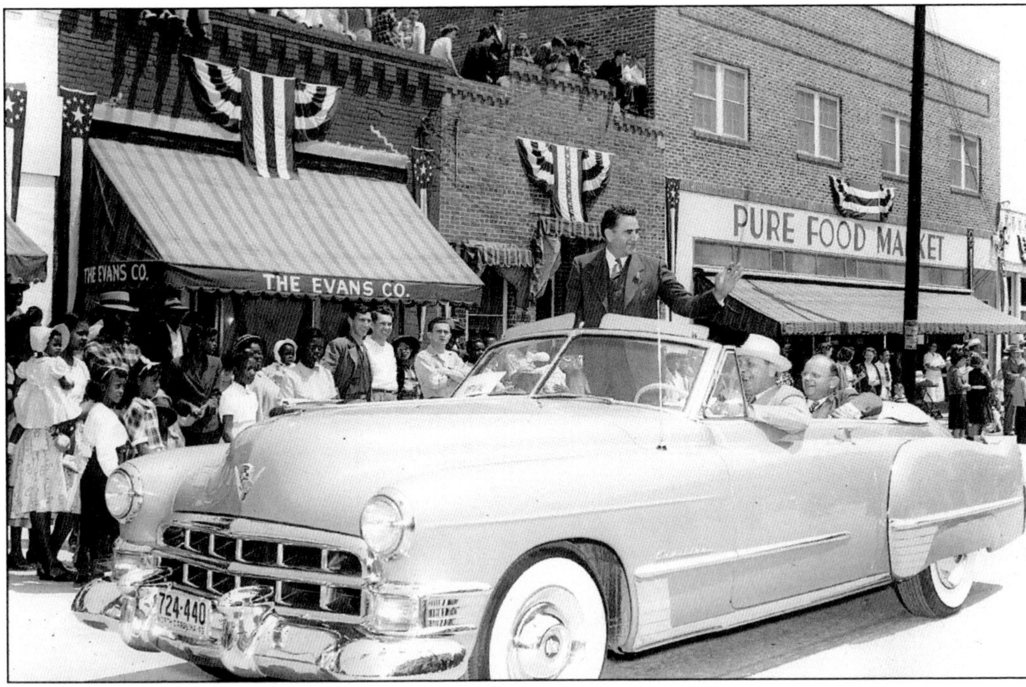

North Carolina governor Kerr Scott, principal speaker for the Chowan College reopening celebration, stands and waves to the crowd lining Murfreesboro's Main Street for the parade. In the backseat, behind the driver, is Dr. B.D. Bunn, president of the college. (Courtesy of Conway Photo and Print Shop.)

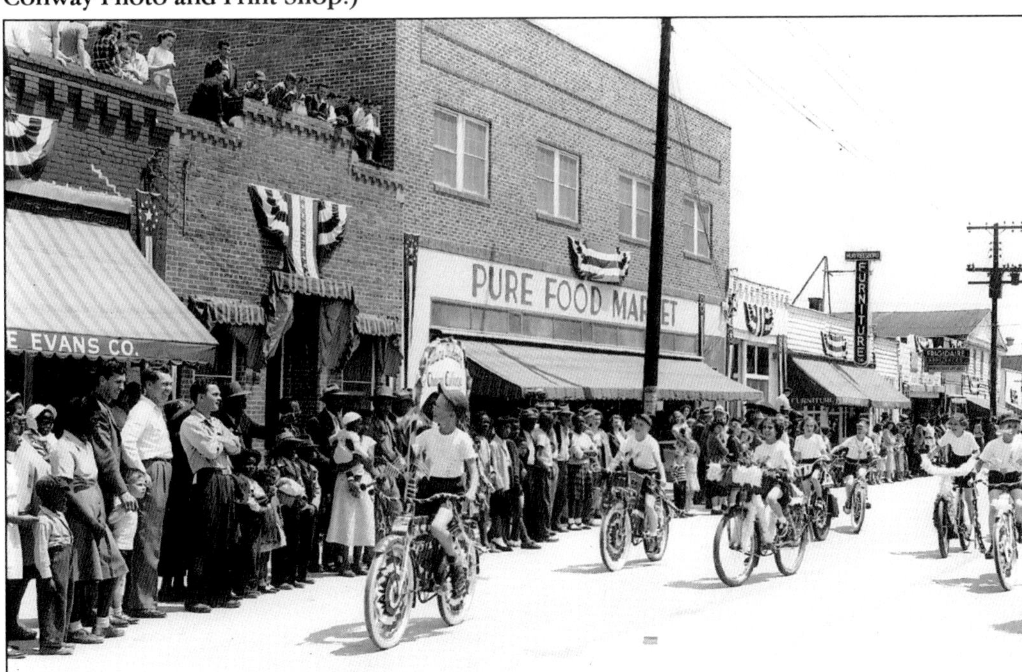

Area youngsters riding their decorated bicycles were part of the Chowan College reopening celebration parade. (Courtesy of Conway Photo and Print Shop.)

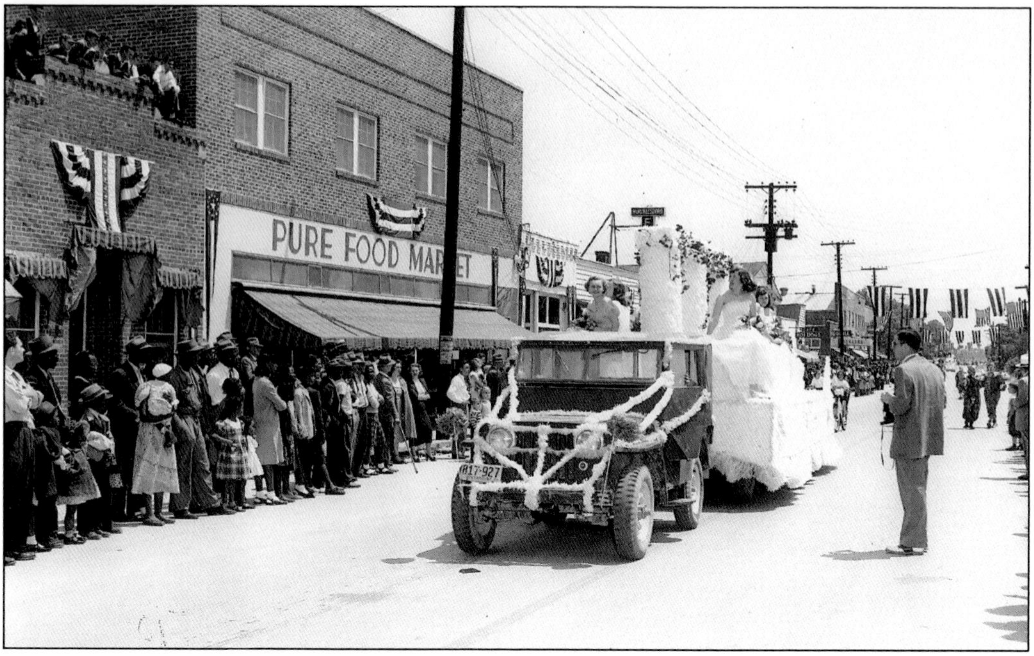

The reopening celebration parade contained a number of floats. (Courtesy of Conway Photo and Print Shop.)

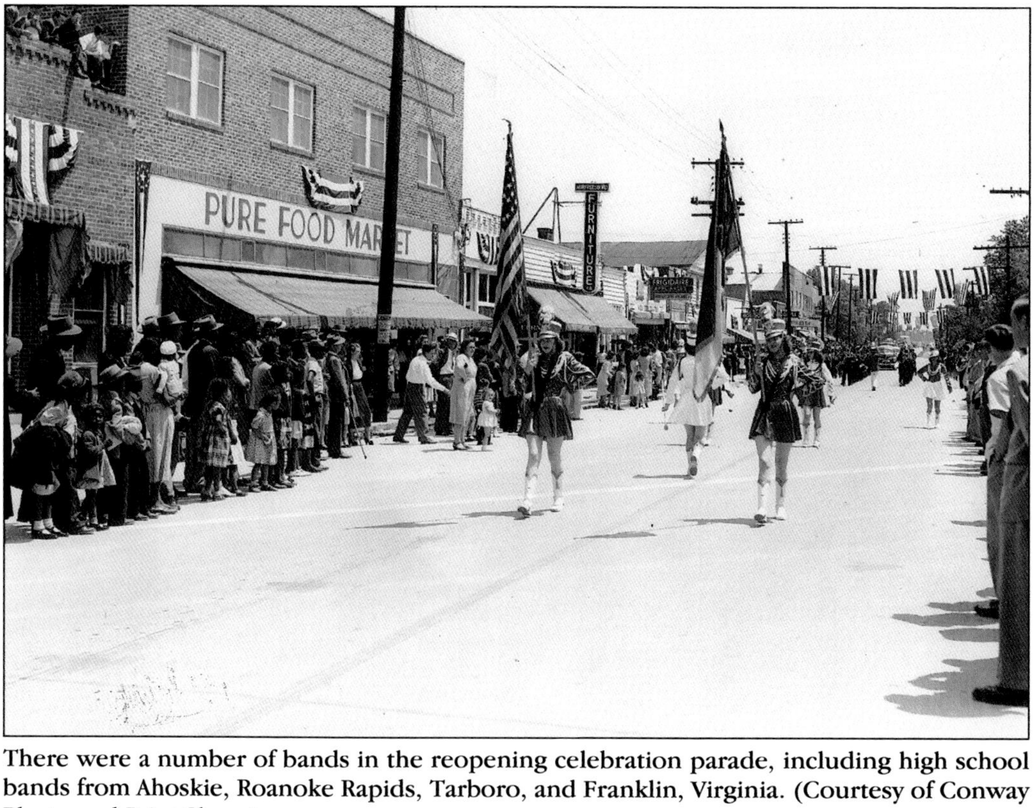

There were a number of bands in the reopening celebration parade, including high school bands from Ahoskie, Roanoke Rapids, Tarboro, and Franklin, Virginia. (Courtesy of Conway Photo and Print Shop.)

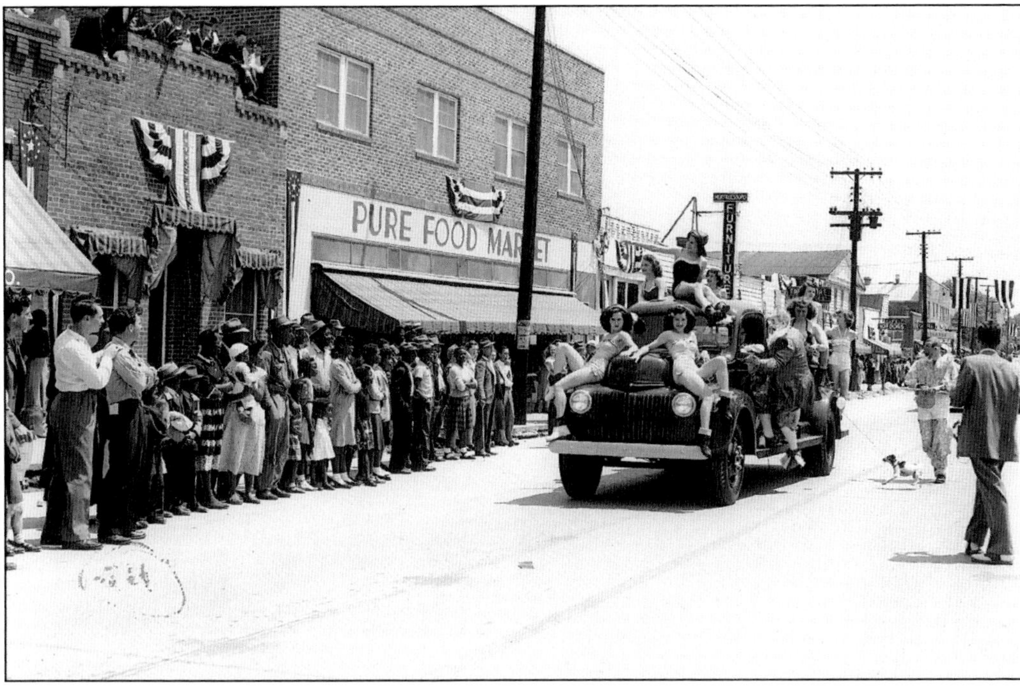

The Murfreesboro Fire Department provided transportation in the reopening celebration parade for a group of bathing beauties, seen here riding of one the fire trucks. (Courtesy of Conway Photo and Print Shop.)

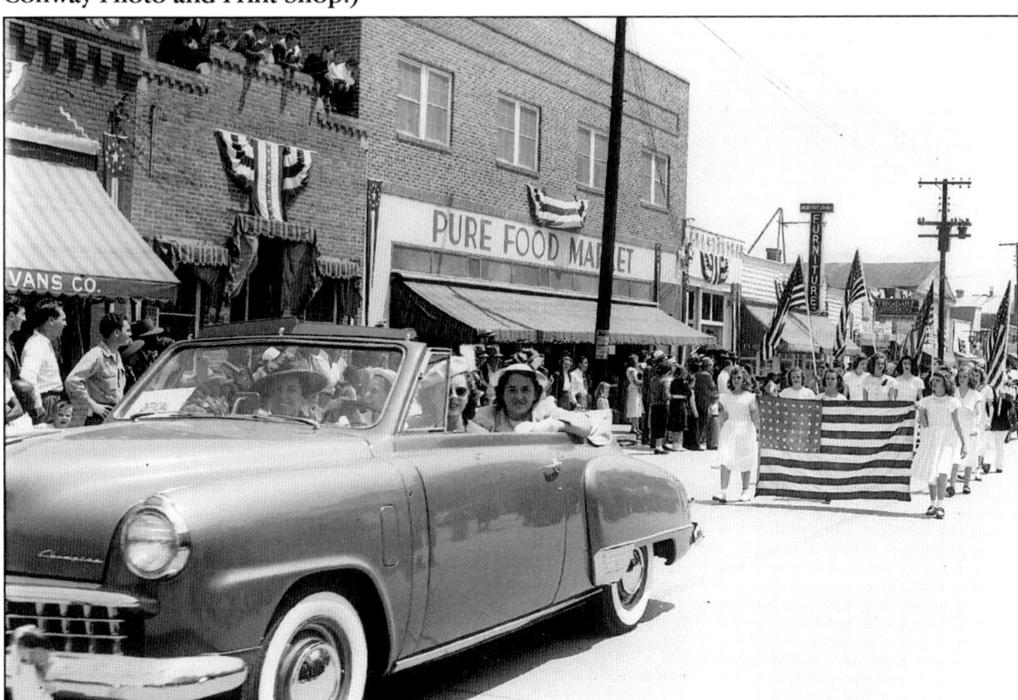

A new car is seen in front of the sixth and seventh grade Murfreesboro flag unit in the reopening celebration parade. (Courtesy of Conway Photo and Print Shop.)

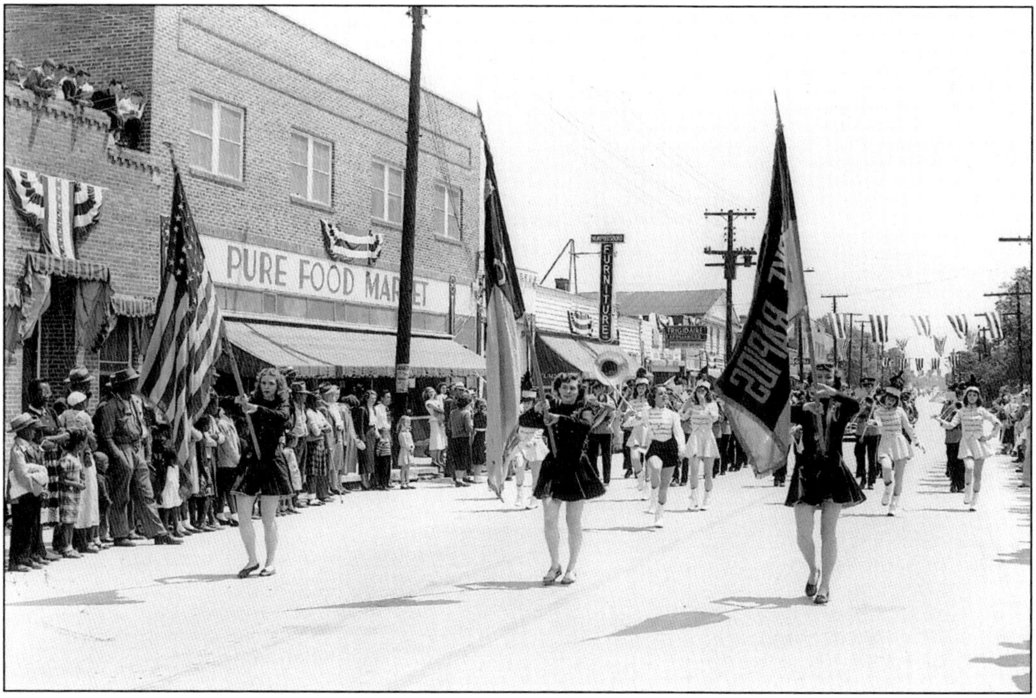

This is the Roanoke Rapids High School band appearing in the reopening celebration parade. (Courtesy of Conway Photo and Print Shop.)

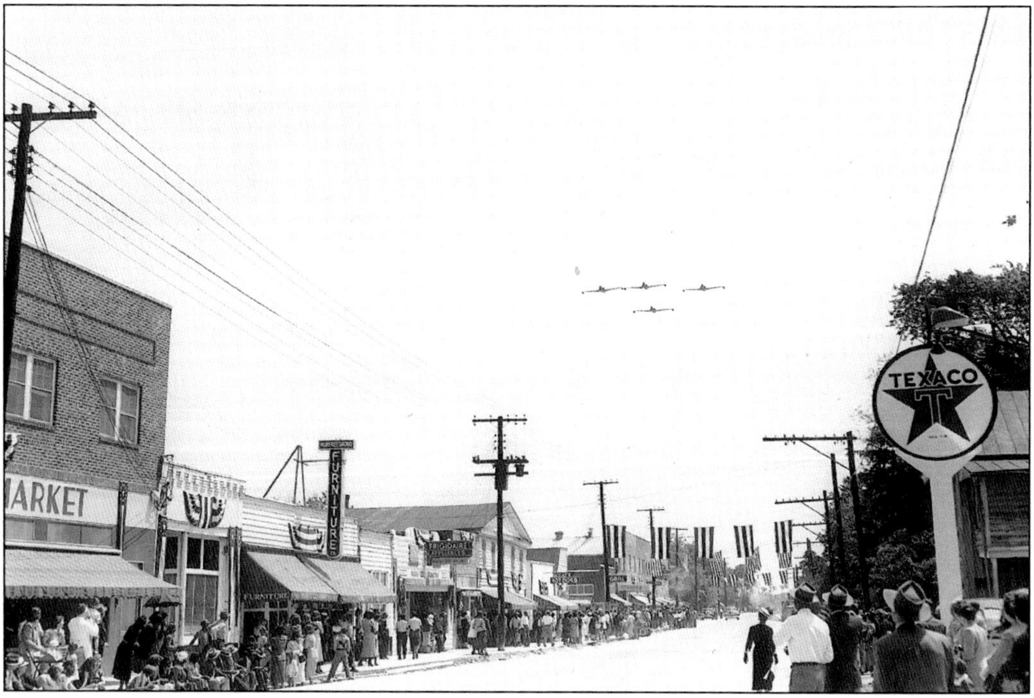

One of the highlights of the Chowan College reopening celebration parade occurred when four jets from Langley Air Force Base of Hampton, Virginia, flew over Main Street at 800 feet and 400 miles per hour. (Courtesy of Conway Photo and Print Shop.)

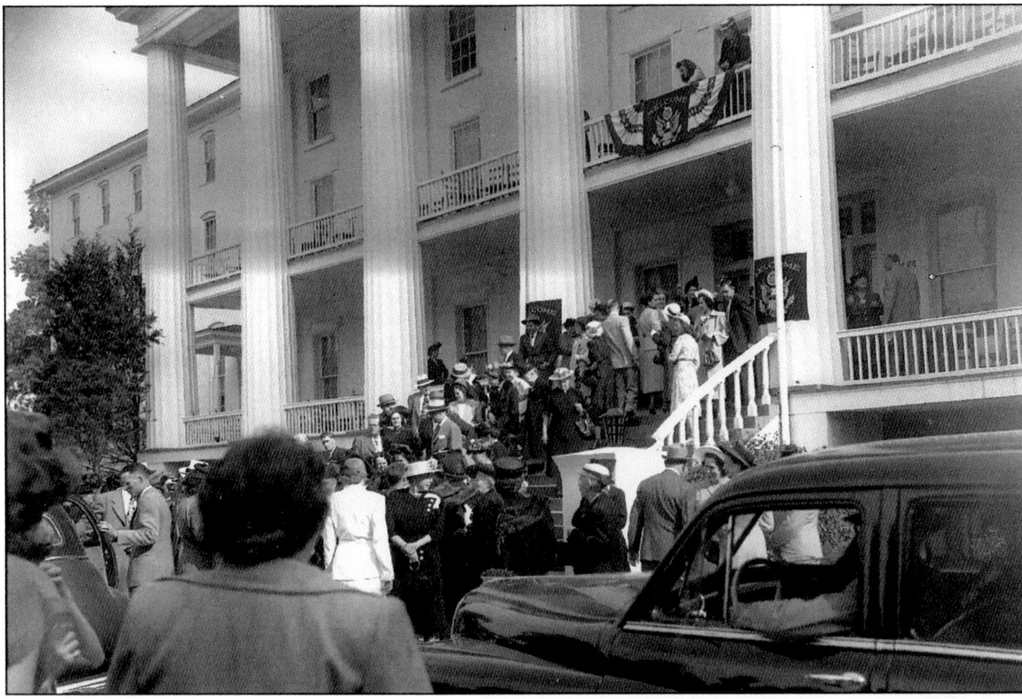

A standing room crowd turned out for the Chowan College reopening celebration on May 13, 1949. The crowd was so large that not everybody could get into the auditorium to hear the speakers. (Photograph by Joel C. Holland.)

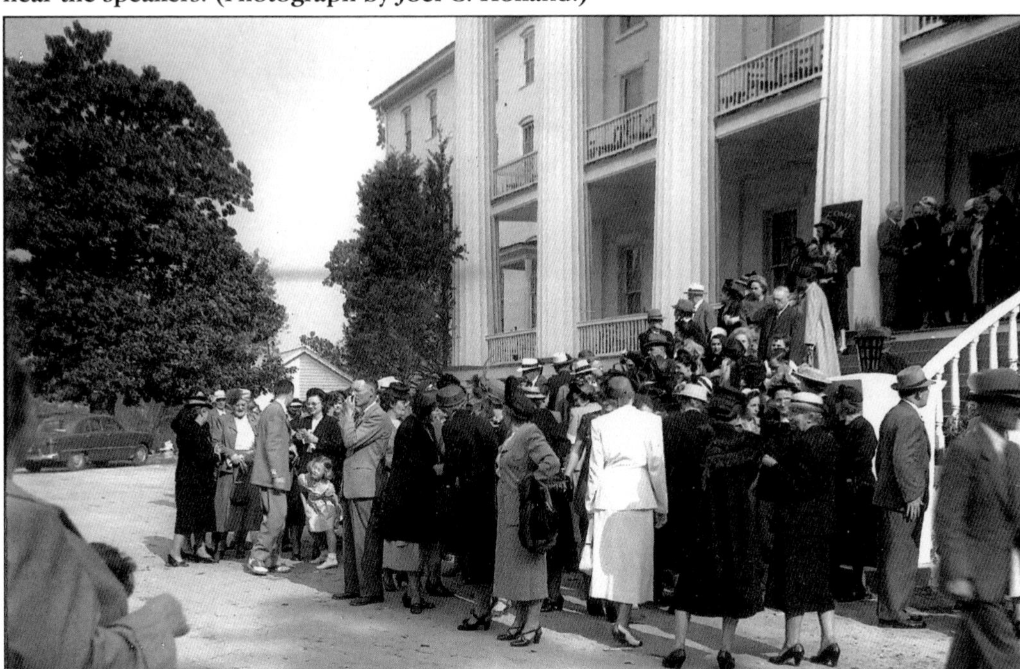

People from all walks of life attended the Chowan College reopening celebration, as it was a momentous occasion for the community.

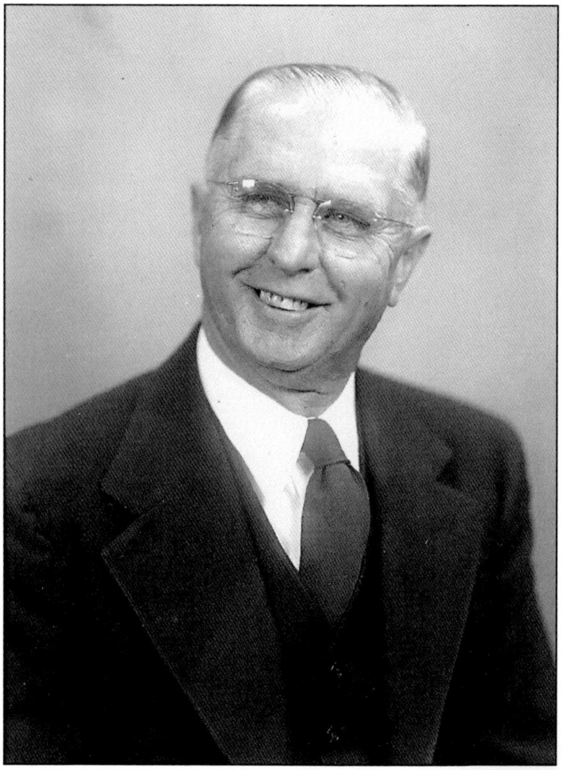

Many people played key roles in the reopening of Chowan College and none more so than Rev. Lonnie Sasser of Murfreesboro. Reverend Sasser was appointed director of the fund-raising campaign to reopen the college, and his efforts were exemplary. This author remembers as a young boy when Reverend Sasser visited Buckhorn Baptist Church and made an elegant plea for the church to support the reopening of Chowan College. The church and many members made financial contributions in support of the reopening of the college. (Photograph by Joel C. Holland.)

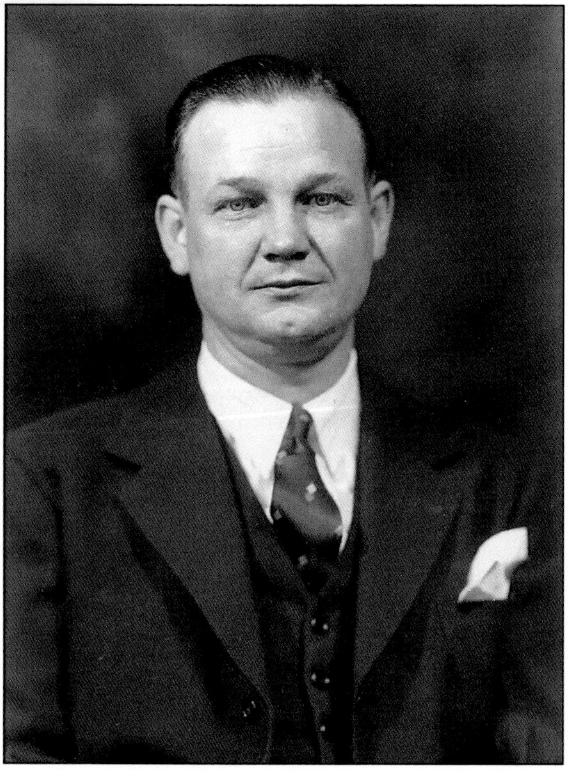

Chowan College has had many influential friends throughout its long history. Included in this group is the late Edwin Pierce Brown of Murfreesboro. Mr. Brown, an industrialist and Quaker, played a key role in the reopening of Chowan College. He used his influence and prestige to raise funds at crucial times to help the college. Mrs. Dorothy Heath Brown, a 1933 graduate of Chowan College, and her four children funded Friendly Place in front of Camp Hall in 1974 in honor of Mr. Brown, who died in 1972. (Photograph by Joel C. Holland.)

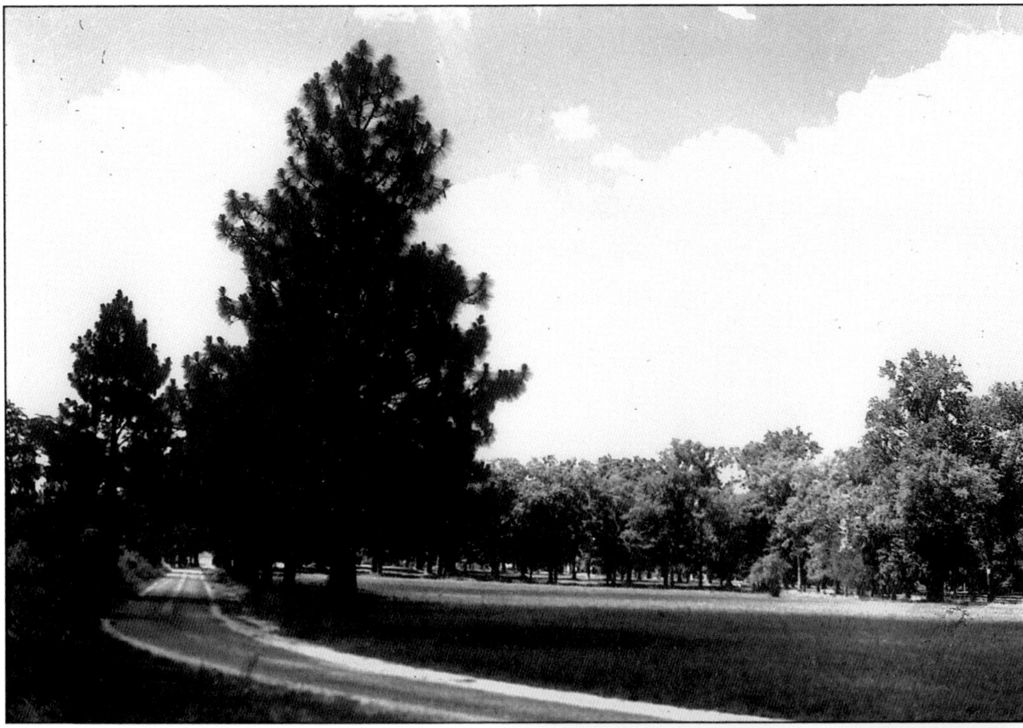

This is a 1950 view of Pine Drive on the left side of the front campus.

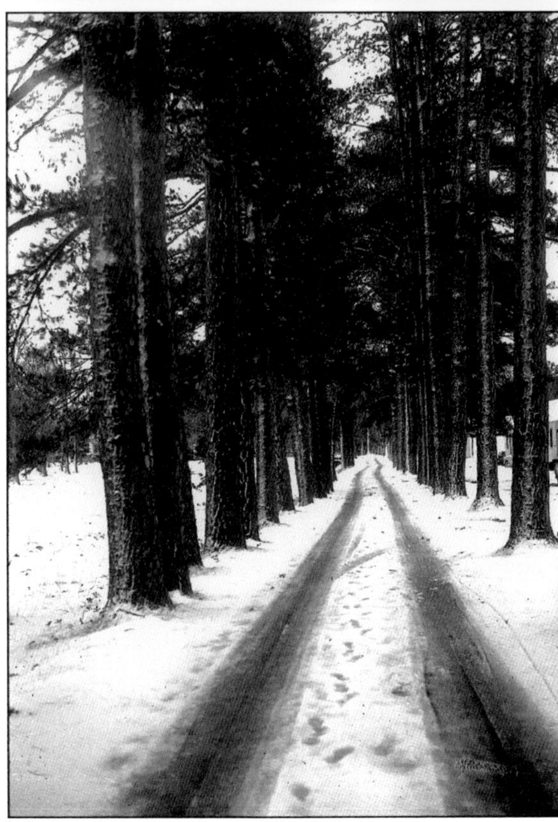

This 1950 view of Pine Drive on the right side of the front campus shows the location of four cottages that were built in 1948–1949 to house boys. Funds for the construction of the four cottages were loaned to the college by three Murfreesboro residents: Mr. Elwood W. Parker, Dr. Lokie M. Futrell, and Dr. Wilson Fleetwood Britt. The cottages were later moved to provide space for the construction of Mixon Hall. (Photograph by F. Roy Johnson.)

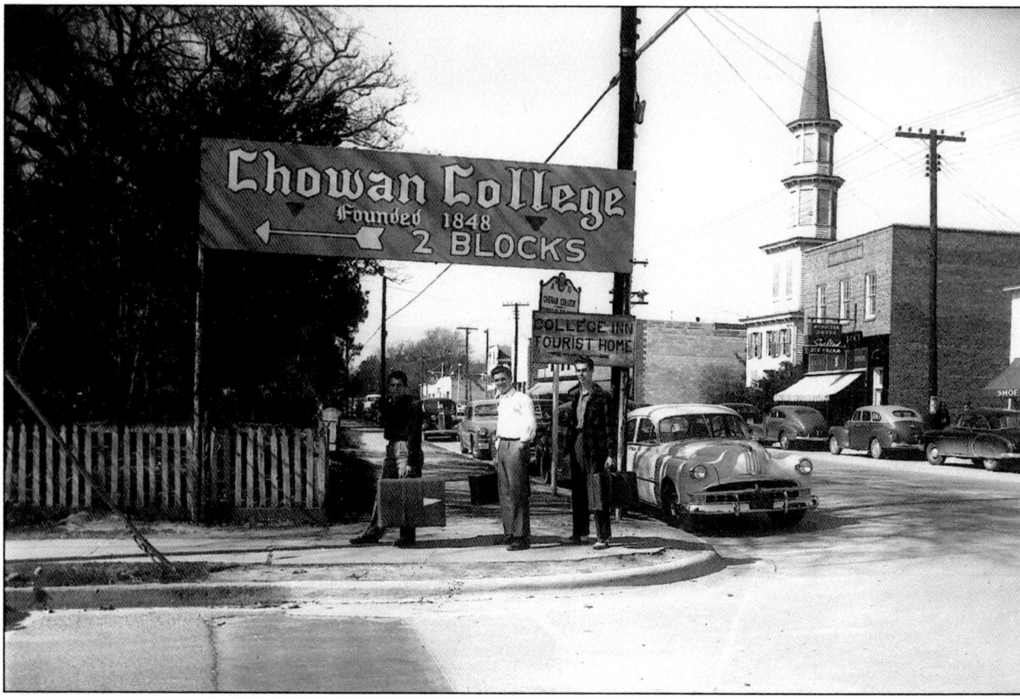

This sign, which stood at the corner of Main and College Streets, was erected by the Murfreesboro Board of Trade in October 1949. (Photograph by F. Roy Johnson.)

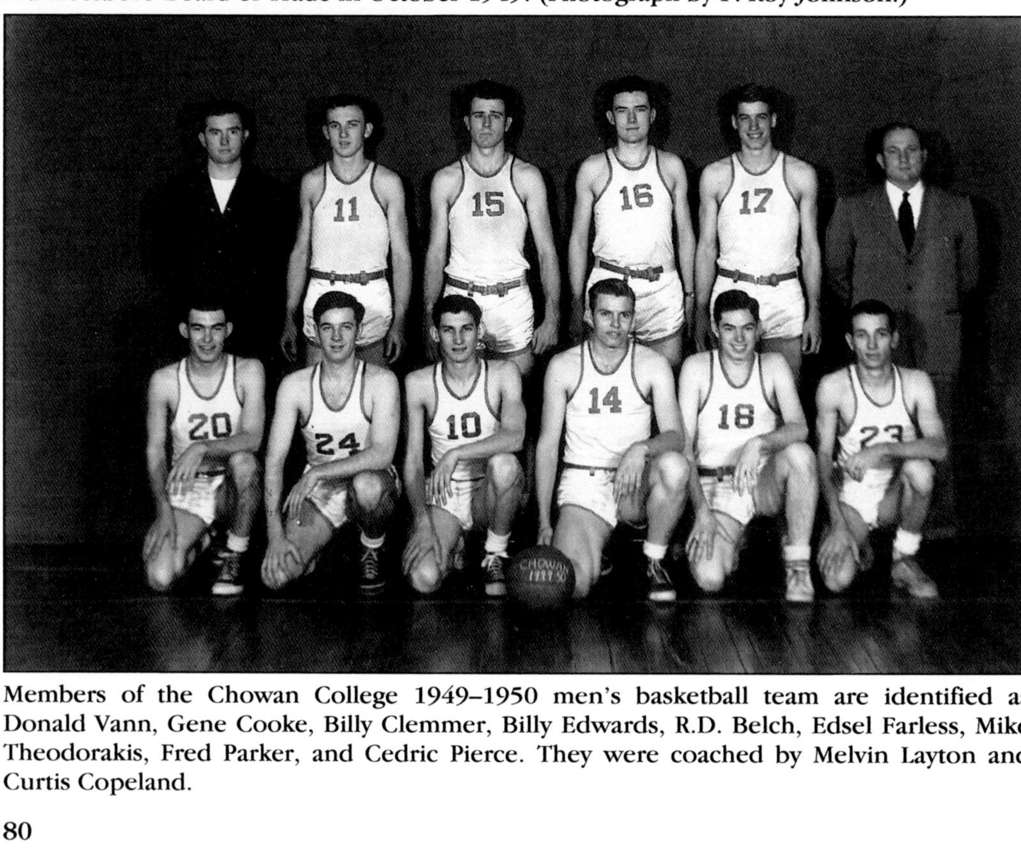

Members of the Chowan College 1949–1950 men's basketball team are identified as Donald Vann, Gene Cooke, Billy Clemmer, Billy Edwards, R.D. Belch, Edsel Farless, Mike Theodorakis, Fred Parker, and Cedric Pierce. They were coached by Melvin Layton and Curtis Copeland.

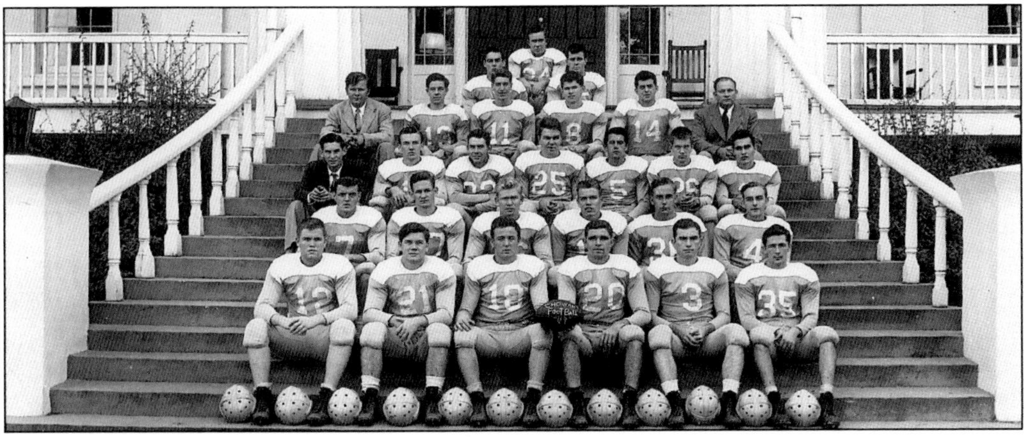

The 1949 Chowan College football team members are, from left to right, (first row) Lu White, Joe Butler, Louis Ivey, Lonnie Harrell, Edsel Farless, and Edward Harper; (second row) Vance Stewart, Clarence Alexander, Billy Midget, Cedric Pierce, Fred Williams, and E.B. Sherrin; (third row) Jay Wilcox, Fred Parker, Thomas Brown, David Edwards, Raymond Bass, Jimmy Coker, and Bobby Dough; (fourth row) Willie Wiggins, Curtis Copeland, Billy Clemmer, Earl Rock, Herman Hooker, and Coach Melvin Layton; (fifth row) Jack Spivey and Gene Cooke.

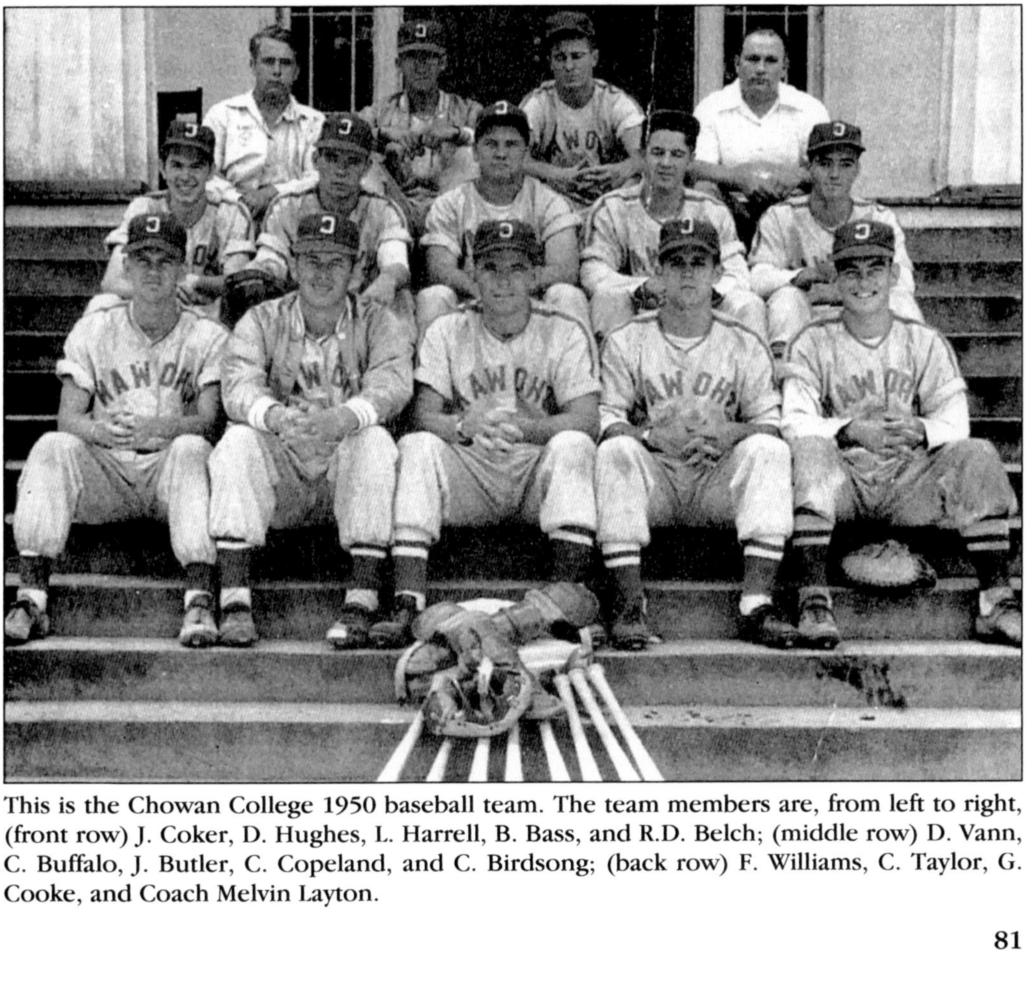

This is the Chowan College 1950 baseball team. The team members are, from left to right, (front row) J. Coker, D. Hughes, L. Harrell, B. Bass, and R.D. Belch; (middle row) D. Vann, C. Buffalo, J. Butler, C. Copeland, and C. Birdsong; (back row) F. Williams, C. Taylor, G. Cooke, and Coach Melvin Layton.

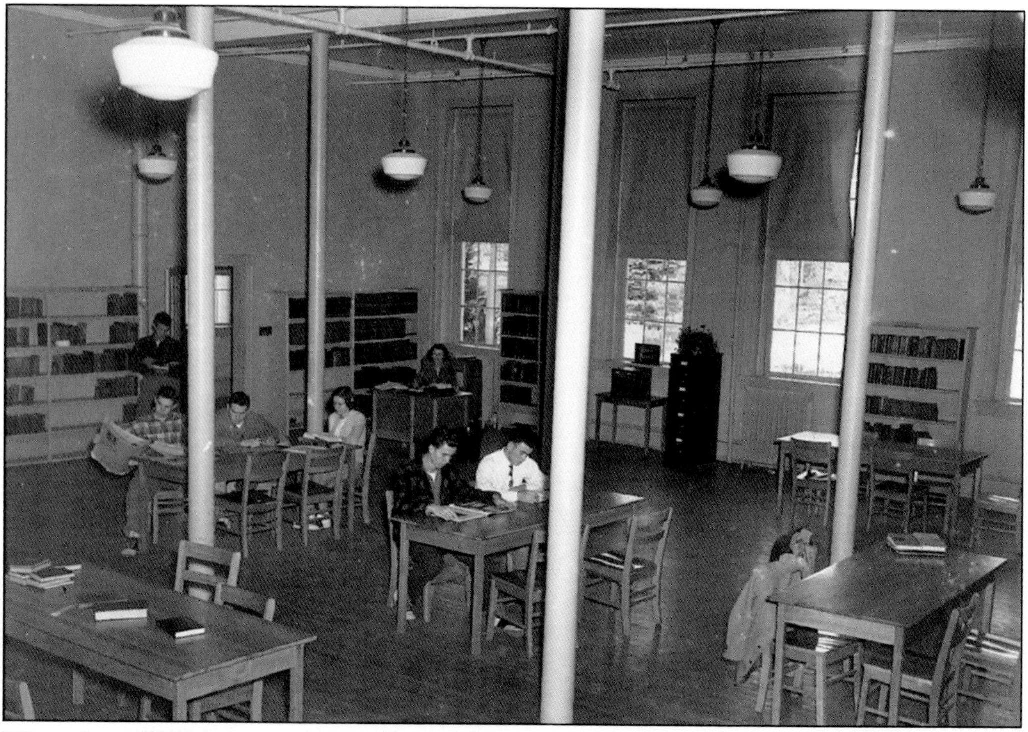

When the college reopened in 1949, the library was located in the 1906 East Wing.

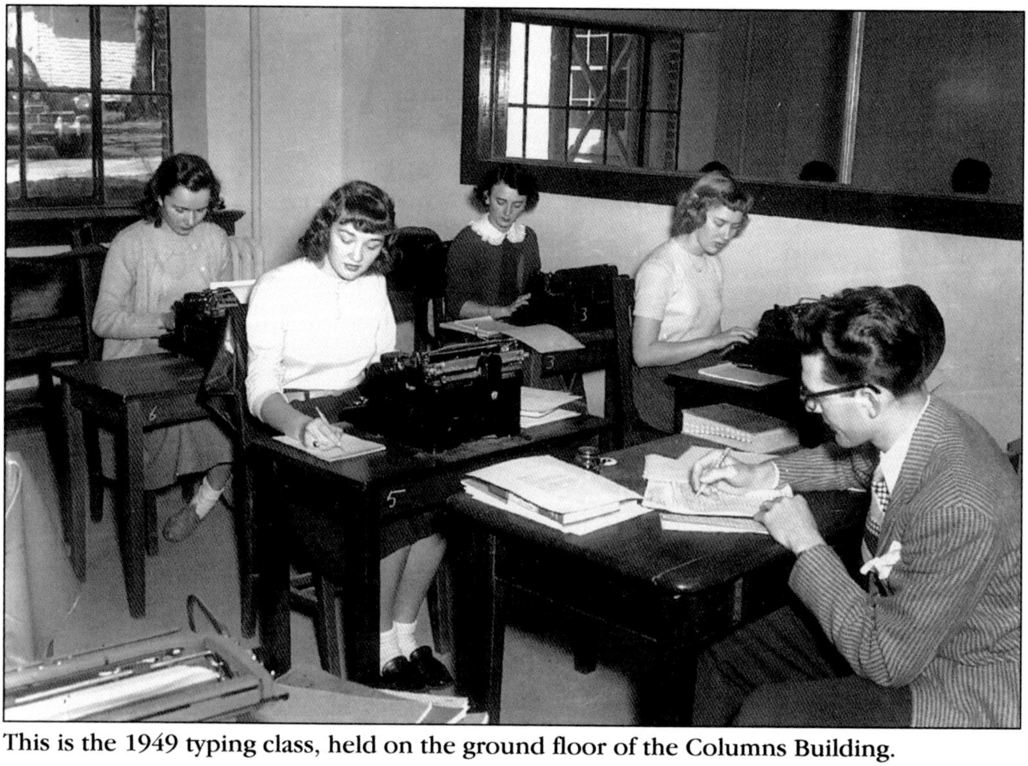

This is the 1949 typing class, held on the ground floor of the Columns Building.

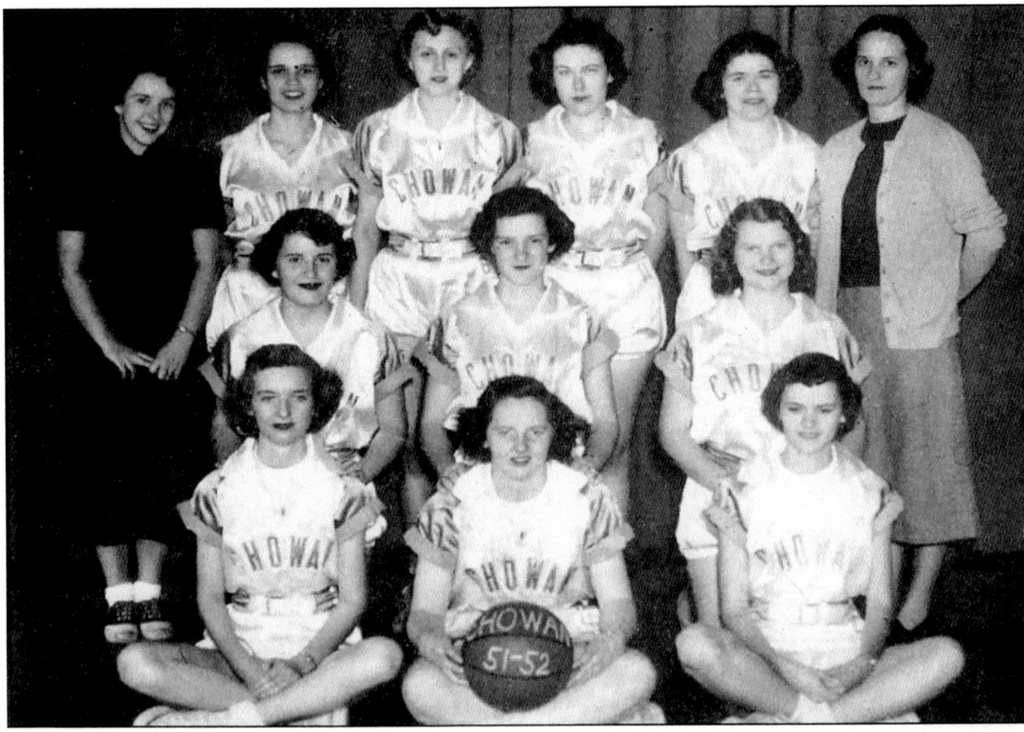

Here is the Chowan College 1951–1952 girl's basketball team. They are, from left to right, (front row) Peggy Turner, Babara Guyton, and Maybelle Bryant; (middle row) Jean Spruill, Marjorie Jenkins, and Josephine Futrell; (back row) Peggy Wiggins, Anne Edwards, Bois Bobbitt, Pearl Edwards, Margaret Pruden, and Coach Josie Keeter.

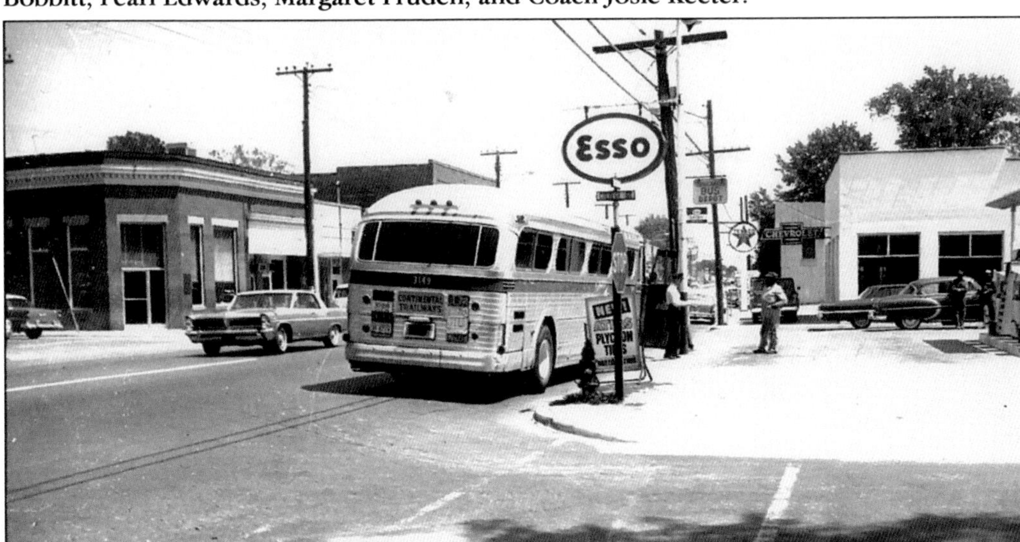

After the college reopened in 1949, the Trailways bus was a popular means of transportation for students coming to Murfreesboro. For many years, the bus station was located in Mr. Harry Underwood's Esso service station, which stood on the corner of Main and College Streets. When that station closed, the bus station moved to Mr. Walter Burke's Texaco Station, on the corner of Main and Liberty Streets. (Photograph by F. Roy Johnson.)

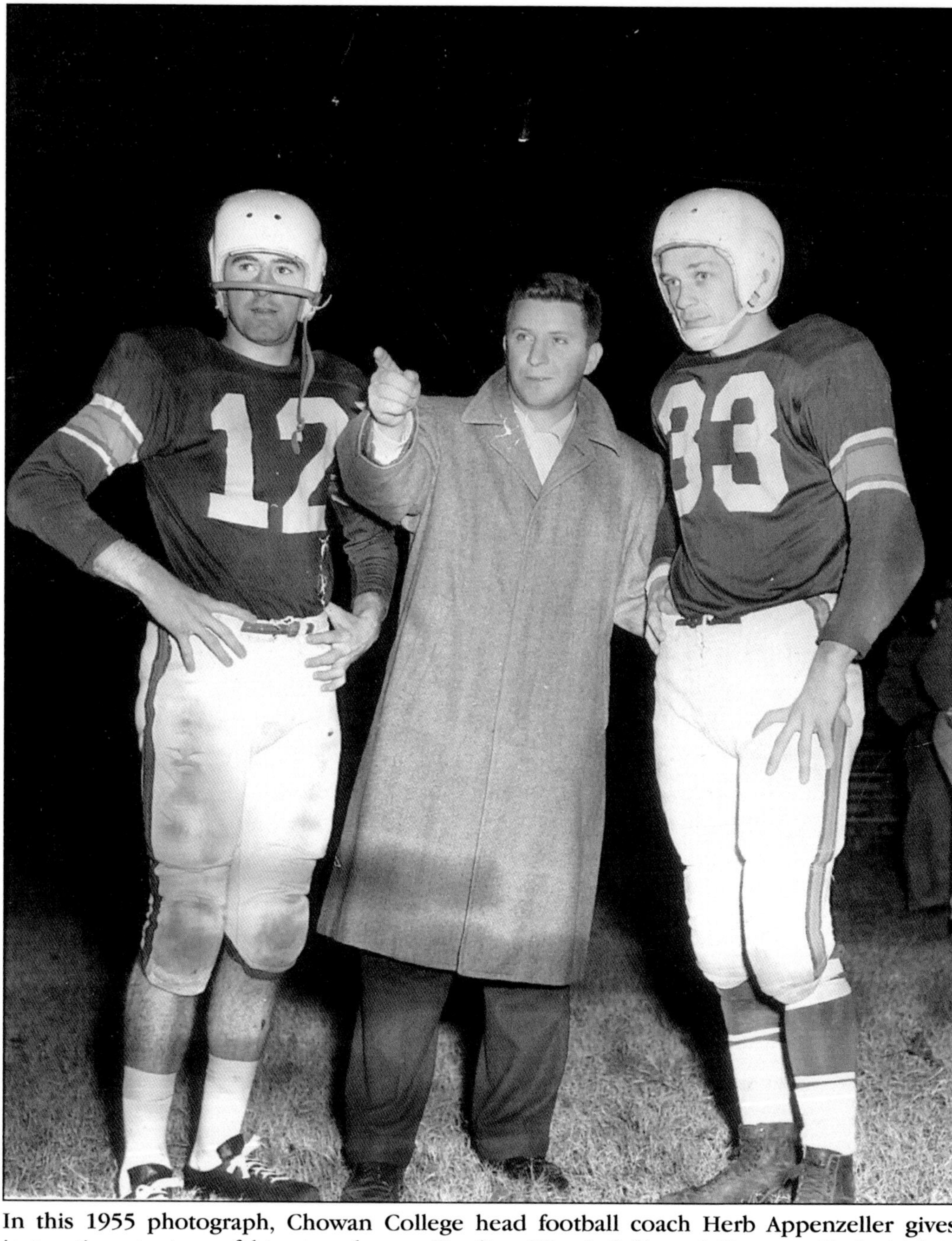

In this 1955 photograph, Chowan College head football coach Herb Appenzeller gives instructions to two of his star players, Harding Wood (left) and Herman Clark (right). Coach Appenzeller left Chowan in 1957 to become head football coach at Guilford College. He later became Guilford's athletic director. Herman Clark and several of Coach Appenzeller's Chowan players transferred to Guilford, where they started for the Guilford College football team.

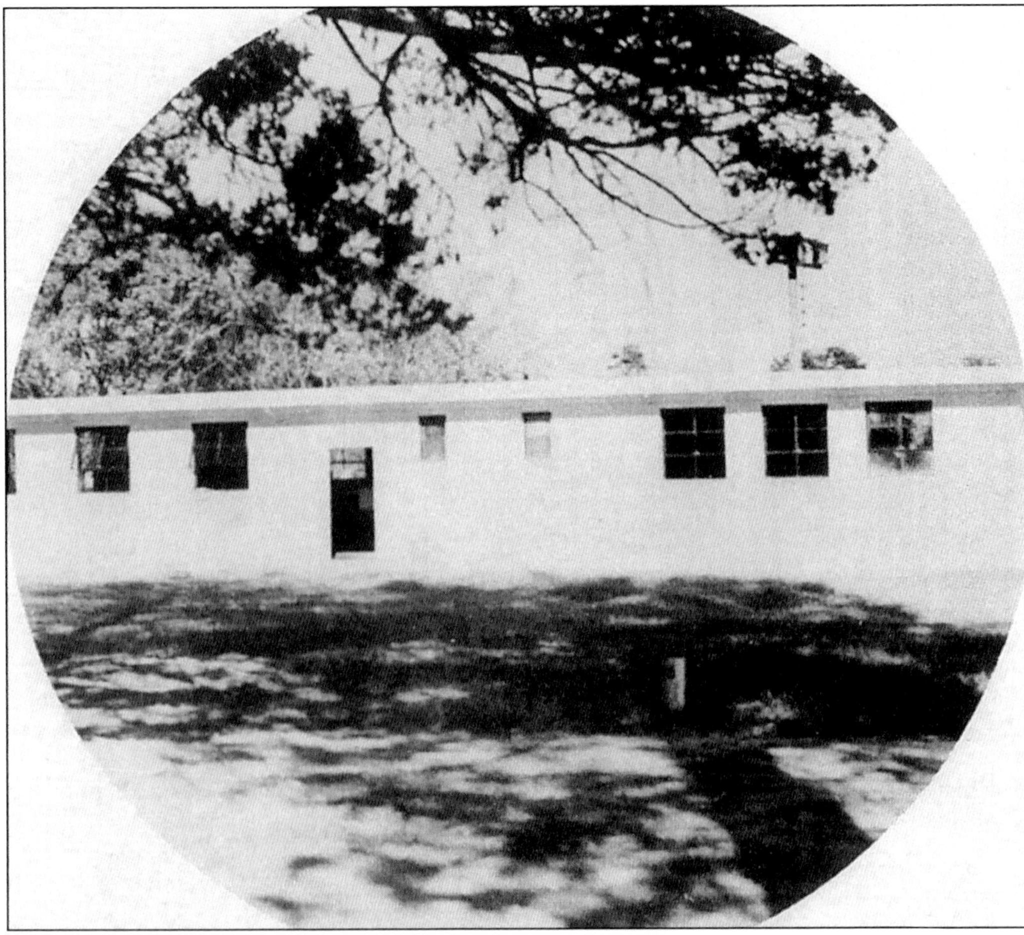

This is a 1954 photograph of the original graphic arts building, constructed in 1953.

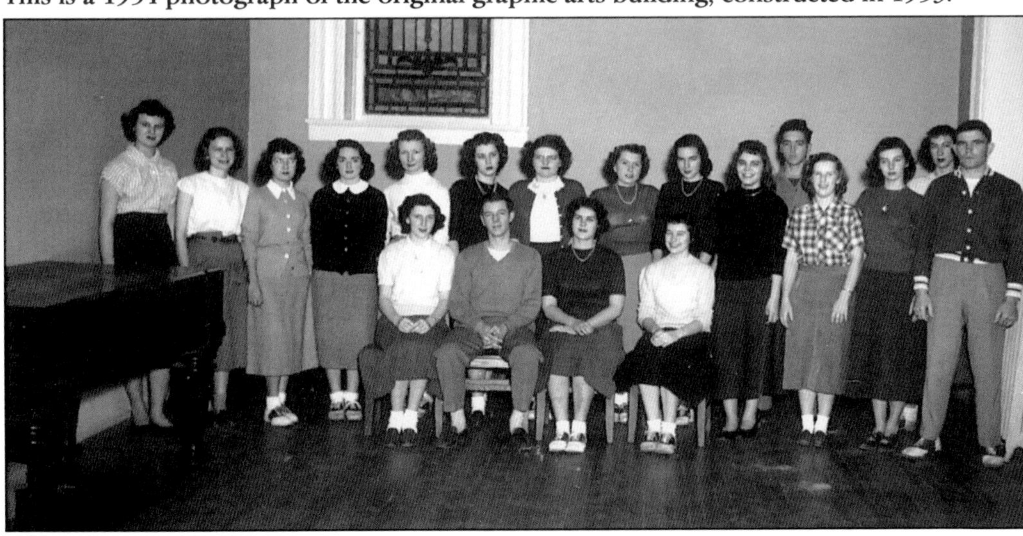

This is a mid-1950s photograph of a group of students in one of the parlors on the second floor of the Columns Building. (Photograph by Joel C. Holland.)

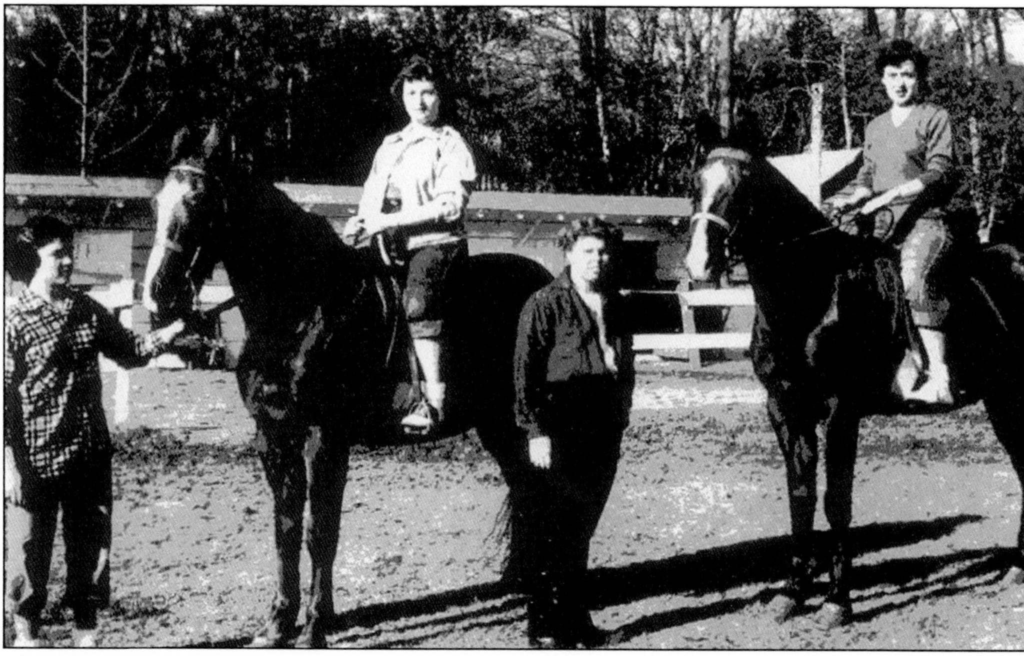

This is a 1955 photograph of some of the students enrolled in the college's horseback riding program. They are, from left to right, Eva Wrenn Williams, Barbara Thorne, Judy English, and Barbara Edwards. The horse stables were located in a wooded area to the left of the Helms Center. This area has since been covered by a parking lot associated with the proposed new football stadium. The horseback riding program was discontinued in the 1960s.

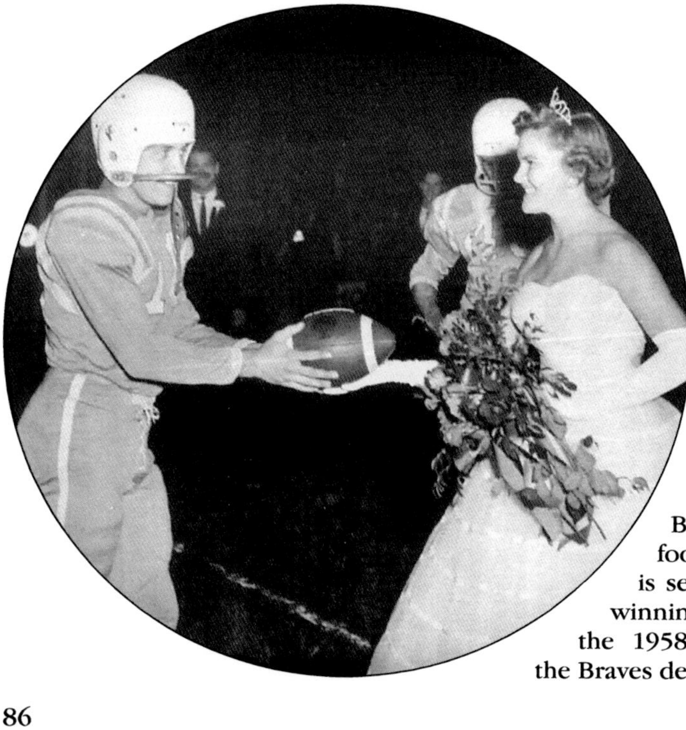

Bill McCants, a Chowan football player from Delaware, is seen here presenting the game winning football to Reba Hale, the 1958 Homecoming Queen, after the Braves defeated Wesley College 21–7.

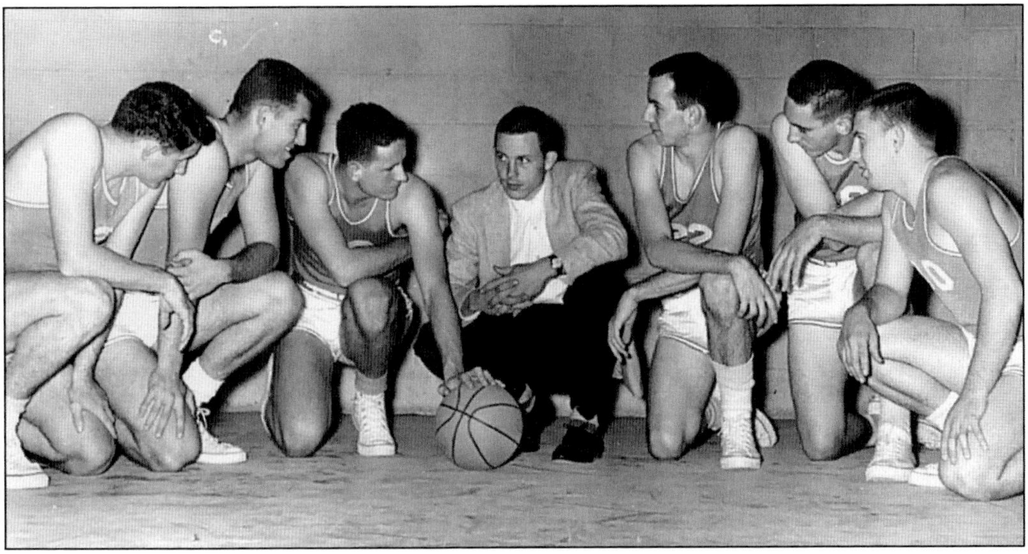

Chowan College 1959 men's basketball team was coached by Jim Garrison, who joined the Chowan faculty the previous year.

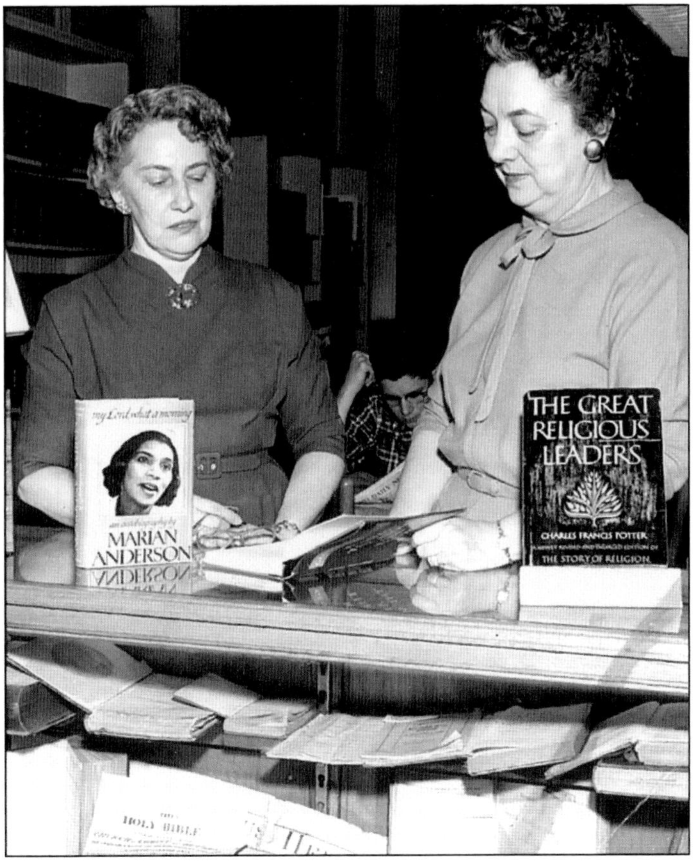

In 1960, the Chowan library was still housed in the 1906 East Building. The librarians were, on the left, Mrs. Lois Cadle, assistant, and Mrs. Neva Campbell, librarian.

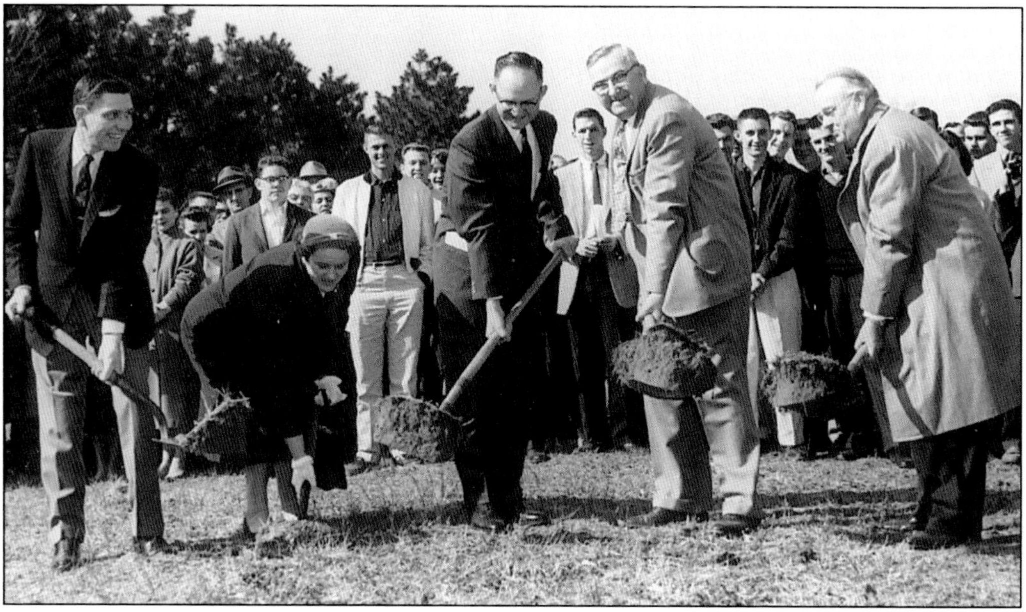

In the fall of 1957, ground was broken for Jenkins Hall, a dormitory for girls. The participants involved in this ground breaking ceremony, from left to right, are Mr. L.H. Hollingsworth, president of the General Board of the Baptist State Convention of North Carolina; Mrs. J. Grady Bridgers, president of the Chowan Alumni Association; Dr. Bruce E. Whitaker, Chowan president; Dr. W. Raleigh Parker, chairman of Chowan College Board of Trustees; and Mr. Thomas P. Pruitt, chairman of the Baptist State Convention's Committee of 25. Jenkins Hall was completed in time for the 1958 fall semester.

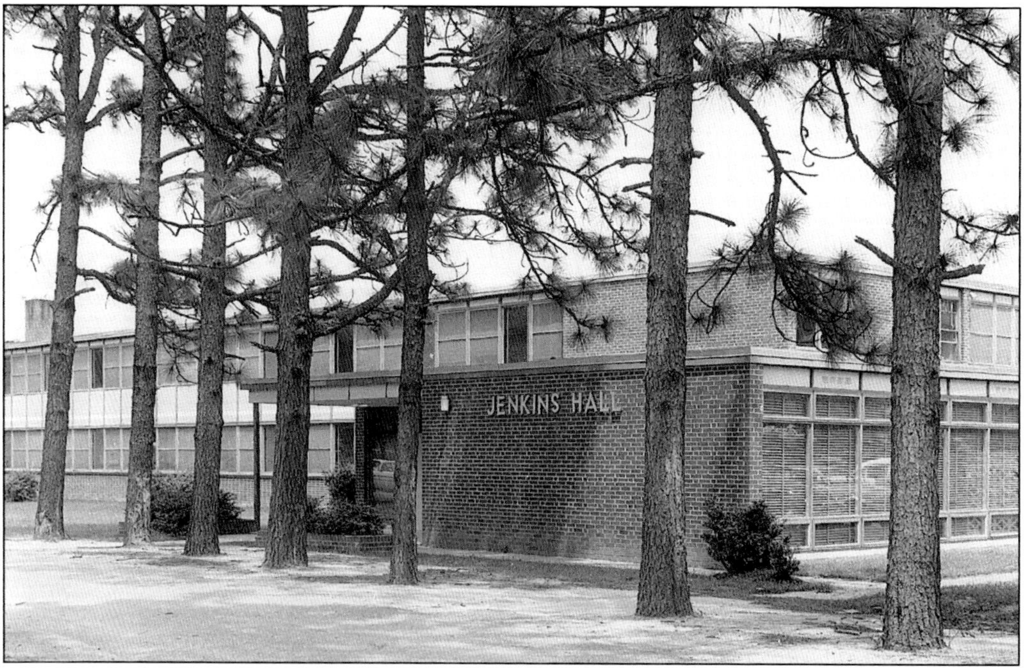

This is Jenkins Hall, a residence hall for women, which was built in 1958. Jenkins Hall was the first residence hall built solely for women since the Columns Building opened in 1852.

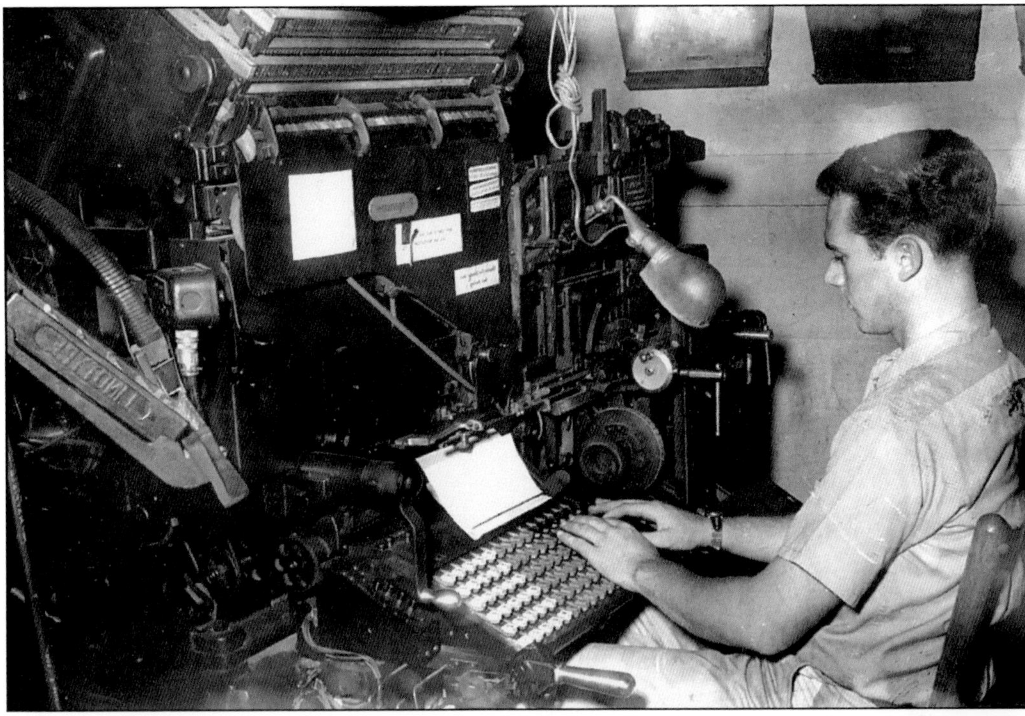

This is a 1958 photograph of a graphic arts student learning how to run a linotype machine.

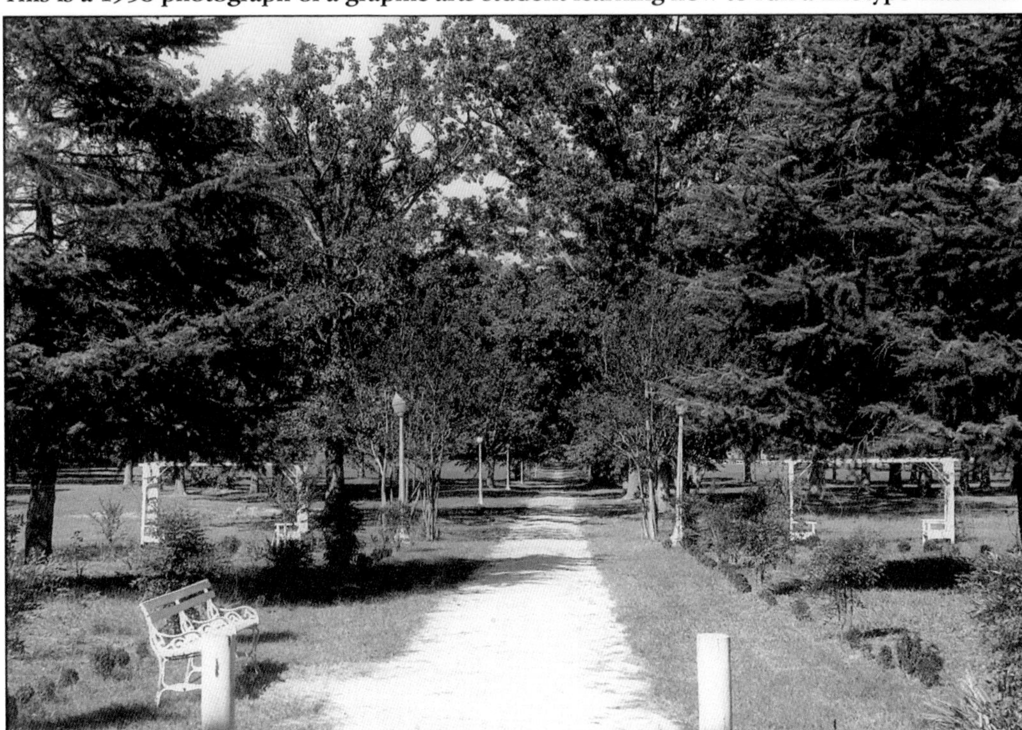

In 1959, John McSweeney, director of the Chowan College Department of Graphic Arts, took this photograph of the center walk at the front campus.

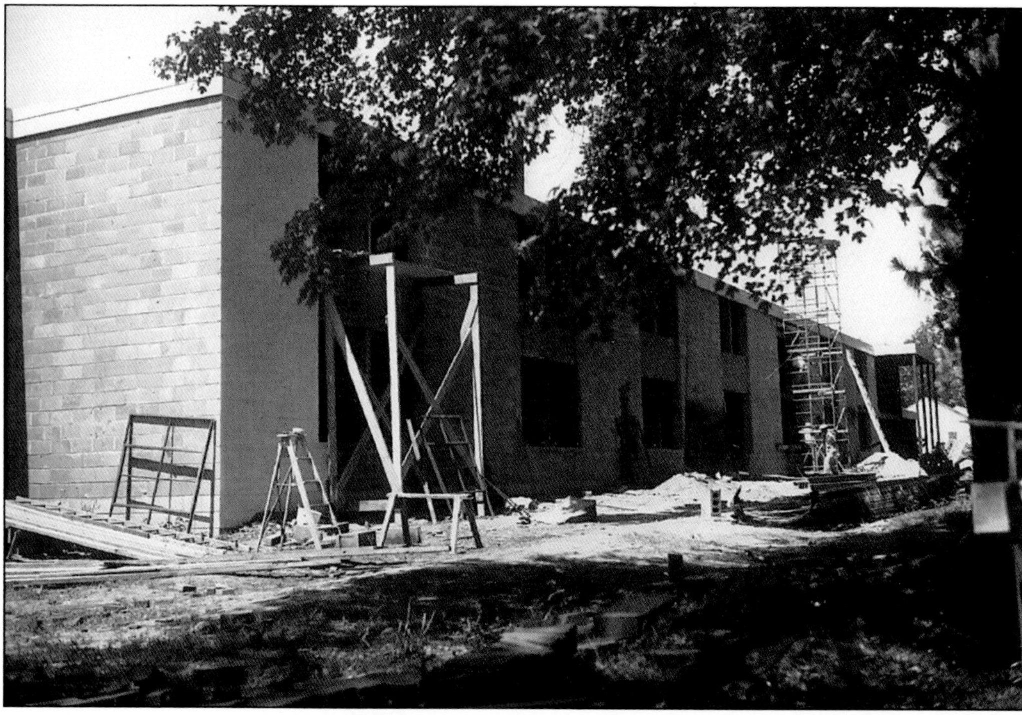

Construction of a residence hall for men is seen in 1954. It was completed that same year and later named Mixon Hall, in memory of Dr. F.O. Mixon, who served as president of the college from 1951 until his untimely death in 1956. (Photograph by F. Roy Johnson.)

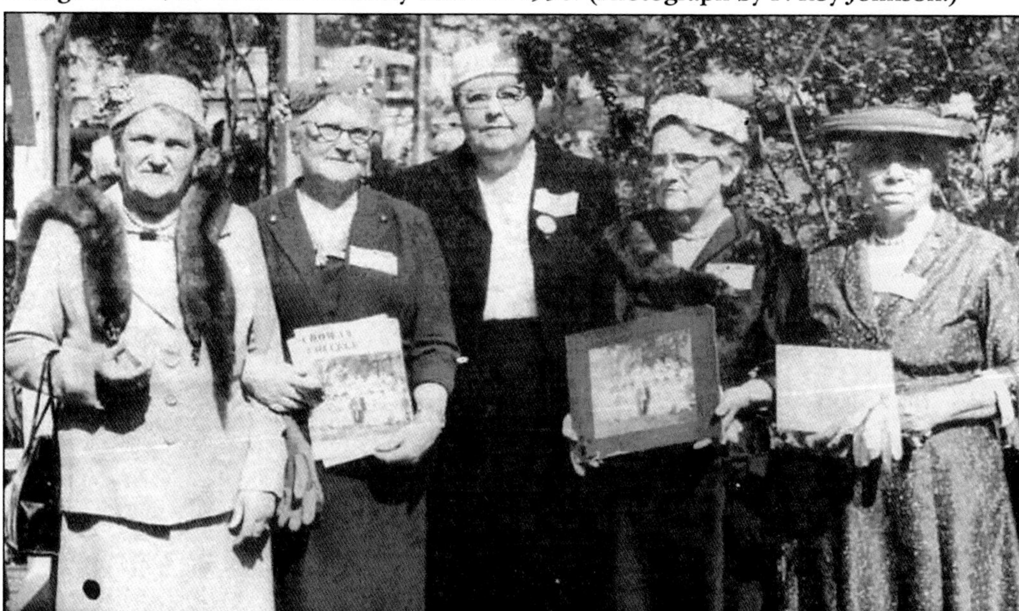

These 1908 Chowan graduates were honored at the 1958 meeting of the Chowan College Alumni Association. They are, from left to right, Mrs. Bessie Lassiter Jackson of Elizabeth City, Mrs. Maude Evans Phelps of Ahoskie, Mrs. Susie Pope Powers of Enfield, Mrs. Nora Benthall Copeland of Woodland, and Mrs. Mary Johnson Woodard of Severn.

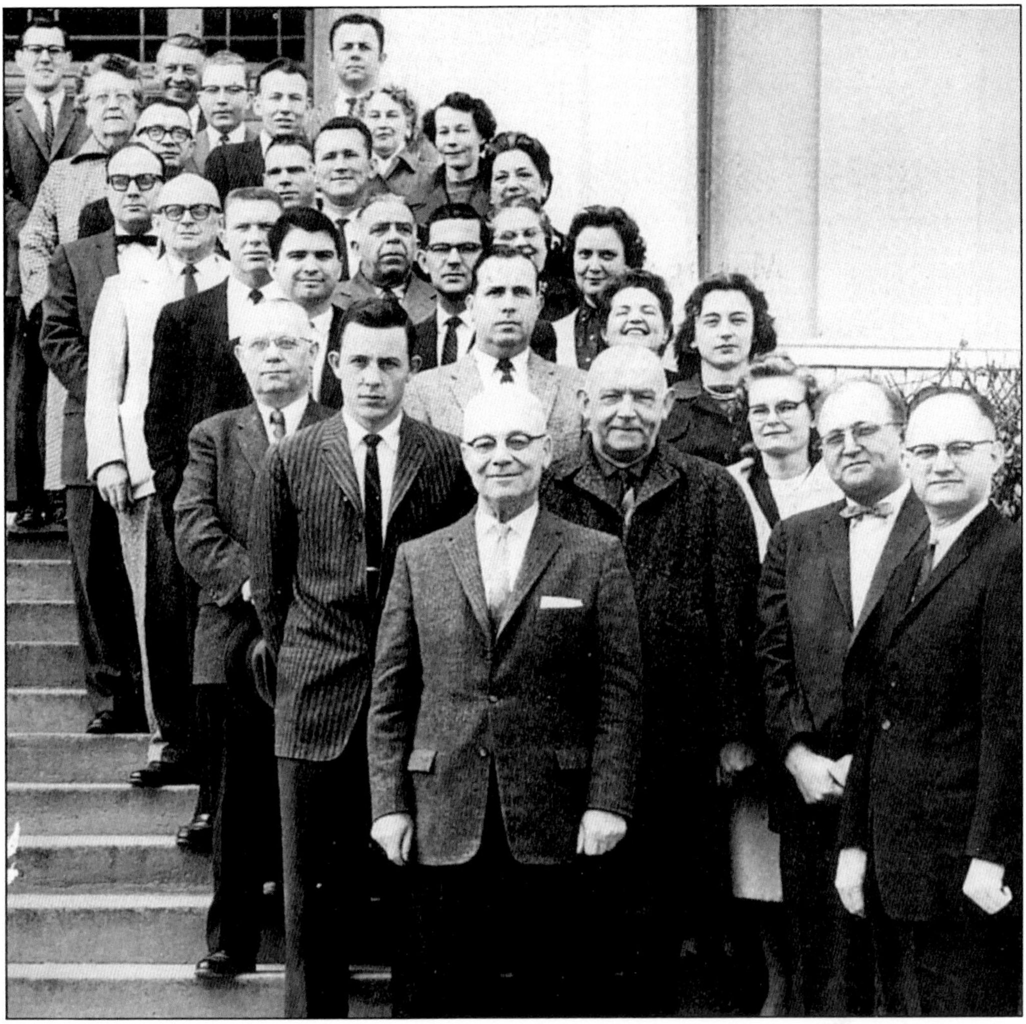

In the fall of 1960, the Chowan College faculty and administrative staff gathered on the front steps of the Columns building for a group photograph. They are, reading up the left row, J. Irving Brooks, dean of the college; James G. Garrison, chairman of Physical Education Department; Dr. Bela Udvarnoki, chairman of Social Sciences Department; James M. Chamblee, chairman of Music Department; Jerry L. Hawkins, physical education; John McSweeney, chairman of Department of Graphic Communications; James Liston, science; Thomas E. Ruffin, chairman of Business Department; Mrs. Sybil Grimes, dean of women; and James Masters, business; (middle row) William I. Marable, English; Milam Johnson, chairman of Science Department; L.L. Bishop, mathematics; Eugene Williams, chairman of Language Department; William B. Sowell, Department of Graphic Communications; Warren Sexton, social sciences; Dr. William Young, college chaplain; L.M. Wallace Jr., business; and Ross Cadle, director of admissions; (right row) Dr. Bruce E. Whitaker, president of the college; Charley Sandifer, English; Mrs. Charley Sandifer, assistant librarian; Mrs. Carla Chamblee, music; Miss Anna Belle Crouch, physical education; Mrs. F.O. Mixon, chairman of Religion Department; Miss Frances White, religion; Mrs. Neva Campbell, librarian; Mrs. Bruce E. Whitaker, religion; Mrs. Ross Cadle, assistant librarian; and Harold Brown, Department of Graphic Communications. Two faculty members were absent when the picture was taken: Levi Gillikin, mathematics, and F.M. Tucker, science.

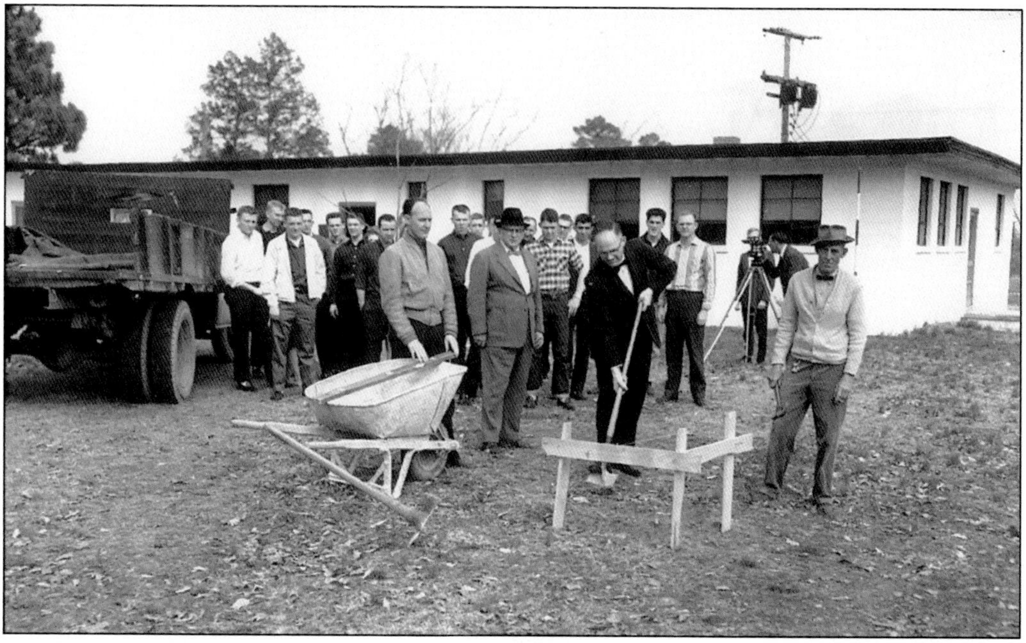

In 1962, ground was broken for a second addition to the original graphic arts building, which was originally constructed in 1953. Dr. Bruce E. Whitaker, center with the shovel, turns the traditional first shovel of dirt as a group of students observe. Also present are, from left to right, Mr. Jack Hassell, superintendent of buildings and grounds; Mr. John McSweeney, director of Department of Graphic Communications; and Mr. Jack Vaughan, retired superintendent of buildings and grounds.

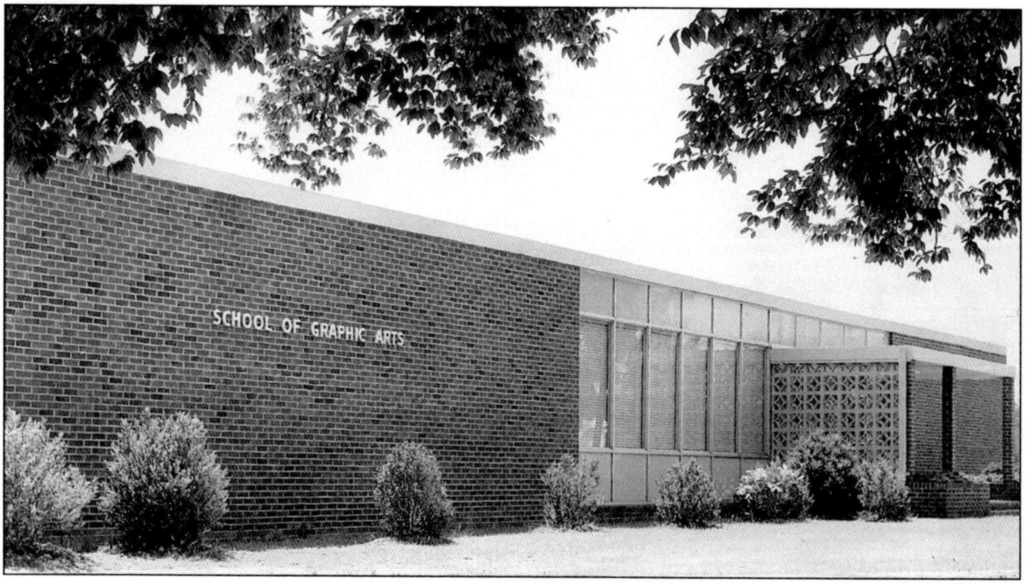

The 1962 addition transformed the graphic arts building into this structure, which remained in use until 1983, when a new graphics building, Horner Graphics Communications Center, was opened. The old graphics arts building was remodeled and named McSweeney Hall, in honor of Mr. John McSweeney, the first director of the Department of Graphic Communications. Today, McSweeney Hall houses the Texie Camp Marks Computer Center.

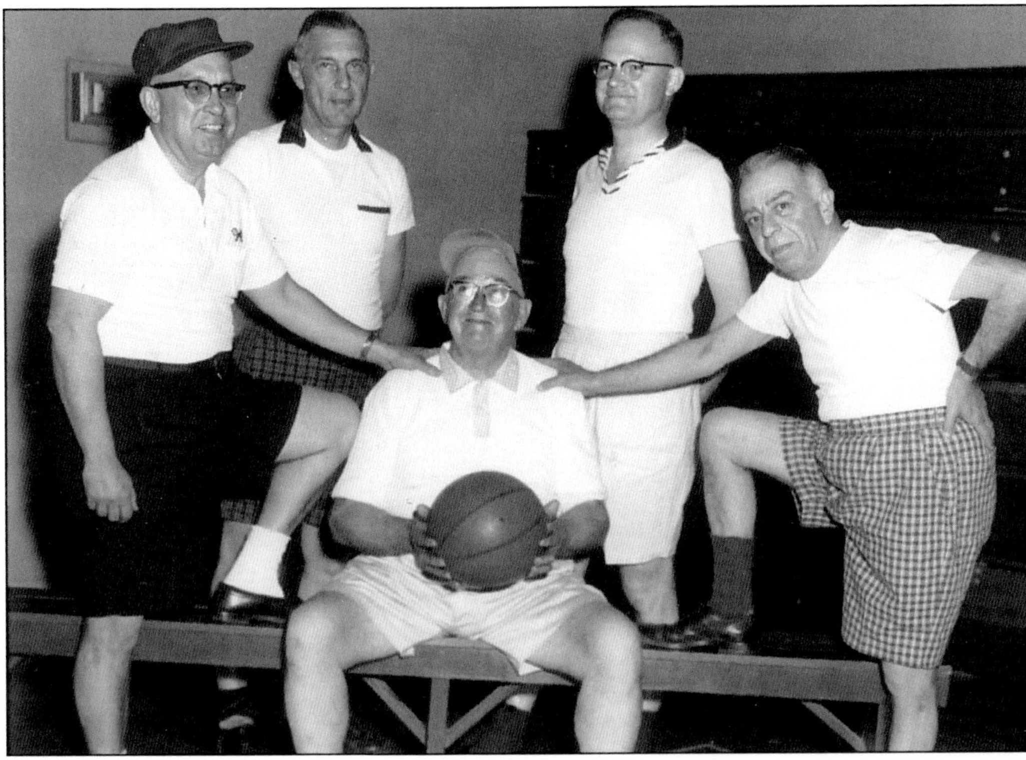

A college president has to be willing to leave the ivory tower from time to time. This mid-1960s image shows Chowan College president Dr. Bruce E. Whitaker with the Murfreesboro Rotary Club basketball team. Team members are, from left to right, (front row) Mr. Eddie Cason, Mr. Will Stephenson, and Mr. Eugene Williams, who taught French at Chowan; (back row) Mr. Archie Parker and Dr. Whitaker. (Photograph by Joel C. Holland.)

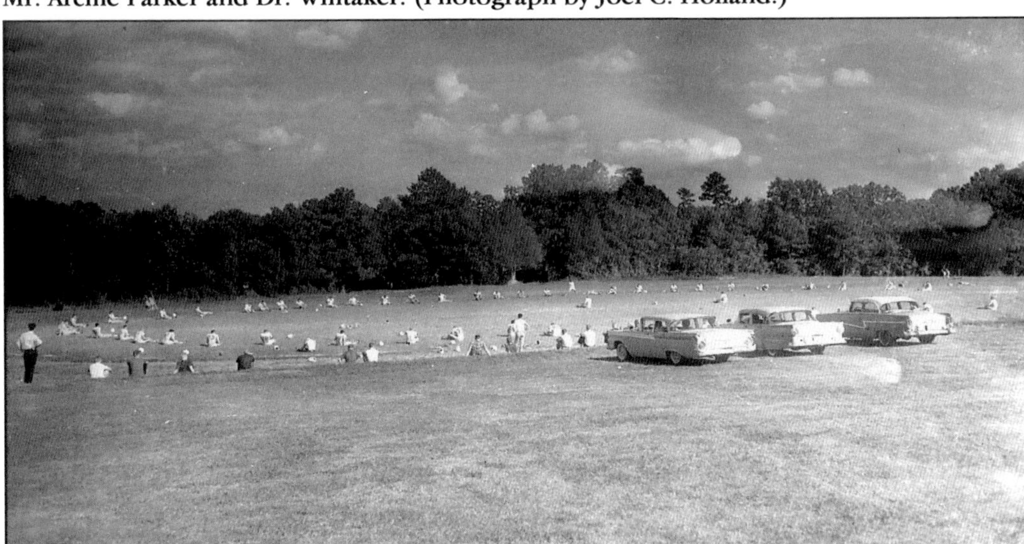

In the early 1960s, the Chowan College football team used this area as a practice field. Today, the upper site is occupied by Camp Hall and the field with players on it is occupied by Horner Graphics Communication Center. (Photograph by F. Roy Johnson.)

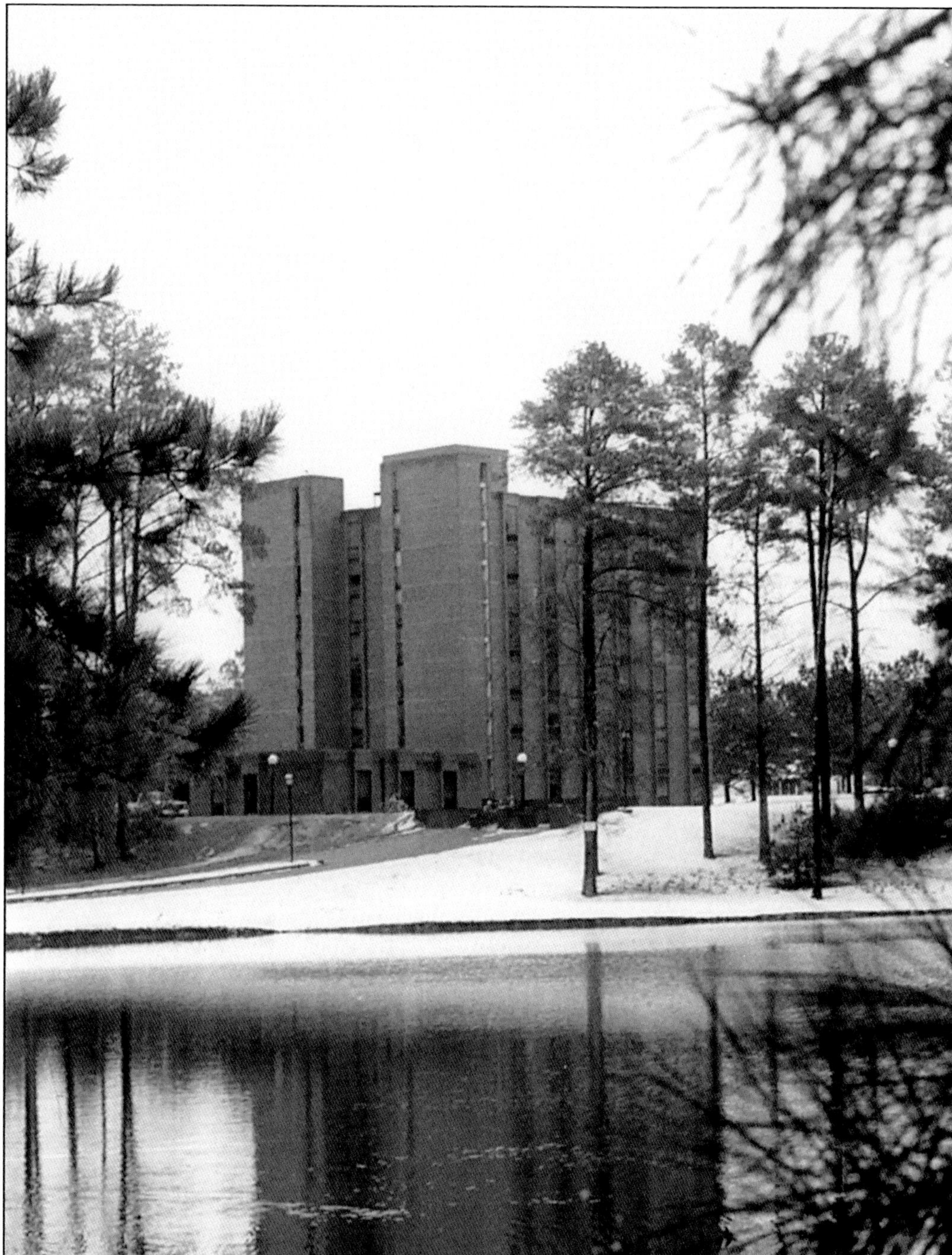

Parker Hall is a nine-story residence hall constructed in 1970. It is named in honor of one of the college's longtime supporters, Mr. Elwood W. Parker of Murfreesboro. Mr. Parker was one of the key persons involved in the reopening of Chowan College in 1949.

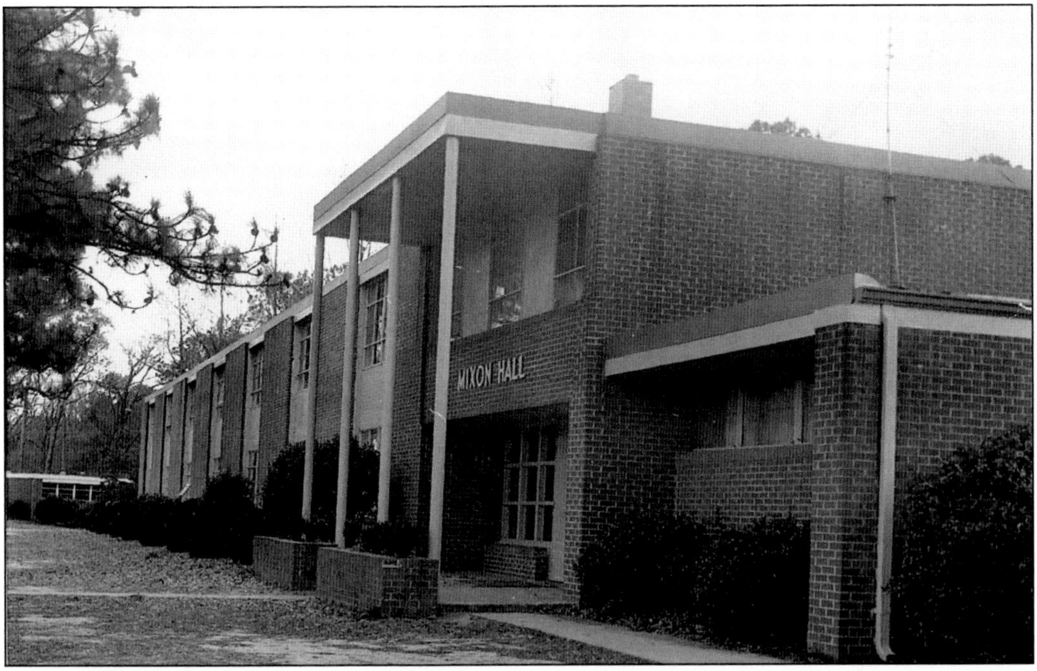

Mixon Hall was constructed in 1954 and named in honor of Dr. F.O. Mixon, who served as president of the college from 1951 to 1956.

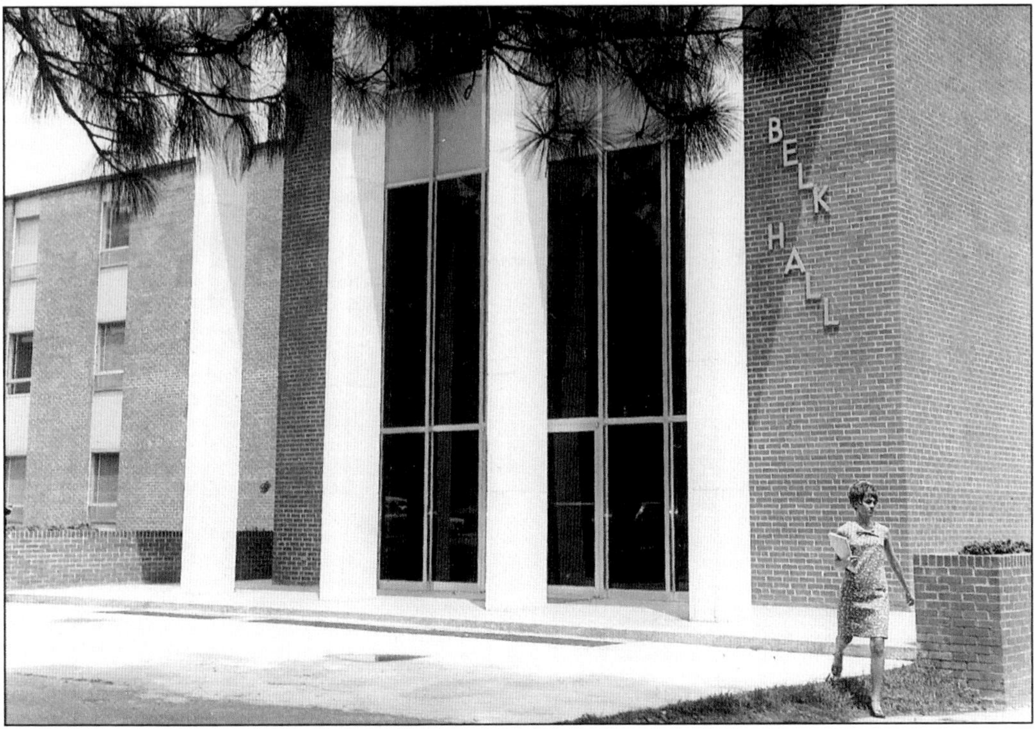

Belk Hall, a three-story residence hall for women, was built in 1964 and named in honor of Mrs. Irwin Belk of Charlotte, North Carolina. The money for this dorm was given by the Belk Foundation in her honor.

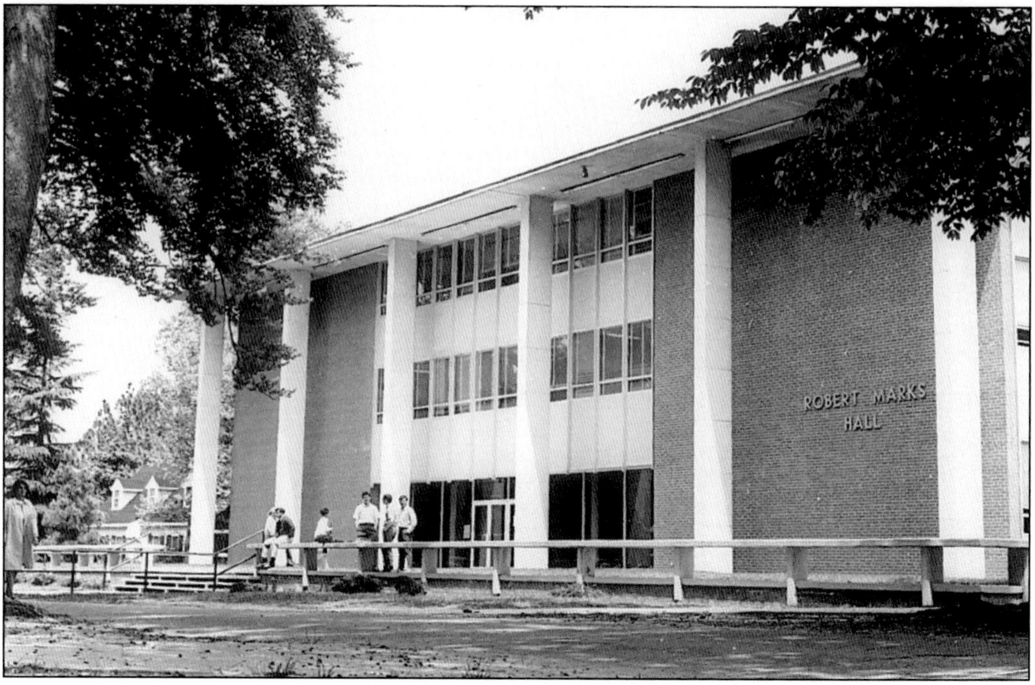

Marks Hall is a three-story classroom building that also houses a number of the college's academic programs. It was constructed in 1962–1964 and is named in honor of Mr. Robert Marks of Boykins, Virginia.

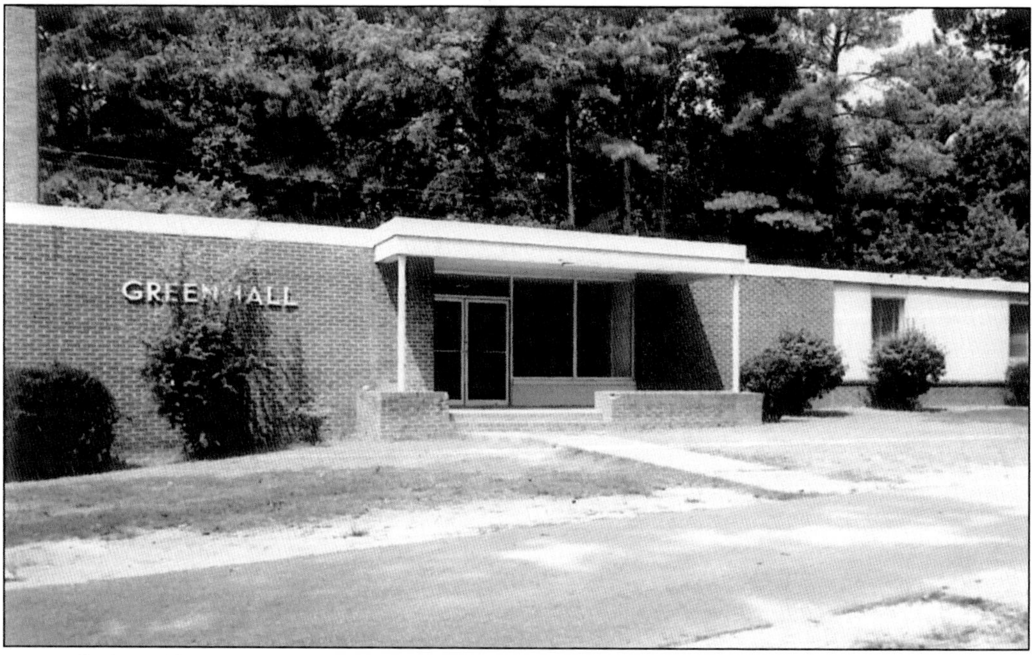

In 1956, the college constructed Green Hall for use as a science facility. This building housed the college's science department until 1974, when the department moved into the newly constructed Carrie Savage Camp Science Building. Green Hall today serves as the home for the college's visual arts programs.

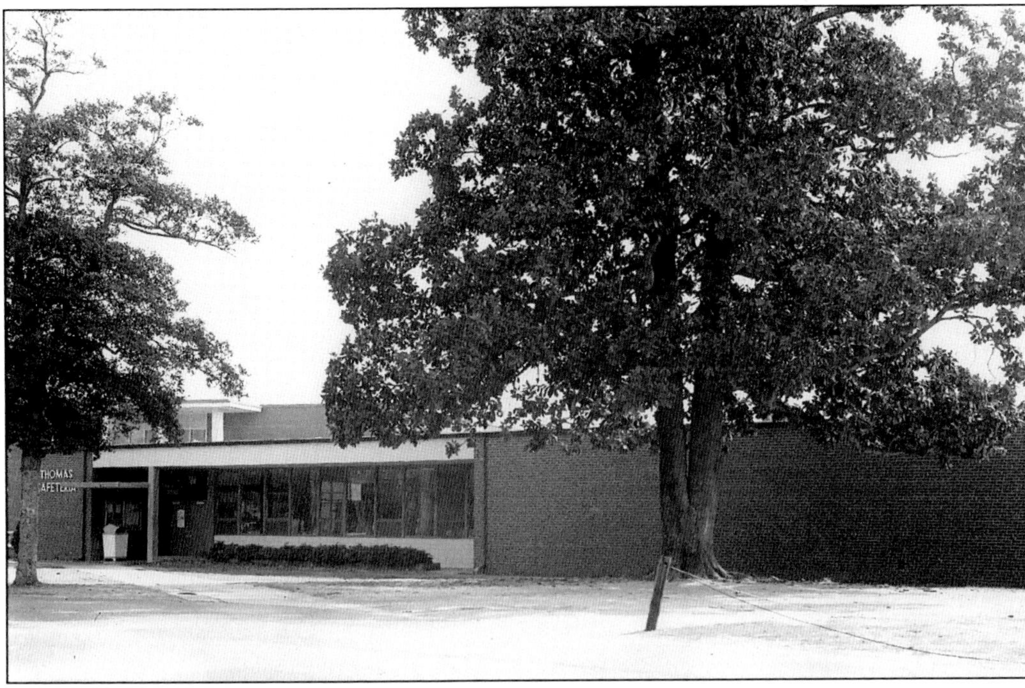

Thomas Cafeteria was constructed in 1959 as the college's main dining facility. It houses the President's Dining Room, used for special meals and meetings. The cafeteria was named in honor of Dr. R.P. Thomas, who served on the college's board of trustees for many years.

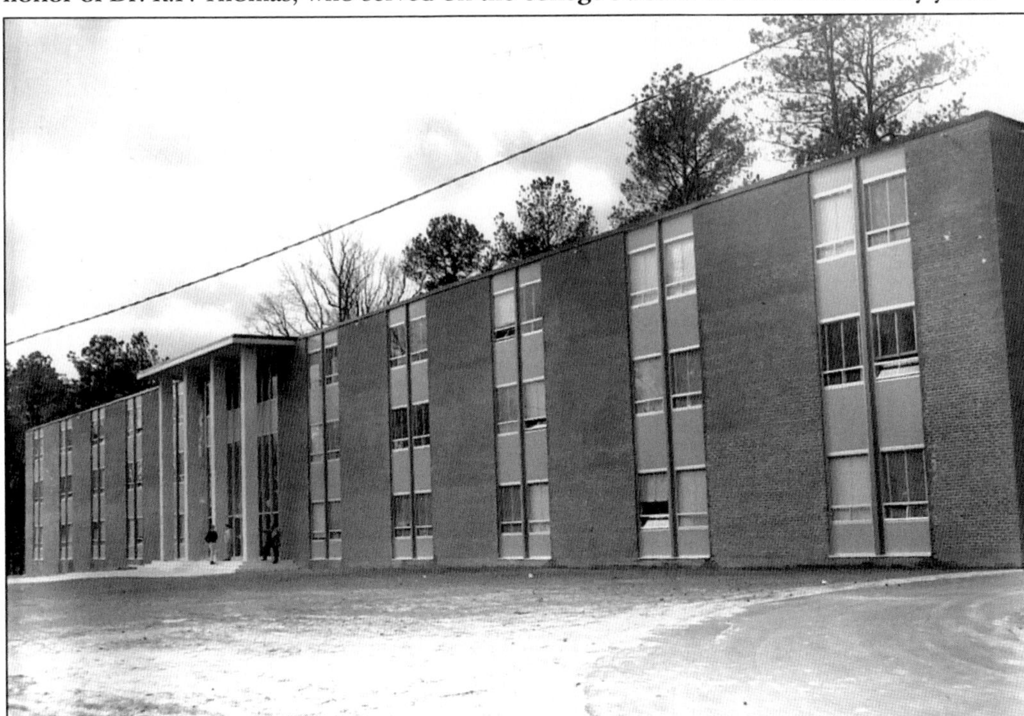

Dunn Hall, a three-story residence hall for men, was constructed in 1963.

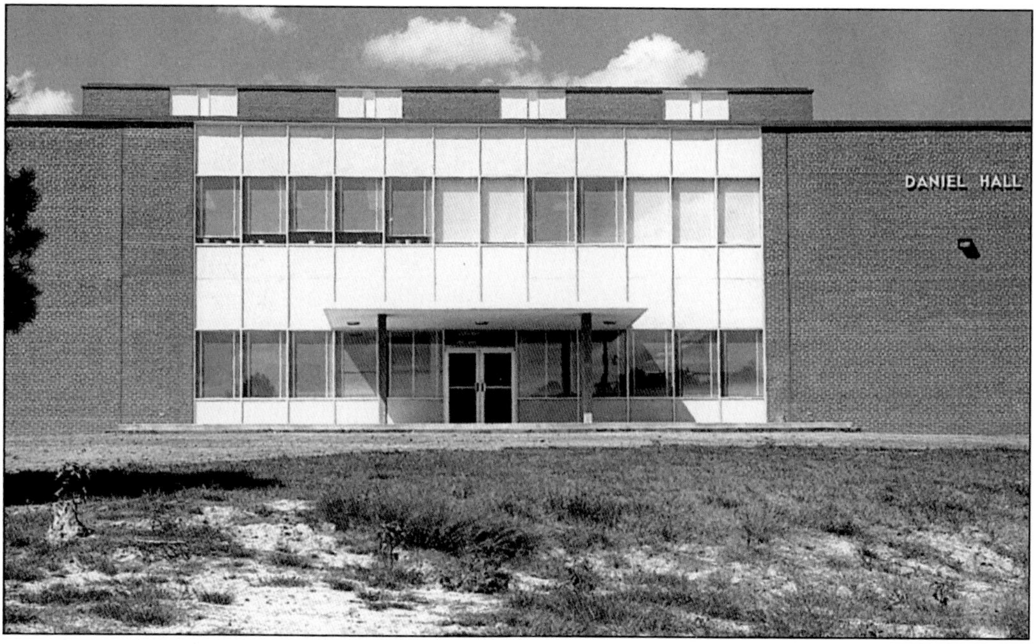

Daniel Fine Arts Building was constructed in 1968 and houses the college's music, drama, and dance programs.

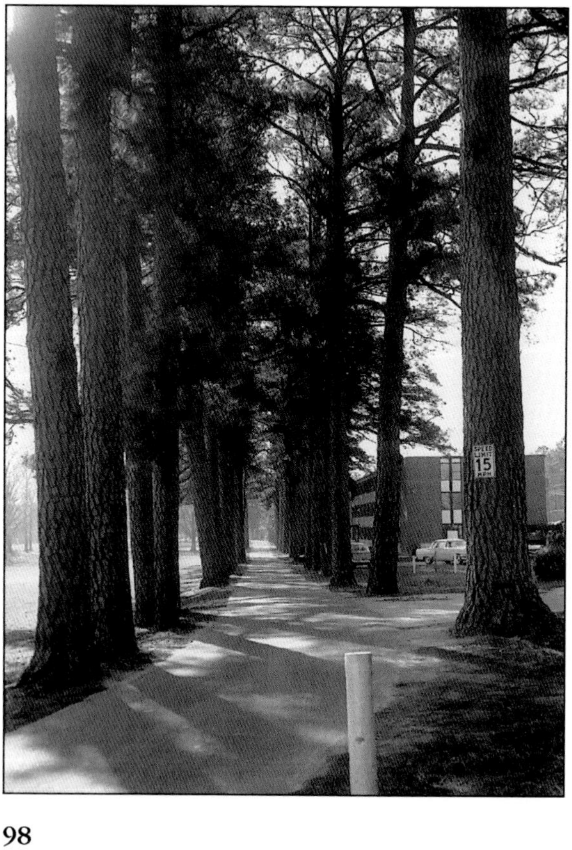

Simons Hall, built in 1960, is a three-story residence hall for men. It is located to the immediate right of Pine Drive, on the right side of the front campus. Simons Hall was named in honor and memory of Mr. W.L. (Roy) Simons.

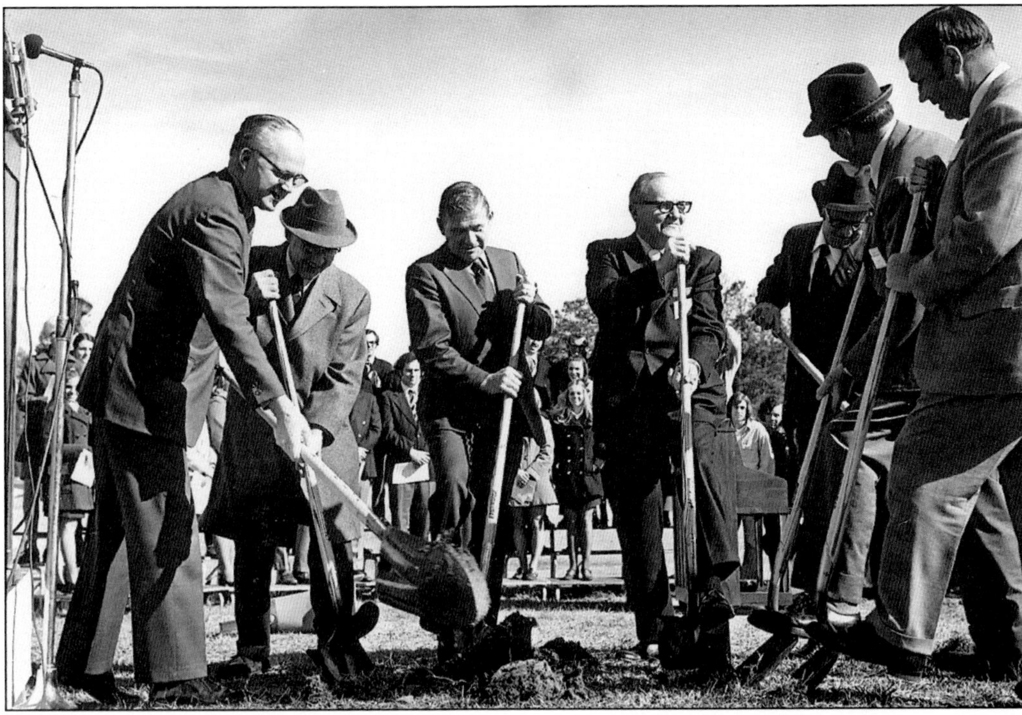

In early 1972, the college broke ground for a new science building, Carrie Savage Camp Hall. At the ground breaking ceremony, those in attendance included, from left to right, Dr. Bruce E. Whitaker, president, Murfreesboro Mayor Billy Hill, Chowan trustee Mr. H.D. White, and on the far right Chowan trustee Mr. Don Mathews Jr.

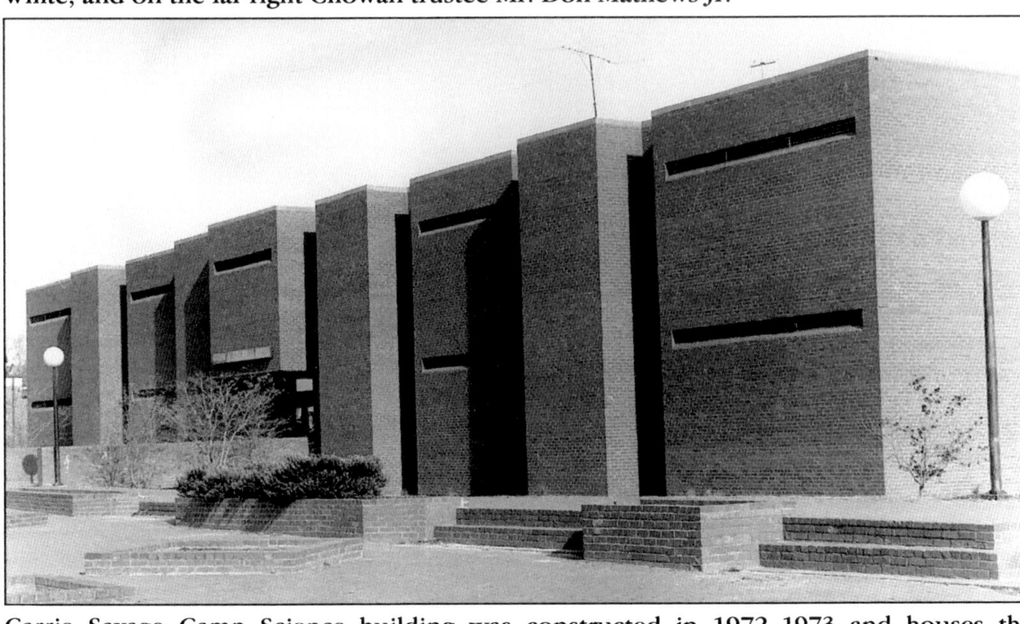

Carrie Savage Camp Science building was constructed in 1972–1973 and houses the college's math, science, physics, teacher education, and academic support programs. It was named in honor of Carrie Savage Camp, Class of 1881, wife of J.L. Camp Sr. of Franklin, Virginia.

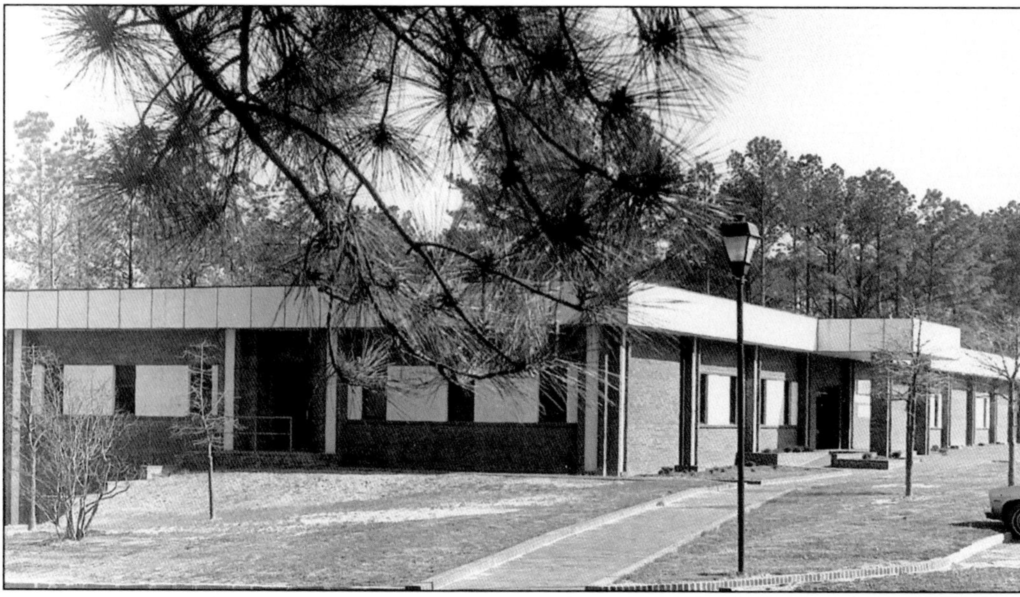

Horner Graphics Communications Center was built in 1982–1983 and houses the college's Department of Graphic Communications. This facility was funded in part by significant contributions from the North Carolina Press Association.

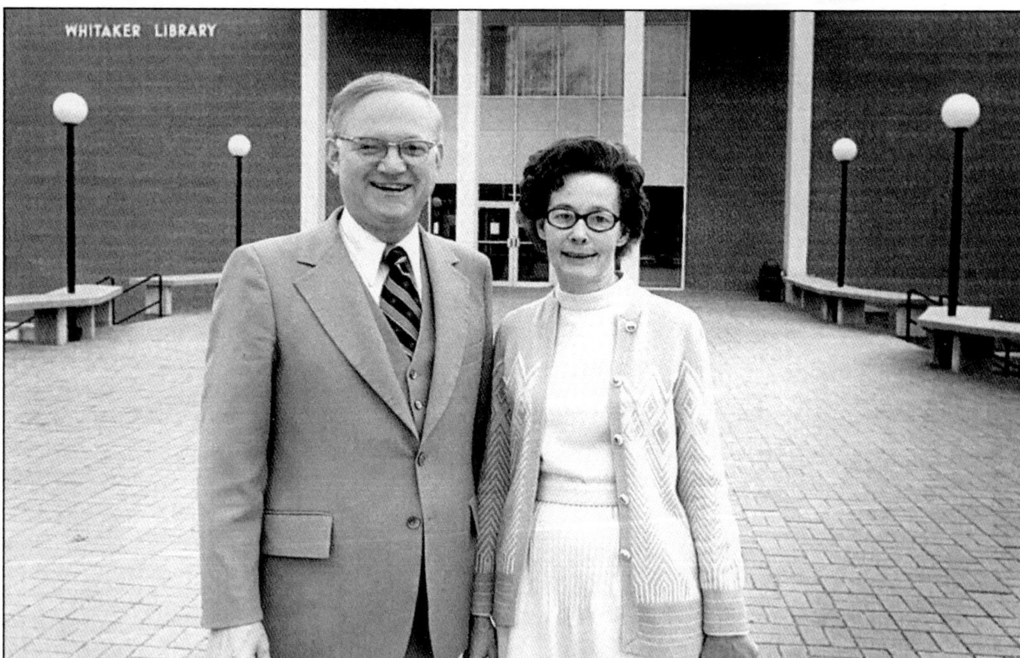

Dr. and Mrs. Bruce E. Whitaker are seen standing in front of the library that bears his name. Dr. Whitaker served as president of the college for 33 years, from 1957 to 1990, while Mrs. Esther Whitaker taught religion and English for many of those years. Dr. Whitaker, like all men who served as president of Chowan College, made his mark through unparalleled growth and construction. Whitaker Library was built in 1968 and houses a number of special collections, along with other numerous resources found in collegiate libraries.

In the fall of 1965, these students are seen taking a break at Marks Hall. They are, from left to right, unidentified, Kathy Smith, Mary Jo Brittle, and unidentified.

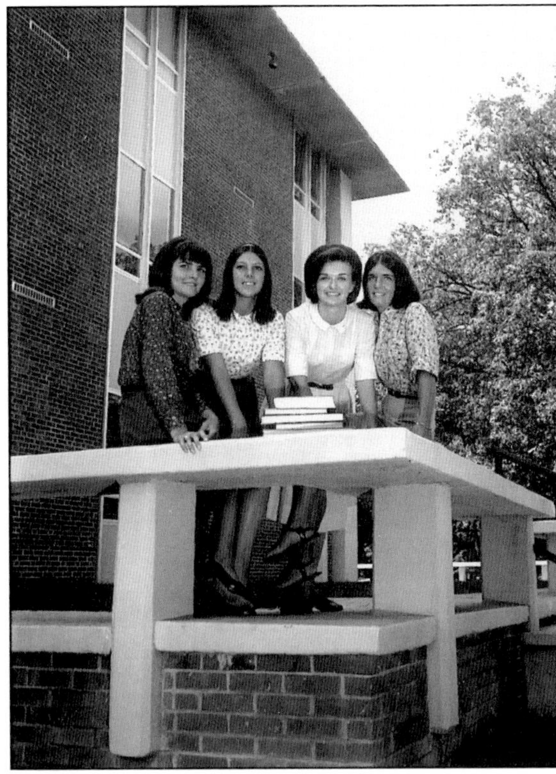

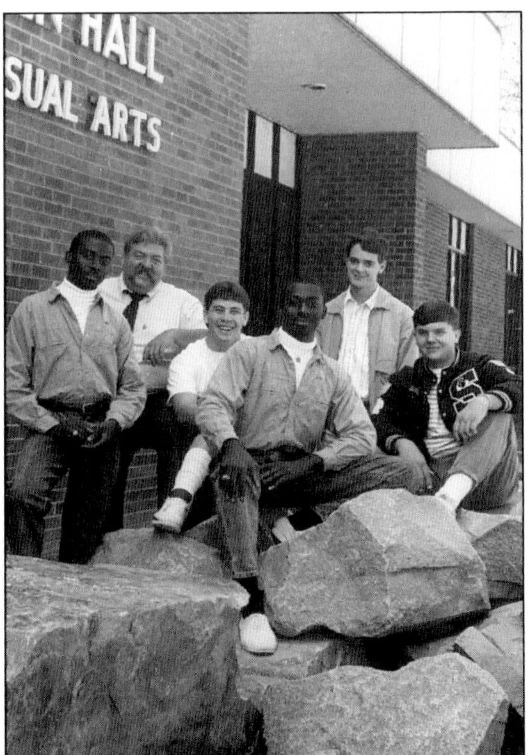

Long-time art professor Douglas Eubank, second from left, is seen in front of Green Hall with a group of his art students in this early 1980s photograph.

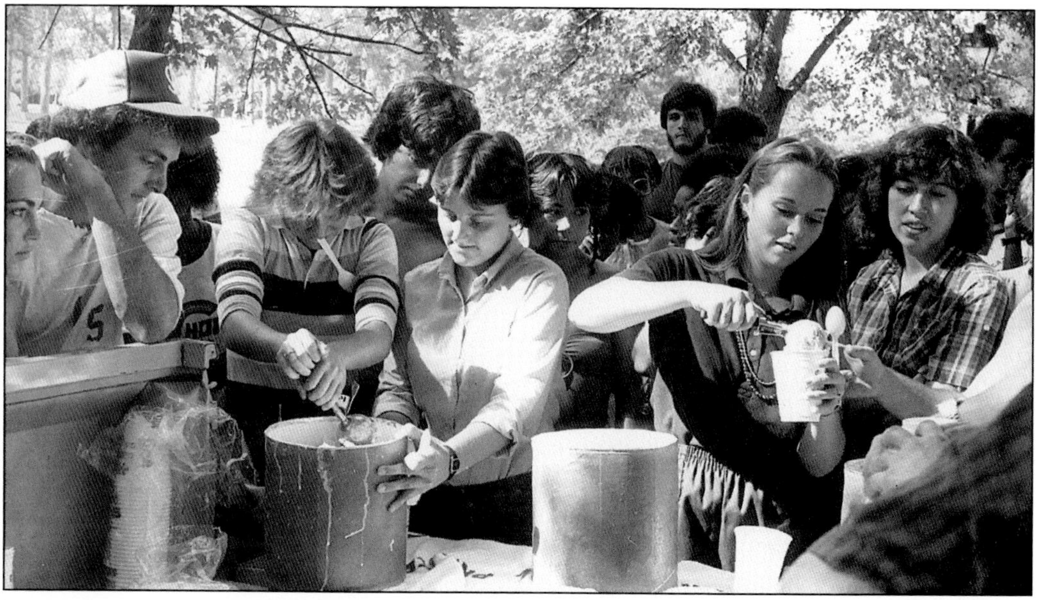

Ice cream parties, as seen in this 1970s photograph, have been a part of student life at Chowan College for many years.

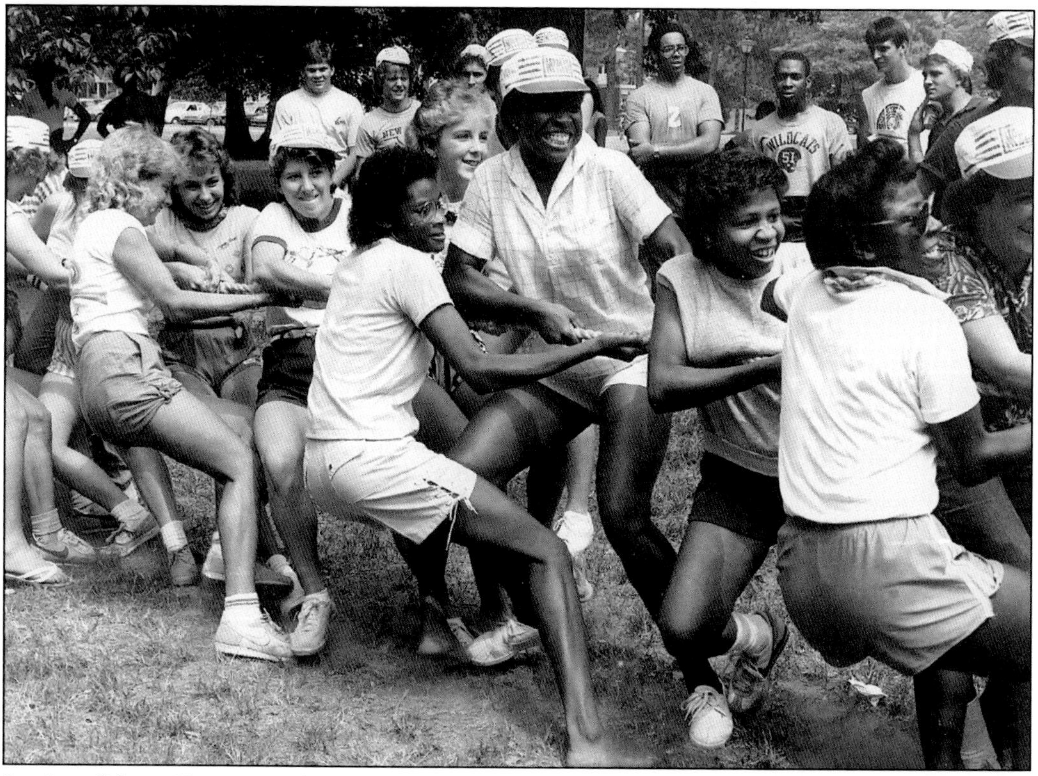

Student life at Chowan College takes the form of many varied activities, such as this 1980s tug-of-war match. Performers such as Charlie Daniels, Charlie Rich, John Denver, Kenny Rogers, the Smothers Brothers, Pat Paulson, and many others have played at Chowan as part of the student activities program.

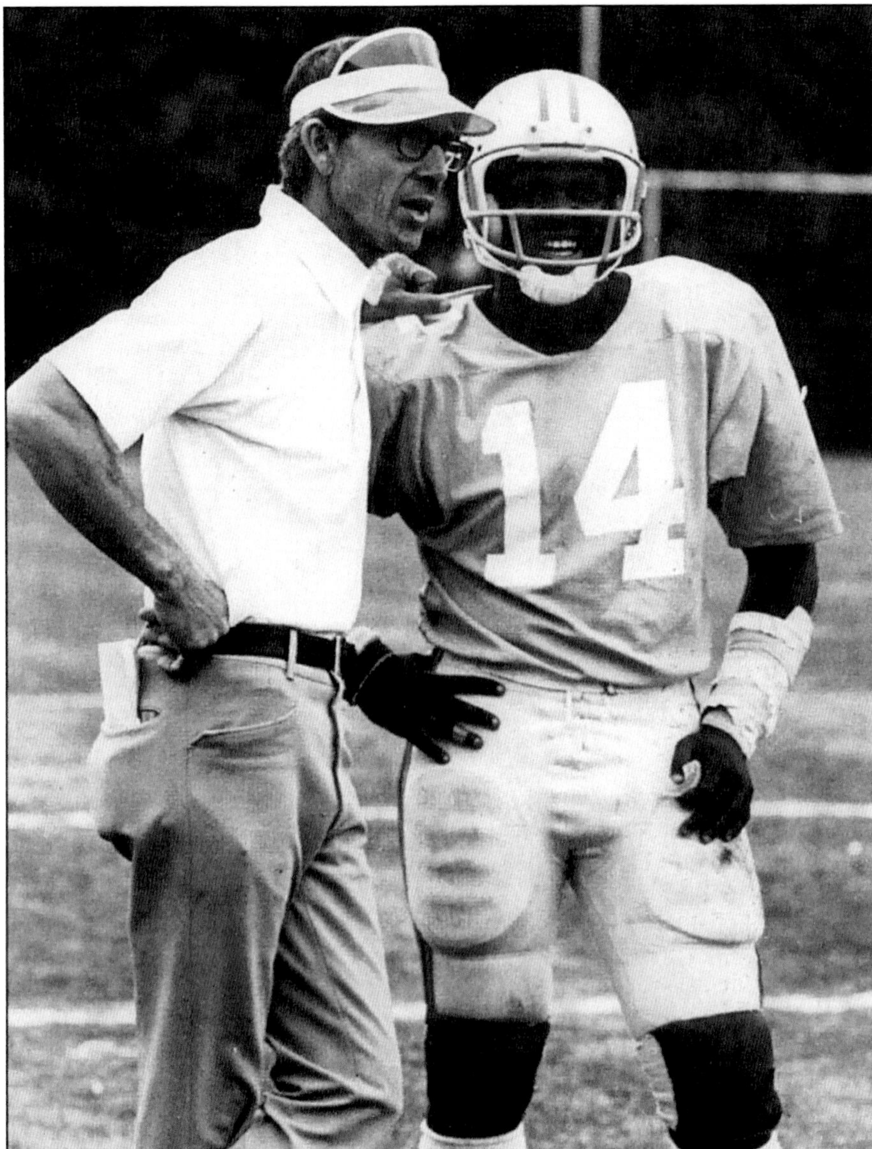

Jim Garrison was head football coach and a familiar figure along the sidelines at Chowan College for 37 years, with 33 years spent on the junior college level. He is seen here giving instructions to quarterback Xavier Love during a game with Lees-MacRae College during the 1979 season. In his 33 years of coaching the Chowan Braves in the junior college ranks, Coach Garrison became a national legend. He ranks third among National Junior College Athletic Association coaches with 182 wins, 27 winning seasons, and 7 Conference Coach of the Year honors. Jim Garrison coached over 3,500 young men at Chowan with 35 of those players earning National Junior College Athletic Association All-American honors. Many of his former players went on to play at the senior college level and in the National Football League. Some of his professional football players are named on page 104. Coach Garrison is a member of the National Junior College Athletic Association Hall of Fame, the North Carolina Sports Hall of Fame, and the Chowan College Sports Hall of Fame. The football stadium at Chowan is named in his honor.

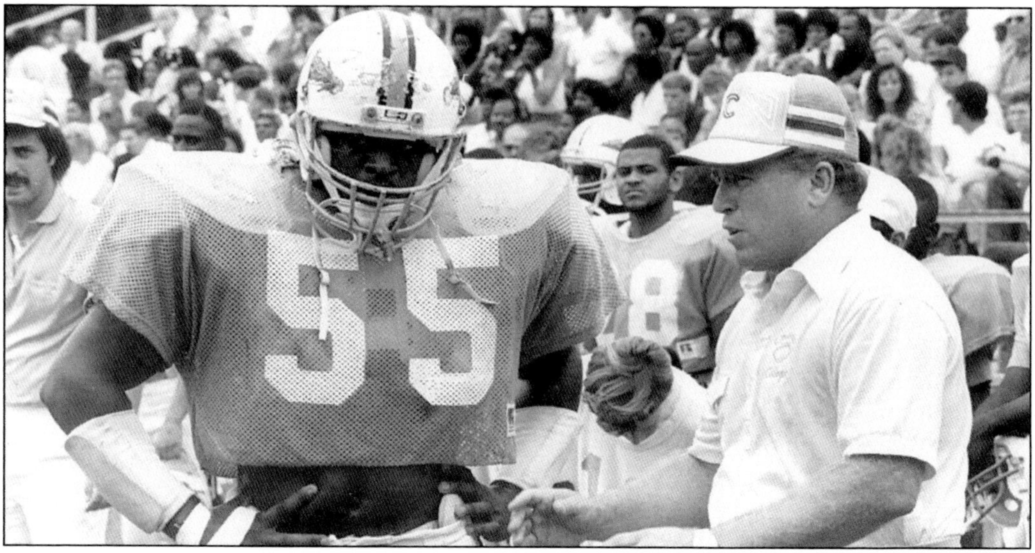

Veteran Chowan defensive coach Dan Surface is seen conferring with All-American linebacker George Koonce during the 1988 Nassau-Chowan football game, which the Braves won 20–14. After graduating from Chowan, Koonce transferred to East Carolina University, where he was a two-year starter. At the end of his career at East Carolina, Koonce was signed by the Atlanta Falcons and was released without playing a game. He was immediately signed by the Green Bay Packers, where he became a 10-year starter and joined another former Chowan star player, Robert Brown, who played 11 seasons with the Packers. Jody Schulz, Curtis Whitley, Freddy Banks, Jerry Holmes, and Mark Royals are among other former Chowan football players who have played in the National Football League. Mark Royals is currently a punter with the Miami Dolphins.

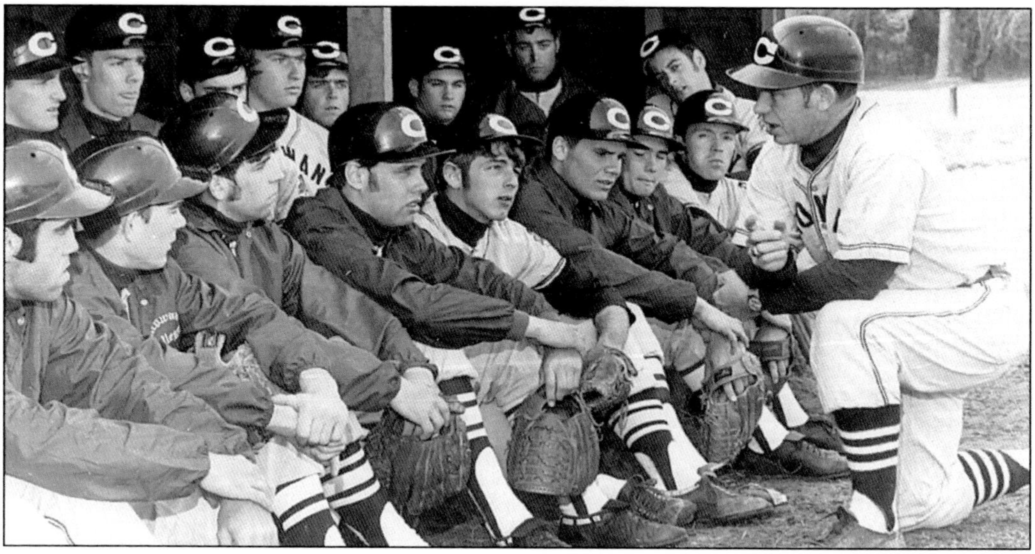

In this late 1970s photograph, Chowan baseball coach Jerry Hawkins is seen going over instructions with his team. Coach Hawkins had many winning seasons, and a number of his players went on to play professional baseball. Chowan College's baseball field is named in his honor for his many years of service. Jerry Hawkins was also line coach for many years with the Chowan Braves football team.

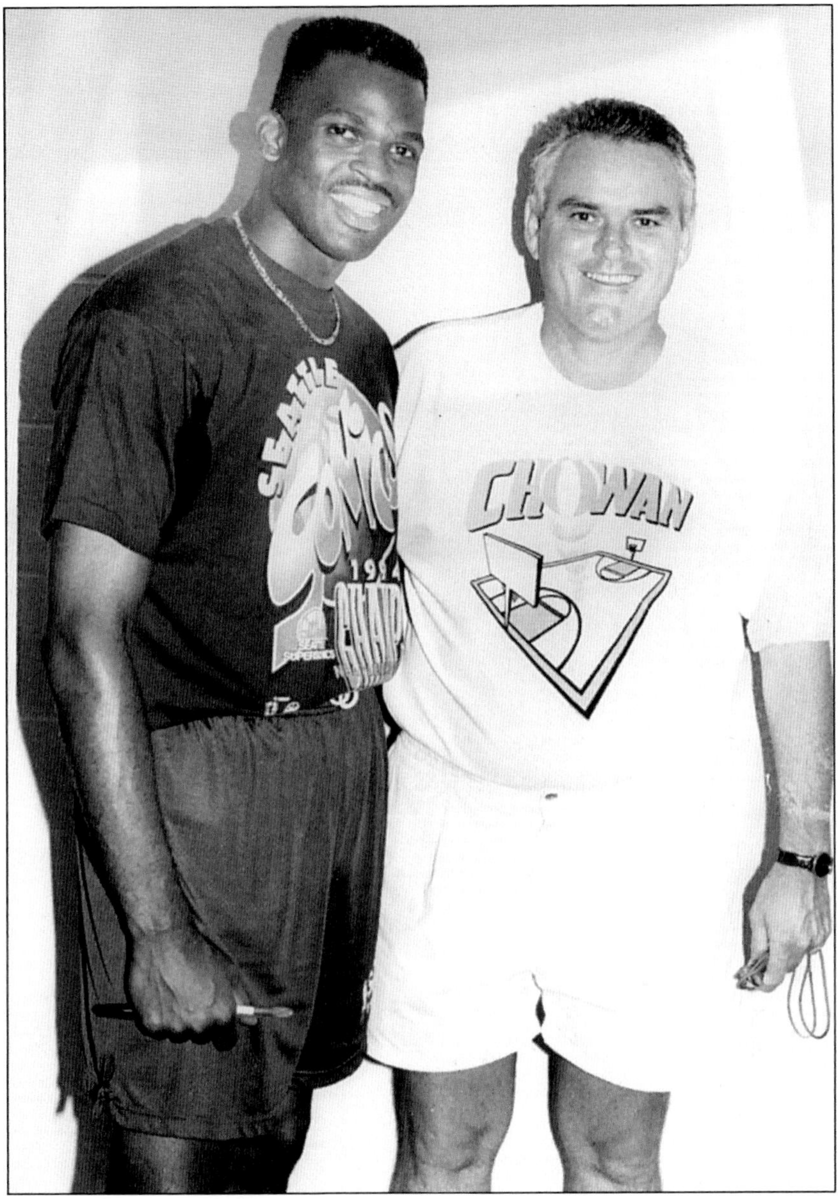

Here are two legends of the Chowan College basketball program: Nate McMillan (left) and Coach Bob Burke (right). Nate McMillan played for two years under Bob Burke at Chowan, from 1982 to 1984, where he led the team to the 1984 NJCAA National Tournament and was named an All-American. He transferred to North Carolina State University, where he played for the next two seasons and was drafted by the Seattle Super Sonics. Nate McMillan played 12 years with the Super Sonics and is now in his fifth year as their head coach. Bob Burke spent 22 years at Chowan College, which he turned into a small-college powerhouse, accumulating a record of 419-217. In 13 years at the junior college level, 70 of his former players received full scholarships, including 35 at Division 1 programs. Fred Vinson, another of Burke's junior college players, played professional basketball for Atlanta and Seattle. In 2000, Bob Burke was inducted into Chowan's Hall of Fame as the school's all-time winning coach. He is now assistant basketball coach at the University of Hawaii.

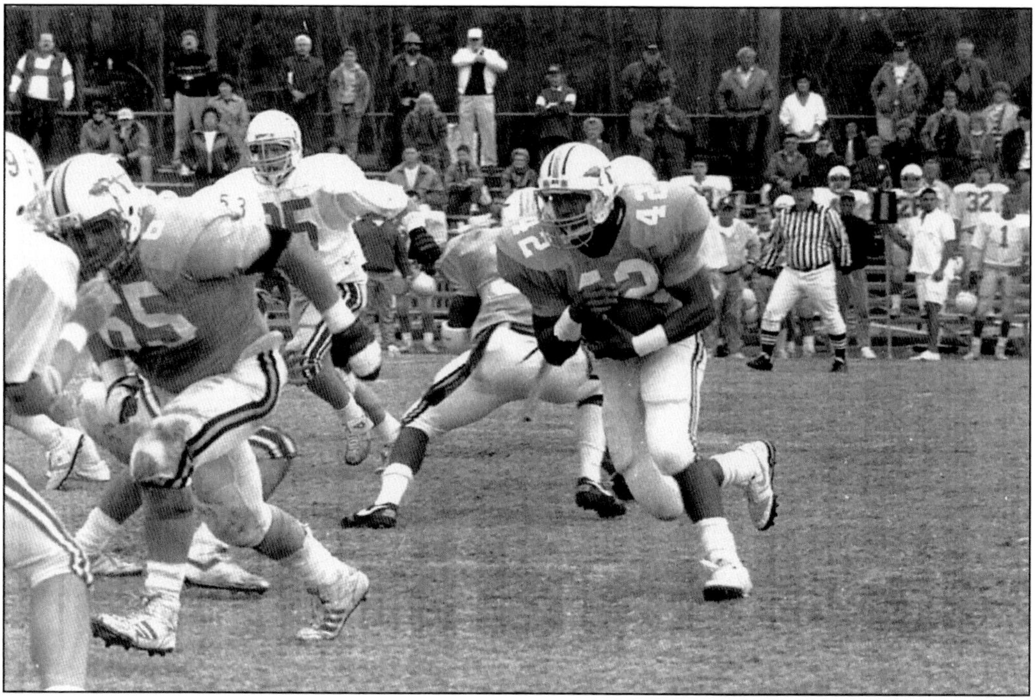

Following blocking by a beefy line, this Chowan running-back picks up considerable yardage in the 1981 Chowan-Montgomery football game. The Braves won 35-14.

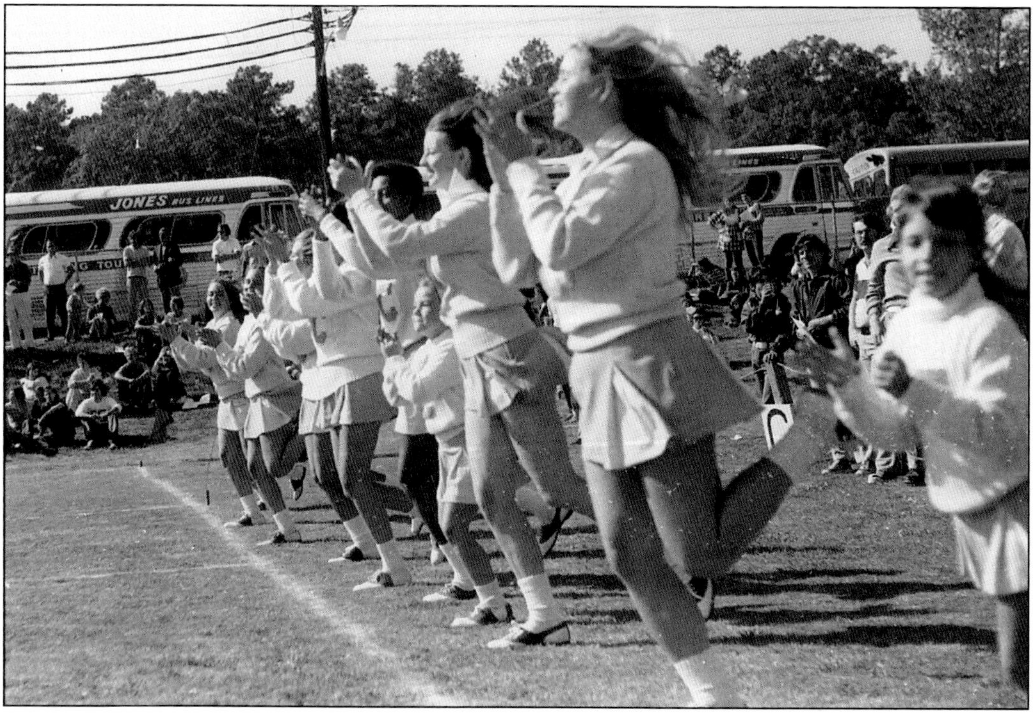

The cheerleading squad cheers the Braves to victory in this 1975 game against Wesley College. (Photograph by Phil Royce.)

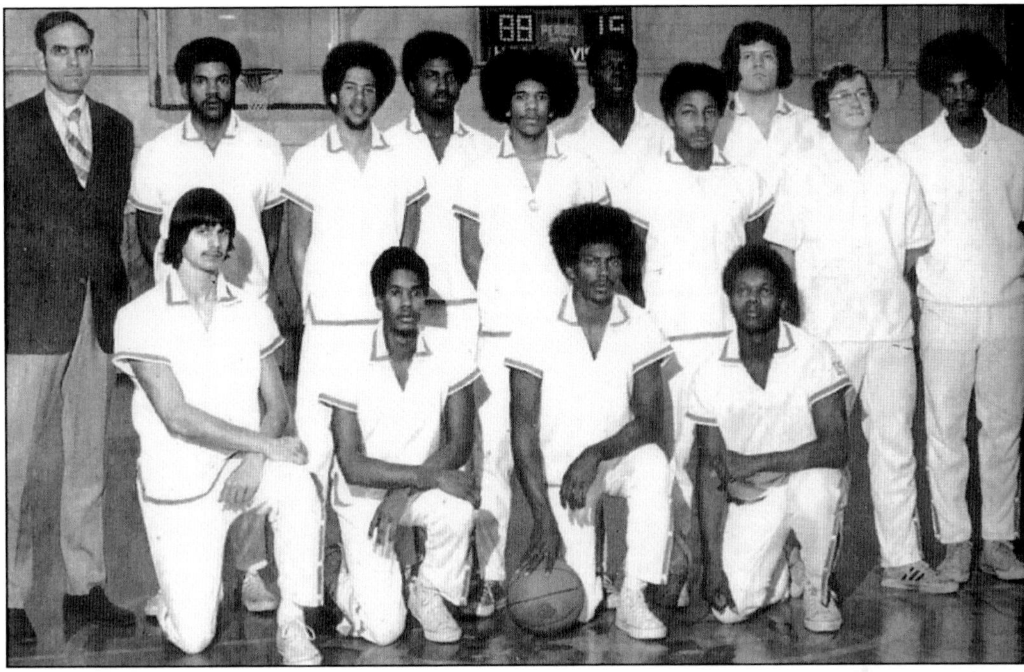

The 1972–1973 Chowan College men's basketball team, coached by Mr. Bill McCraw, included, from left to right, (front row) Greg Wilson, Al Crenshaw, Ray Rawls, and Tim Lyons; (middle row) Coach McCraw, Mike Oliver, Kelvin Barnes, John Spears, Lue Ward, and Pat Callahan; (back row) Keith McClern, James Soard, John Byrd, and Chet Neals.

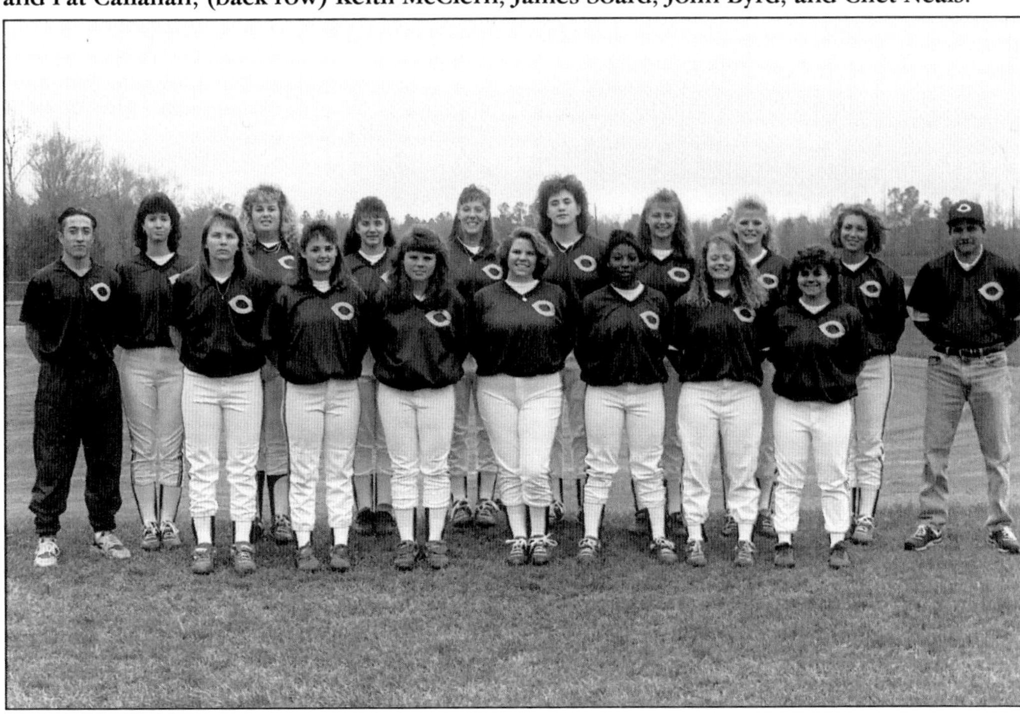

This is the 1984 Chowan College girl's softball team, coached by Mr. Jack Goldberg, pictured on the far right.

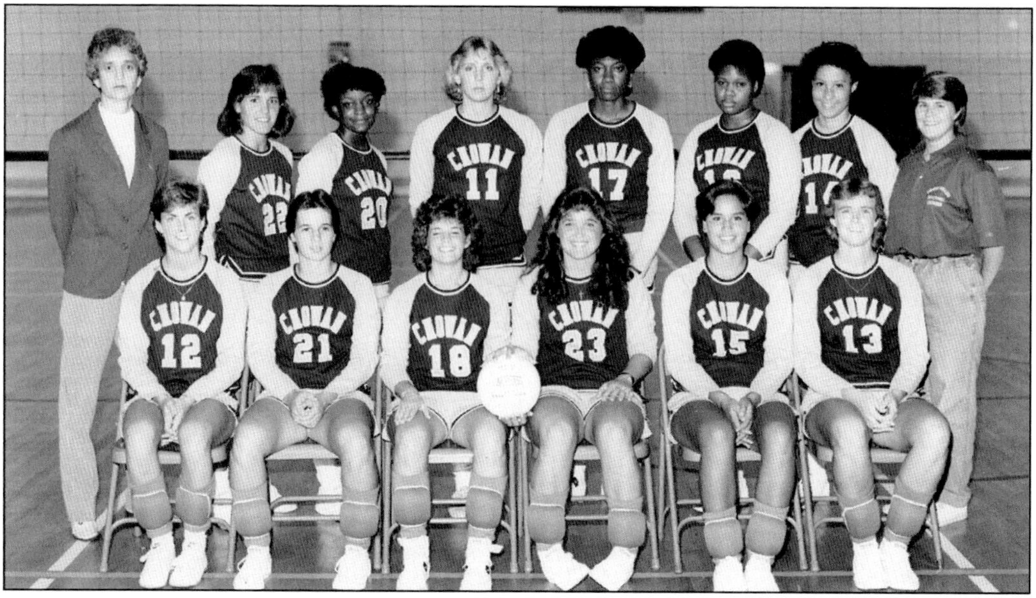

In 1985, members of the Chowan College girl's volleyball team were the region ten champions in national junior college competition. They were coached by Mrs. Janet Collins, longtime women's basketball and volleyball coach, pictured on the far left.

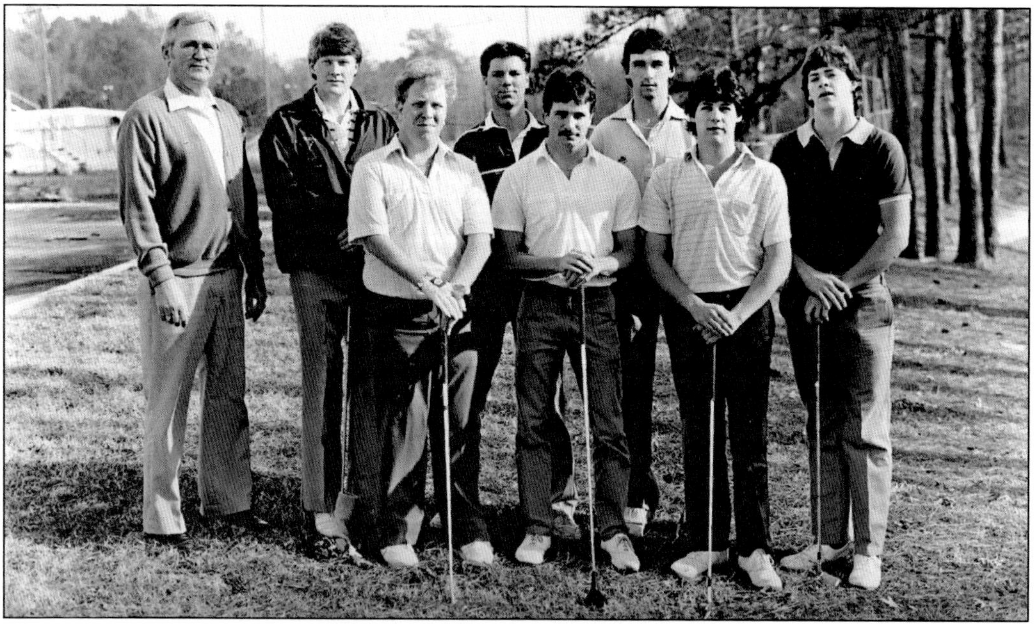

This is the 1986 Chowan College golf team, conference champions that year. Their coach, Mr. William Sowell, is on the left.

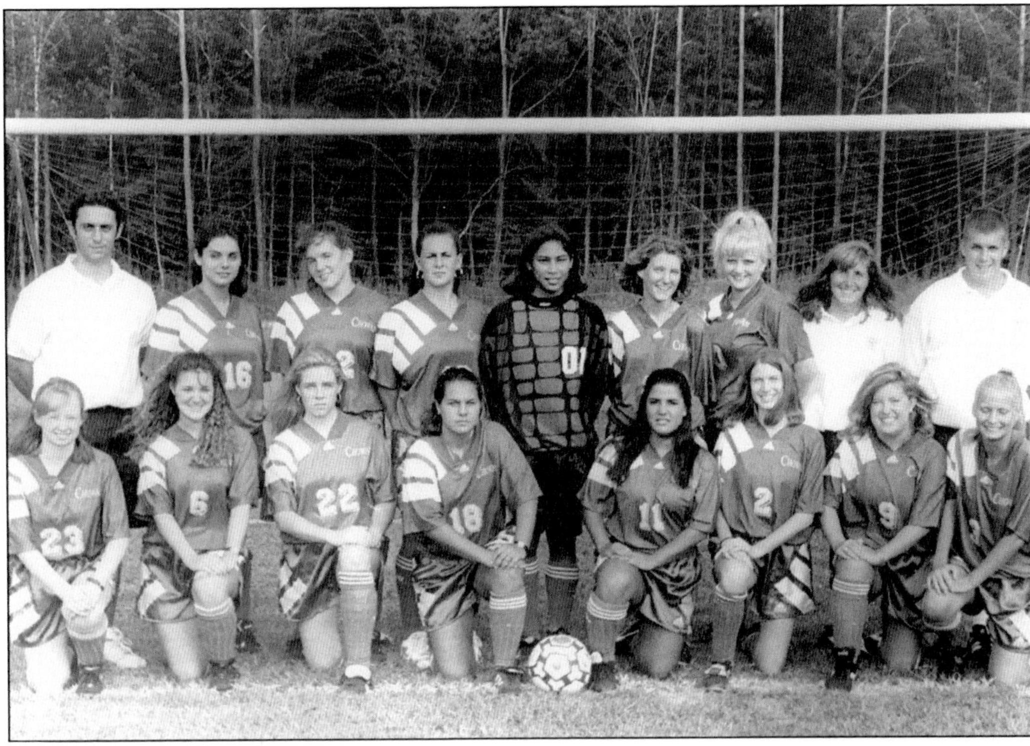

This is the Chowan College girl's soccer team for 1980.

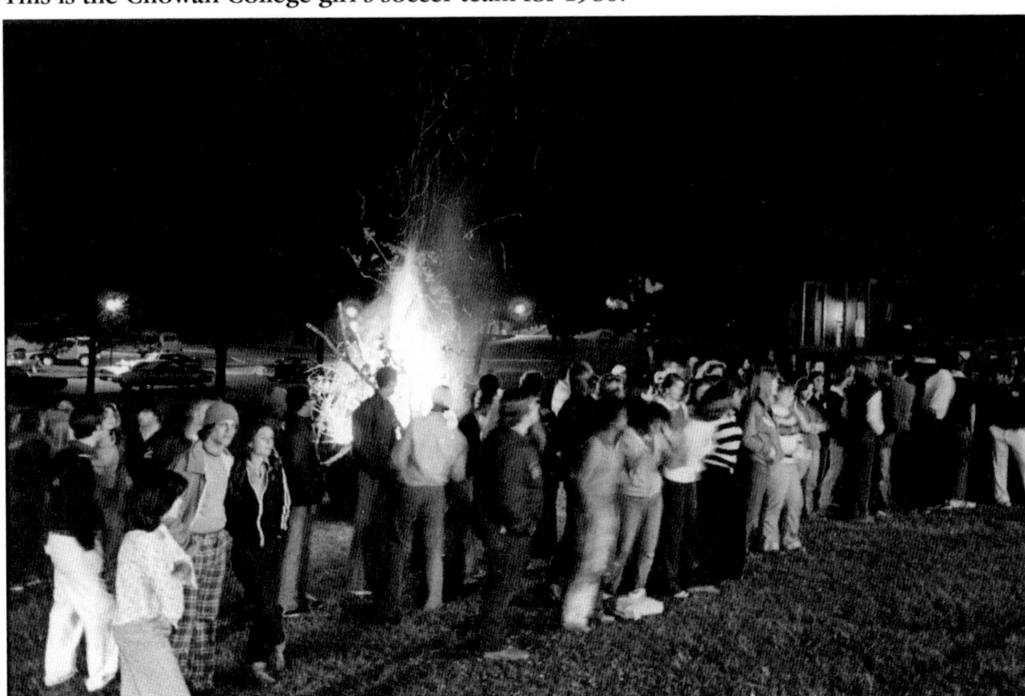

On the eve of a big homecoming football game, a pep rally and bonfire are usually held on the front campus.

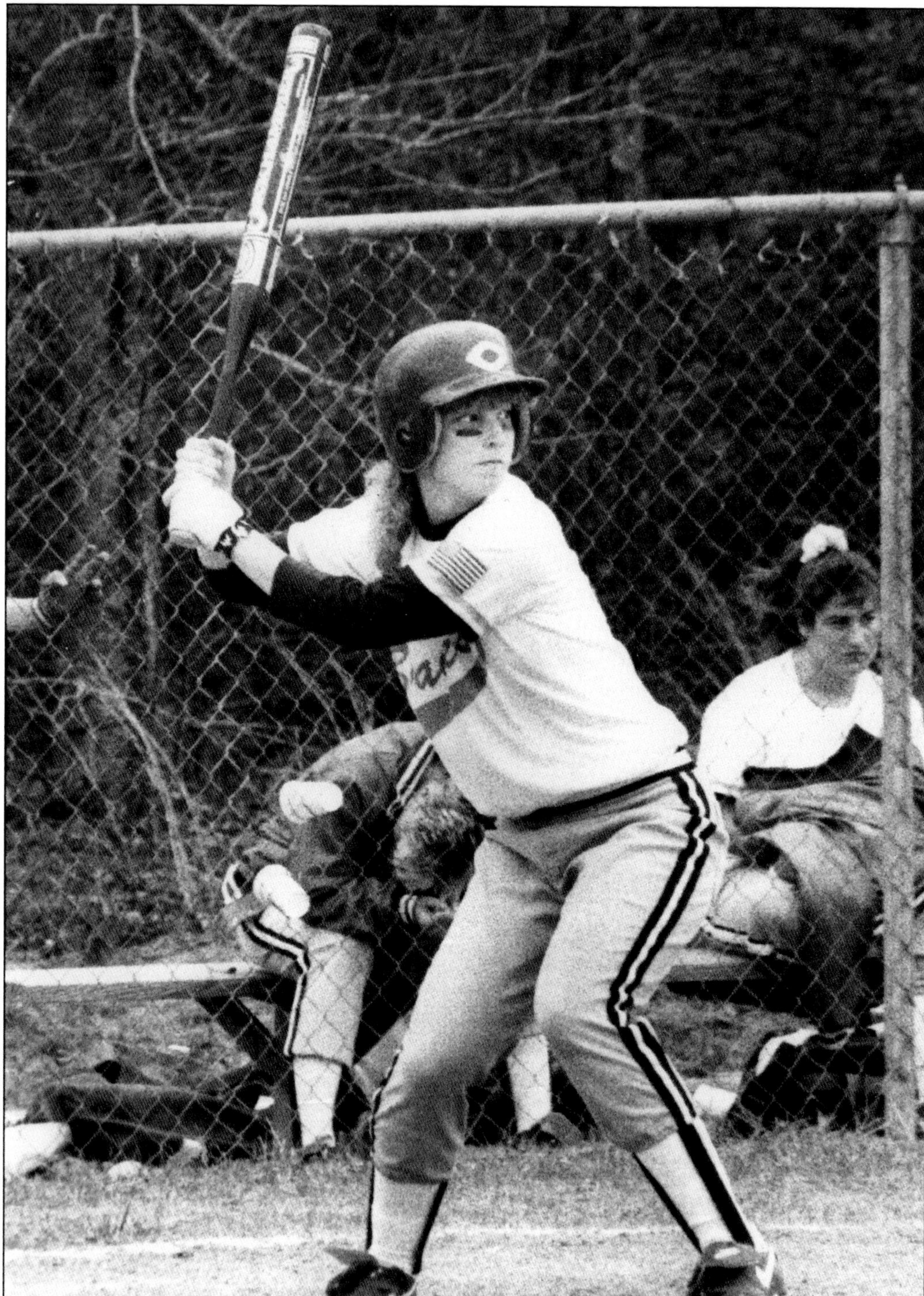

A heavy hitter for the Chowan College women's softball team takes aim at an incoming pitch.

Jerry Holmes was a star cornerback for two years at Chowan College, where he earned an associate's degree in business administration before transferring to the University of West Virginia. There, he lettered for two years and earned a bachelor's degree. He was drafted by the New York Jets and was a 10-year starter for them. Jerry Holmes also played for one year with the Green Bay Packers and the Detroit Lions and has coached for the San Diego Chargers, Washington Redskins, and Cleveland Browns.

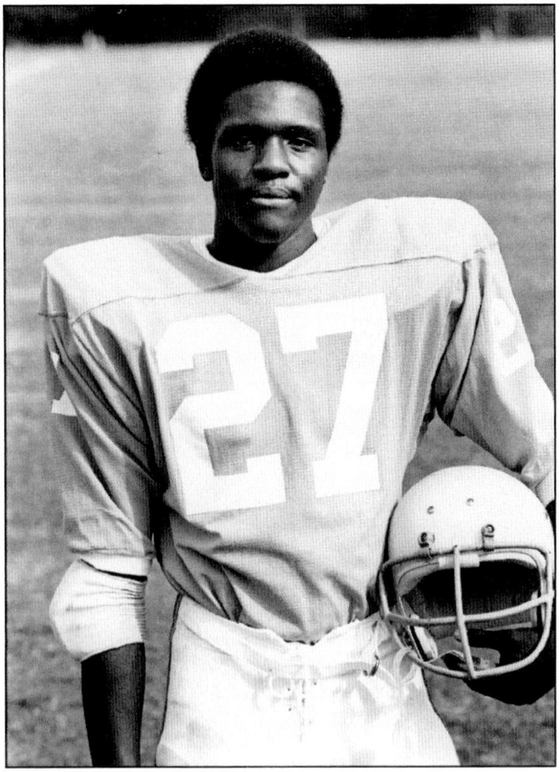

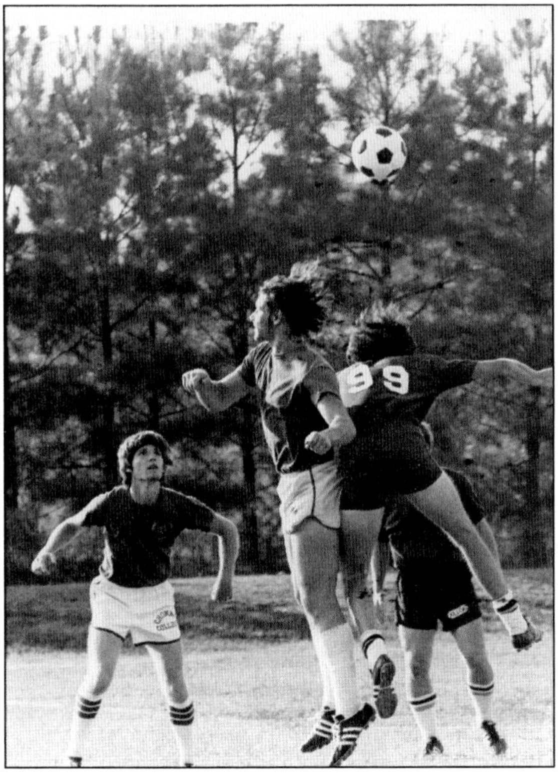

Chowan College soccer teams have been exciting to watch through the years.

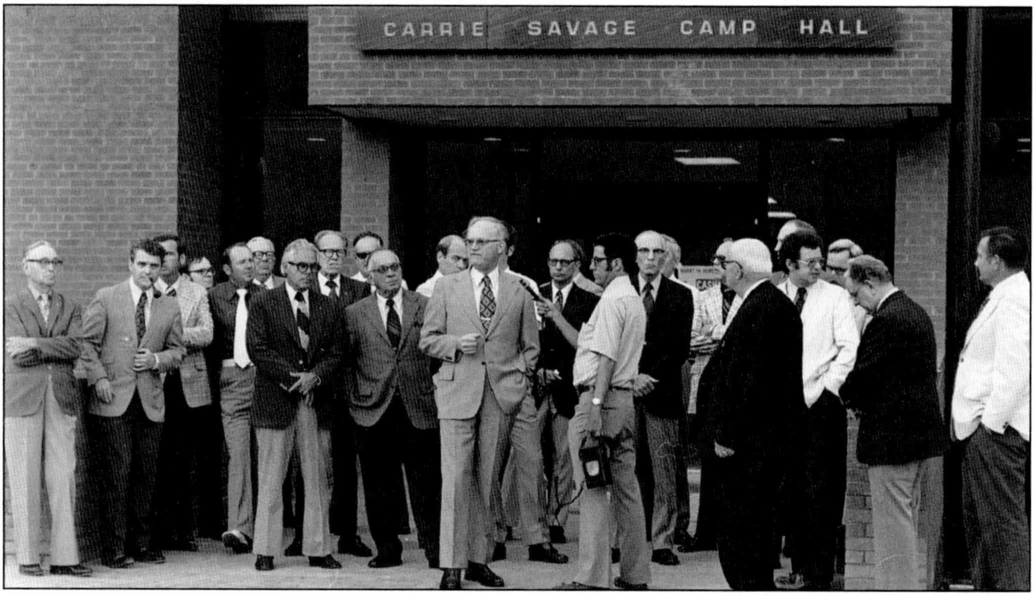

In 1974, members of the Murfreesboro Rotary Club were taken on a tour of Camp Hall, the college's newly constructed science facility. The group included, from left to right, Roger Holloman, Jim Chamblee (Chowan's Music Department chairman), Joe Minton, Cecil Forehand, James Pennington, Pete Whitley, George Gibbs, Ronald Jenkins, Eddie Cason, Dr. Bruce E. Whitaker (Chowan's president), Herman Gatewood, Don Burnette, Robert Parker, Roland Pruitte, George Underwood, Guy Revelle, J.M. Jenkins, Henry Burgwyn, Joel Holland, and Bobby Cross, director of development at Chowan.

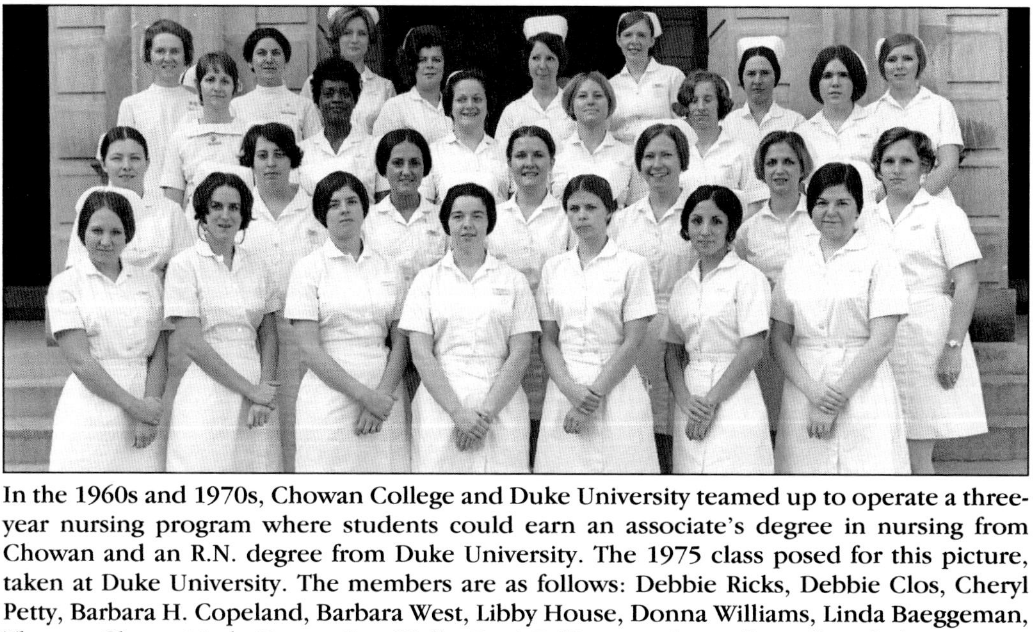

In the 1960s and 1970s, Chowan College and Duke University teamed up to operate a three-year nursing program where students could earn an associate's degree in nursing from Chowan and an R.N. degree from Duke University. The 1975 class posed for this picture, taken at Duke University. The members are as follows: Debbie Ricks, Debbie Clos, Cheryl Petty, Barbara H. Copeland, Barbara West, Libby House, Donna Williams, Linda Baeggeman, Theresa Chees, Marla Burns, Sue Wells, Patti Fallis, Jennifer Miller, Ella Whitley, Juanita Pruitt, Judy Knight, Kathy Moore, Beth Tilley, Mary Carpenter, Carolyn Smigel, Sue Jackson, Deborah Faulkner, Brenda Woodlin, Hilda Escebido, Marlene Miller, Margaret Powell, Katie Parker, Pat Jackson, and Evelyn Nickolson.

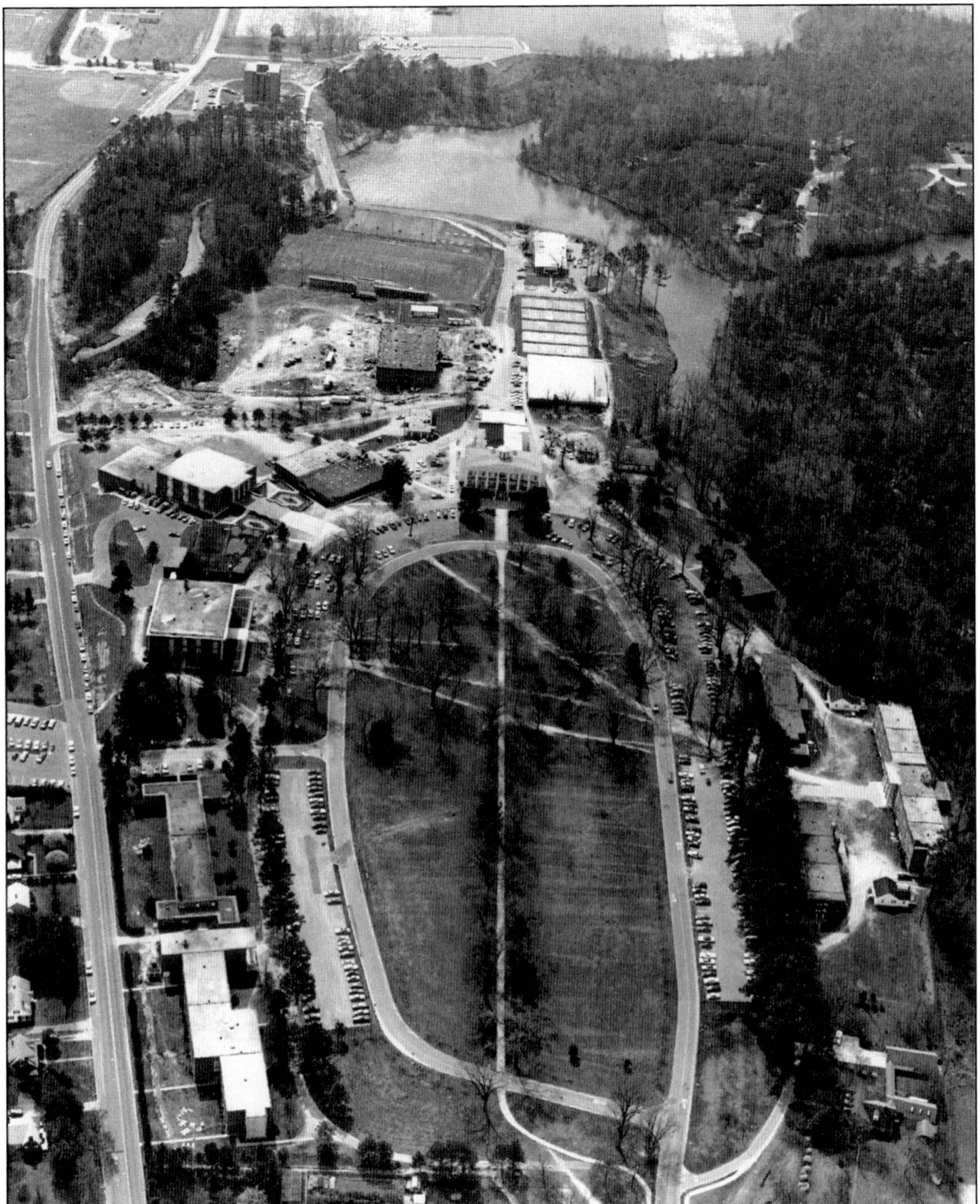

This is a 1973 aerial view of the Chowan College campus.

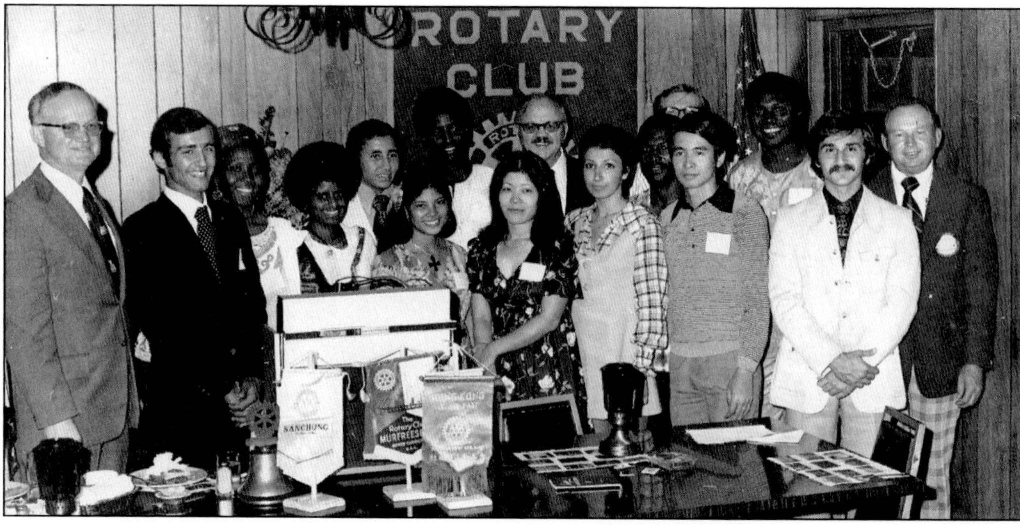

Since 1949, many international students from around the world have attended Chowan College. In the 1950s, a number of students from Cuba attended. In the 1960s and 1970s, the college was popular with students from the Middle East. This late 1970s photograph shows a group of Chowan international students who were guests of the Murfreesboro Rotary Club. The group is identified, from left to right, as Dr. Bruce E. Whitaker (Chowan president), Cumhur Ipek from Turkey, Tonia Okyne from Liberia, Abeba from Ethiopia, Joseph Andrade from Ecuador, Kiki Poll from Micronesia, Sana Ceesay from Gambia, Keiko Hanasato from Japan, Rev. Roland Pruette (Rotary Club member), Parisimi Haghneghadar from Iran, Sheku Mansaray from Sierra Leone, Clayton Lewis (dean of students), Chi Mind Au from Hong Kong, Olumide Kuboye from Nigeria, Jorge Nasasr from Venezuela, and Cecil Forehand of the Murfreesboro Rotary Club.

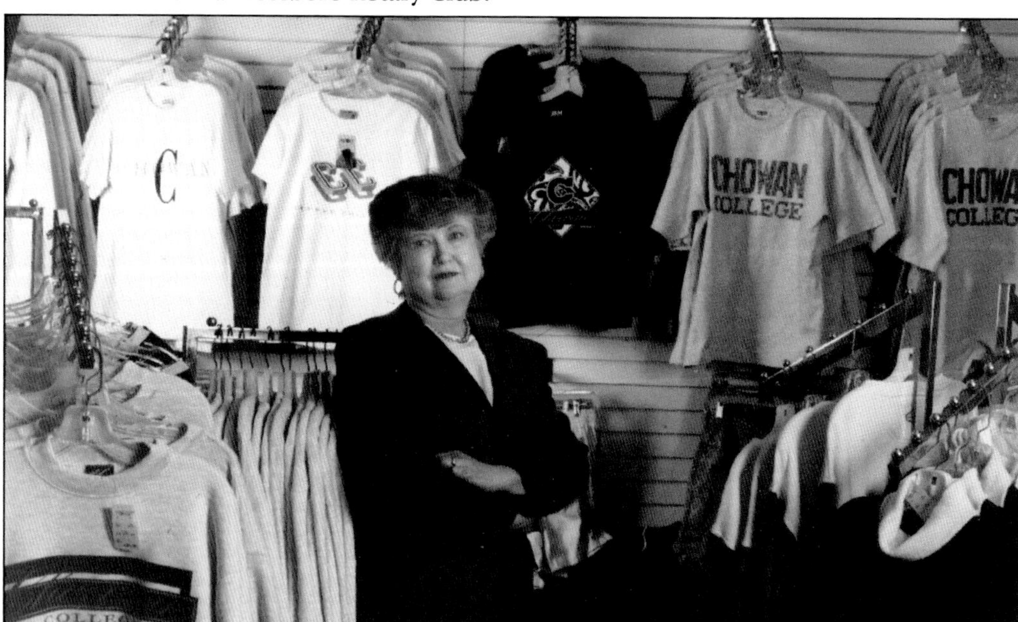

Mrs. Aldeen Gatewood served for many years as the manager of the Chowan College bookstore. She always greeted bookstore patrons with a warm, friendly smile.

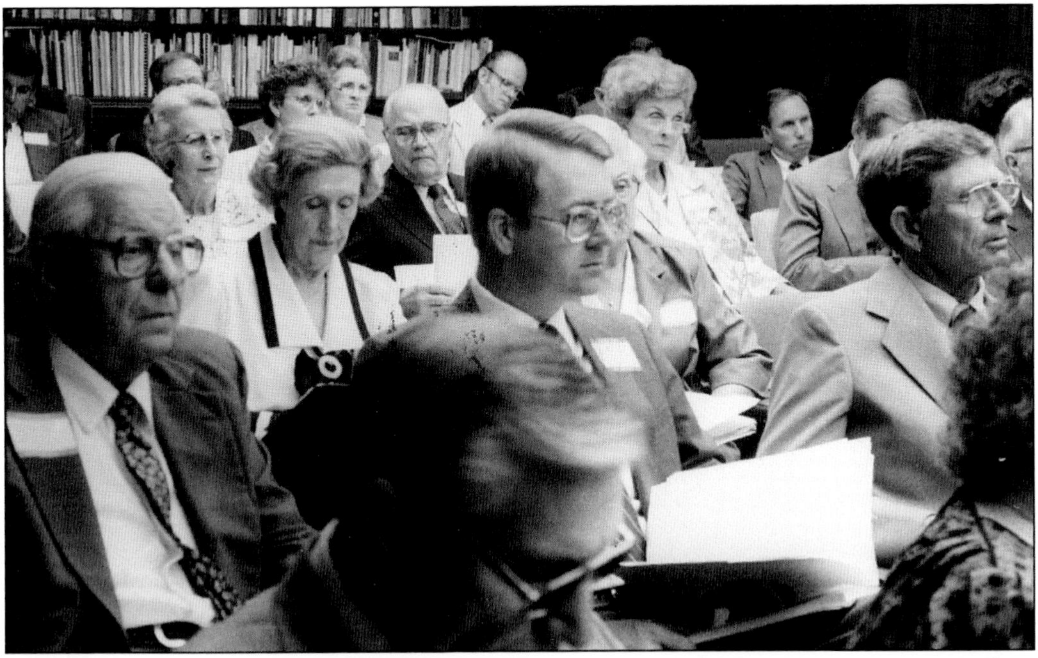

Since the founding of Chowan College in 1848, the men and women who have served on its Board of Trustees and Board of Visitors have given invaluable guidance, leadership, and financial resources in support of the college.

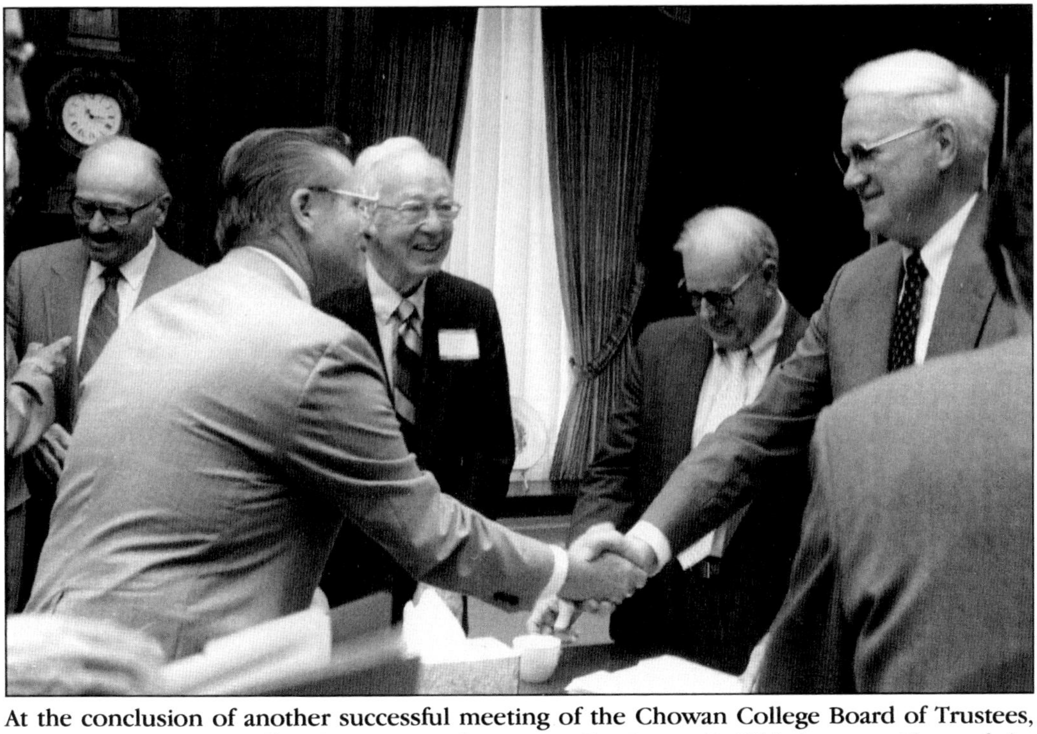

At the conclusion of another successful meeting of the Chowan College Board of Trustees, Rev. Bennie Pledger offers his congratulations to Dr. Bruce E. Whitaker, president of the college. Rev. Felix Arnold and Mr. Robert B. Spivey are among the trustees standing nearby.

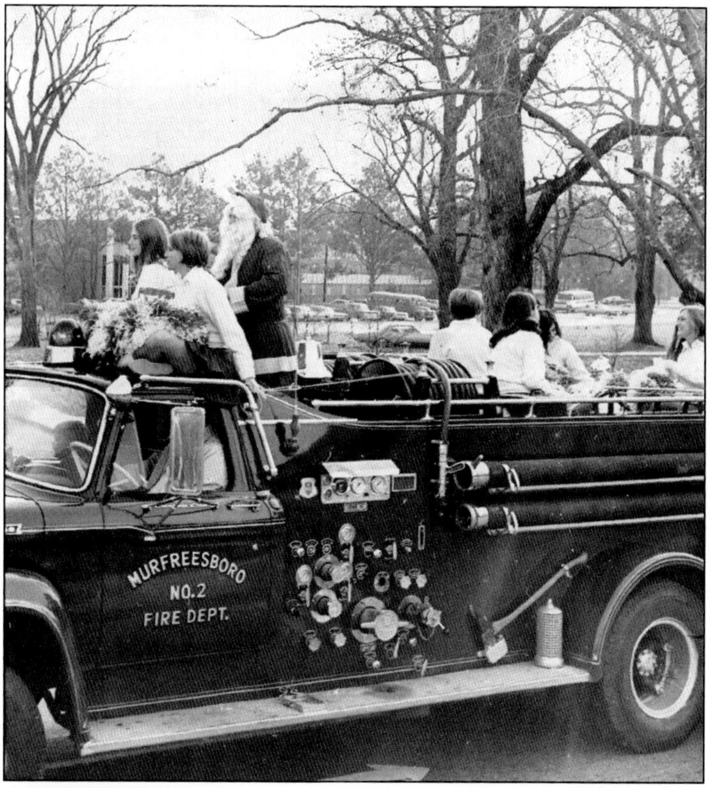

As seen in this 1969 parade, when the town of Murfreesboro holds its annual Christmas parade, the Chowan cheerleaders often ride with Santa Claus on one of the Murfreesboro fire trucks.

An image from the 1969 Chowan yearbook shows that many lifelong friendships and partnerships have been formed on the Chowan College campus.

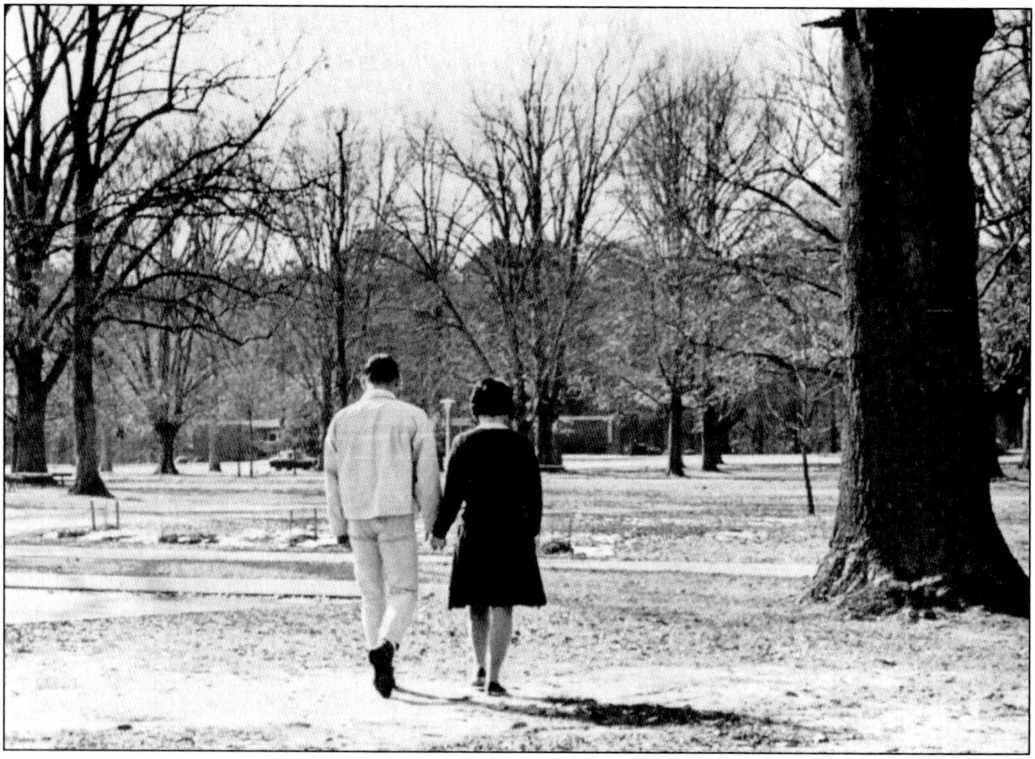

J.M. Jenkins, a native of Murfreesboro, was an educator for 40 years. For 35 of those years, he served in Hertford County, where he was a teacher, school principal, and superintendent. Mr. Jenkins attended Chowan College from 1933 to 1935 and was center on the college's first football team. J.M. Jenkins is a beloved man and it was most fitting for the Chowan College intramural center to be named in his honor. (Photograph from the 1949 Murfreesboro High School yearbook.)

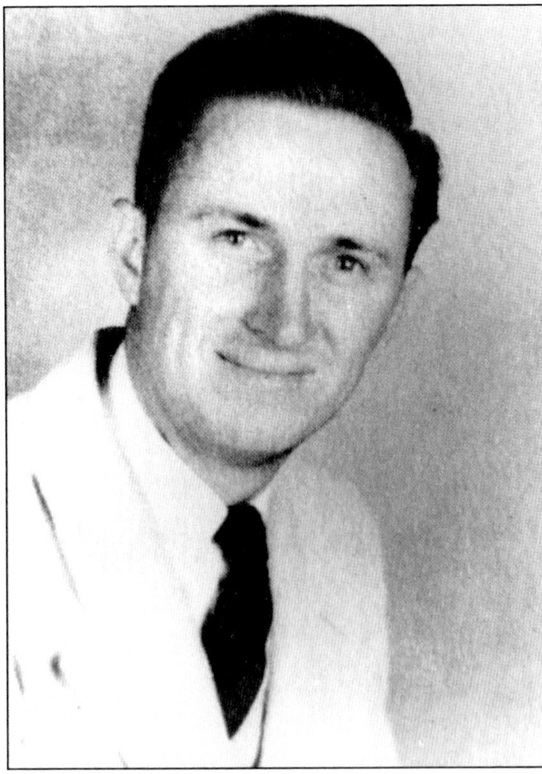

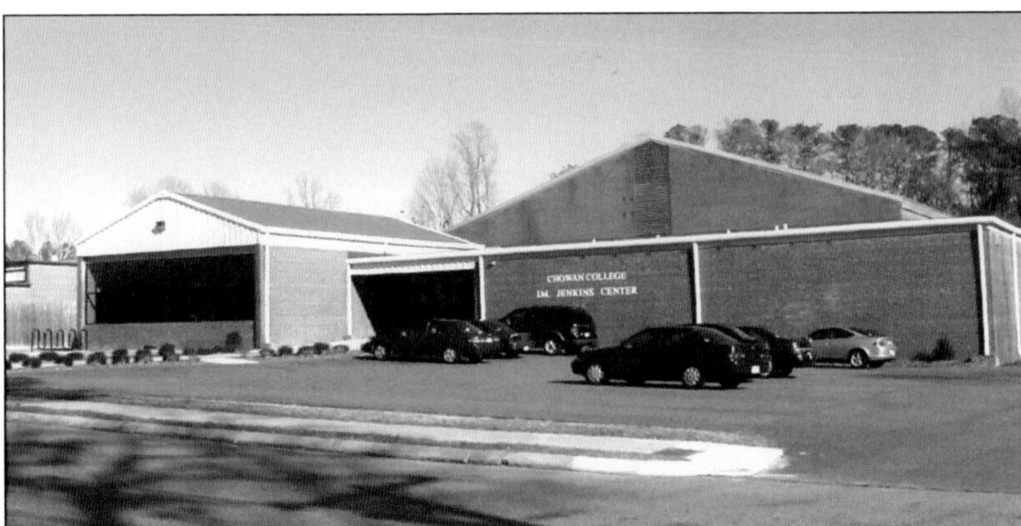

In the spring of 2002, the college dedicated and opened the J.M. Jenkins intramural sports and physical fitness center, which was achieved under the leadership of Chowan president Dr. Stanley G. Lott. The center is named in honor of J.M. Jenkins, who attended Chowan College and Wake Forest University and was the popular principal of Murfreesboro High School from 1947 to 1963. The building that houses the Jenkins Center is actually the former Murfreesboro High School gymnasium, built during the time Mr. Jenkins was principal there. In 1994, the college purchased part of the former Murfreesboro High School property, including the gymnasium.

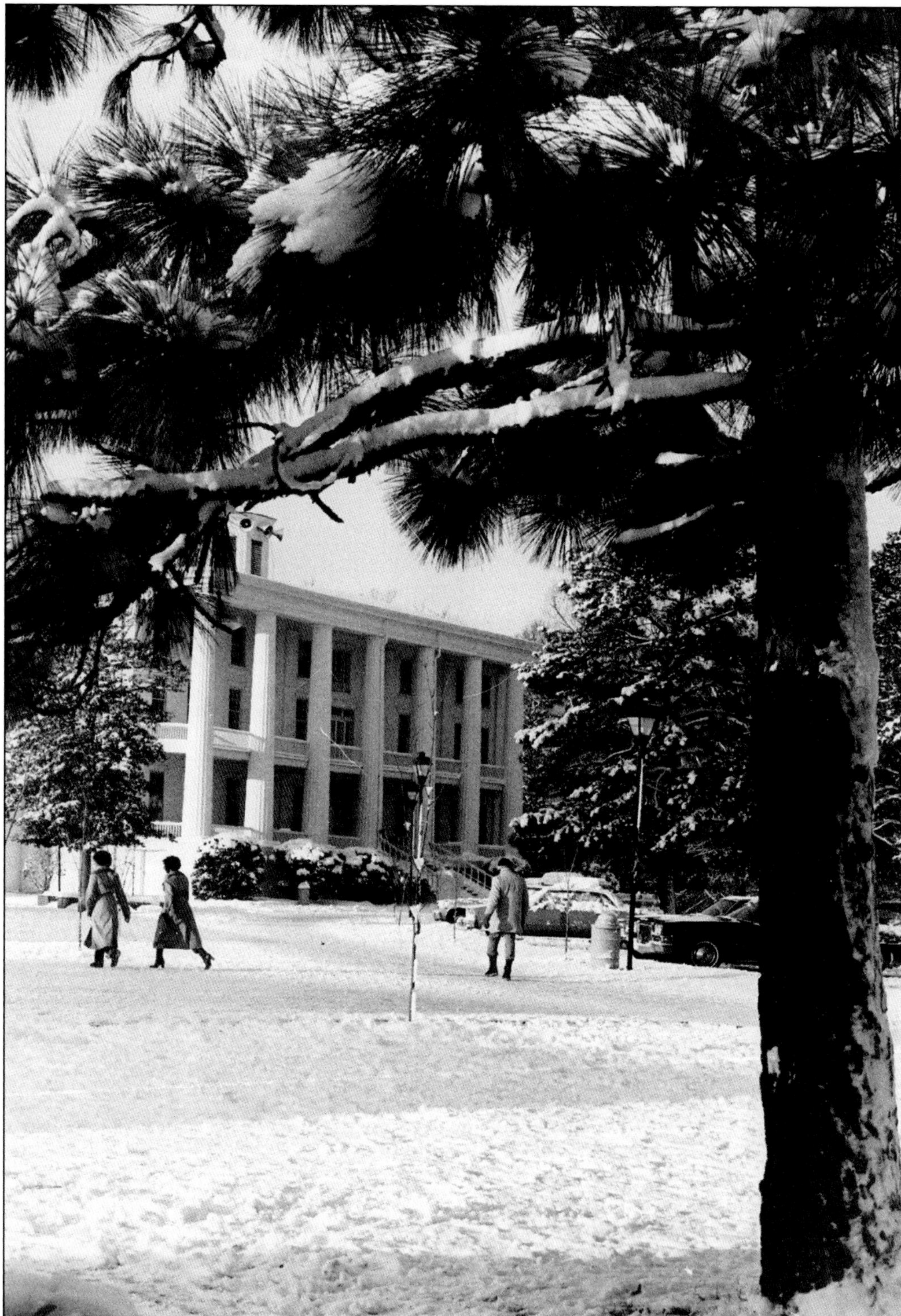

A 1990s winter storm turned the Chowan College campus into a winter wonderland.

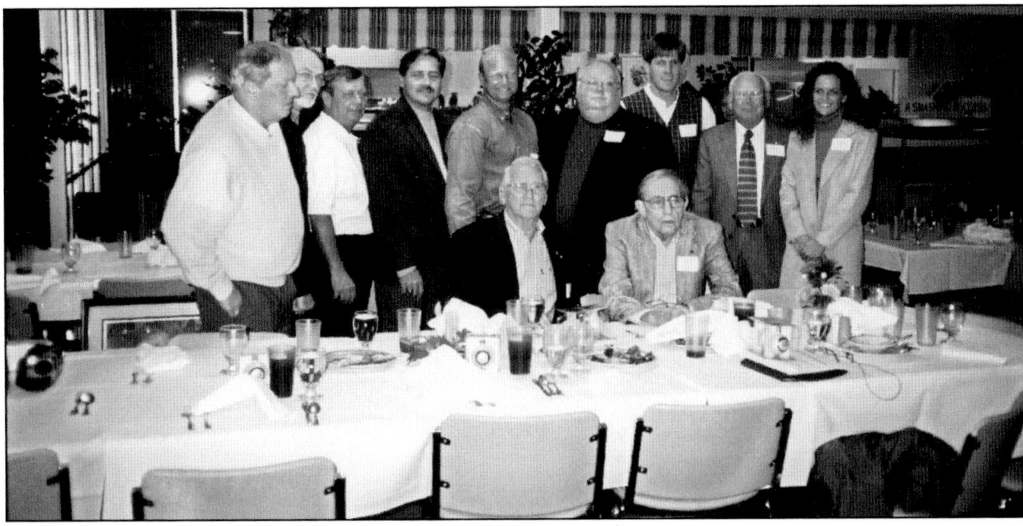

These two retired Chowan College faculty members amassed nearly three-quarters of a century of teaching service between them in the Department of Graphic Communications. The two retired professors, William B. Sowell (left) and Herman W. Gatewood (right), retired in 1995 and 1996 respectively. They are seen here flanked by nine of their former students, all of whom were named Distinguished Alumni by the Department of Graphic Communications in November 2002. It is estimated that the two retired professors taught over 2500 students during their years at Chowan College. Herman W. Gatewood, who served as chairman of the Department of Graphic Communications for 25 years, passed away in March 2003.

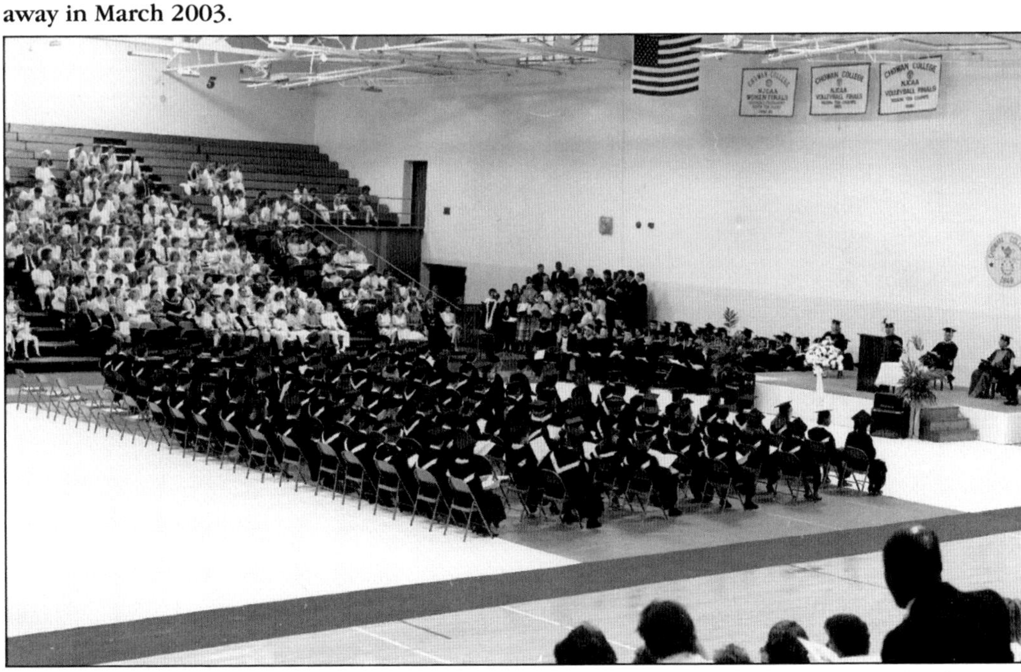

Graduation exercises are occasionally held indoors at the college's physical education complex, the Helms Center, which was constructed in 1979–1980. This state-of-the art facility houses the Department of Physical Education, including a large pool and the Chowan College Sports Hall of Fame.

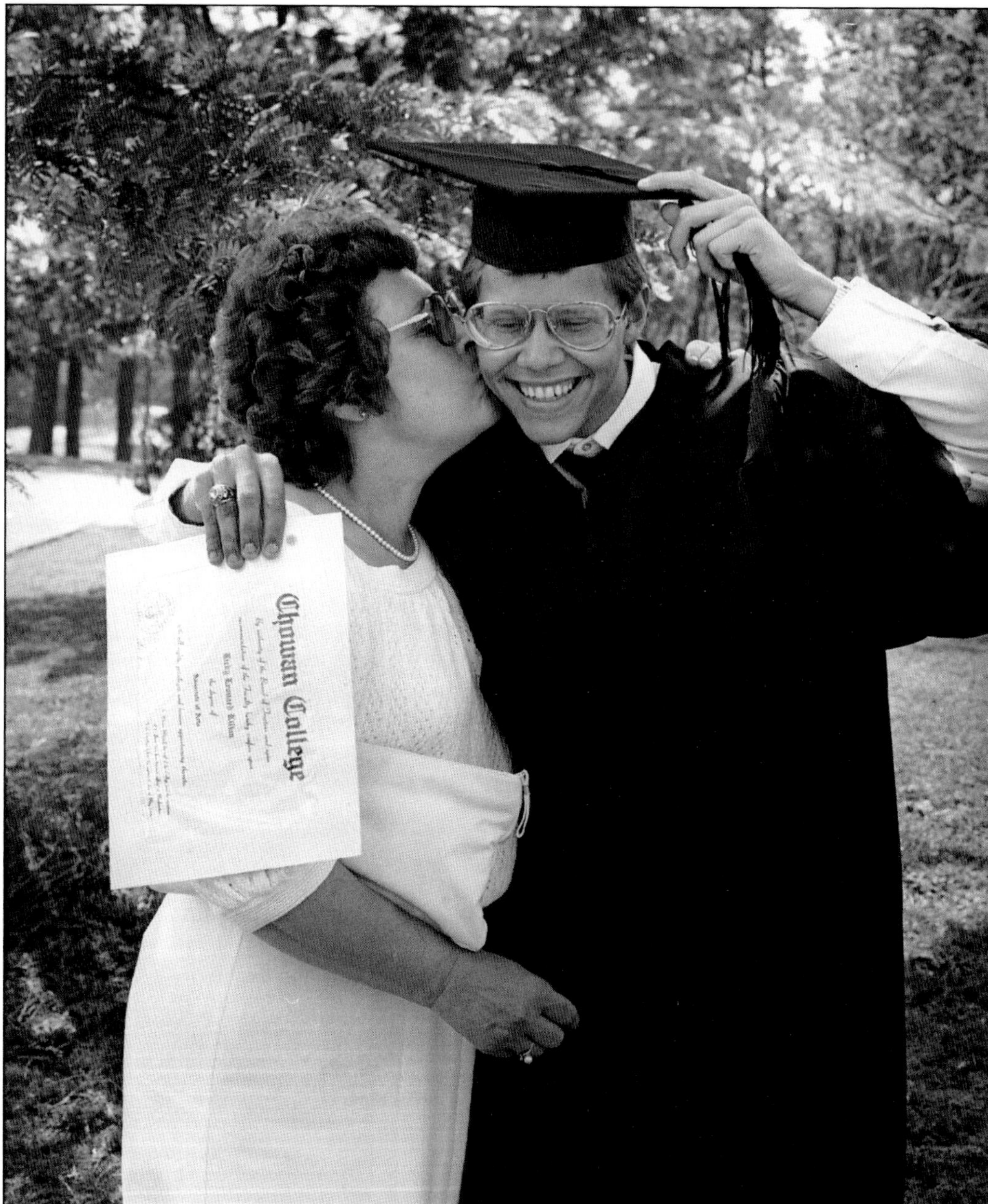

Ricky Killian's mother could not have been any prouder of her son than when he graduated from Chowan College in the spring of 1986.

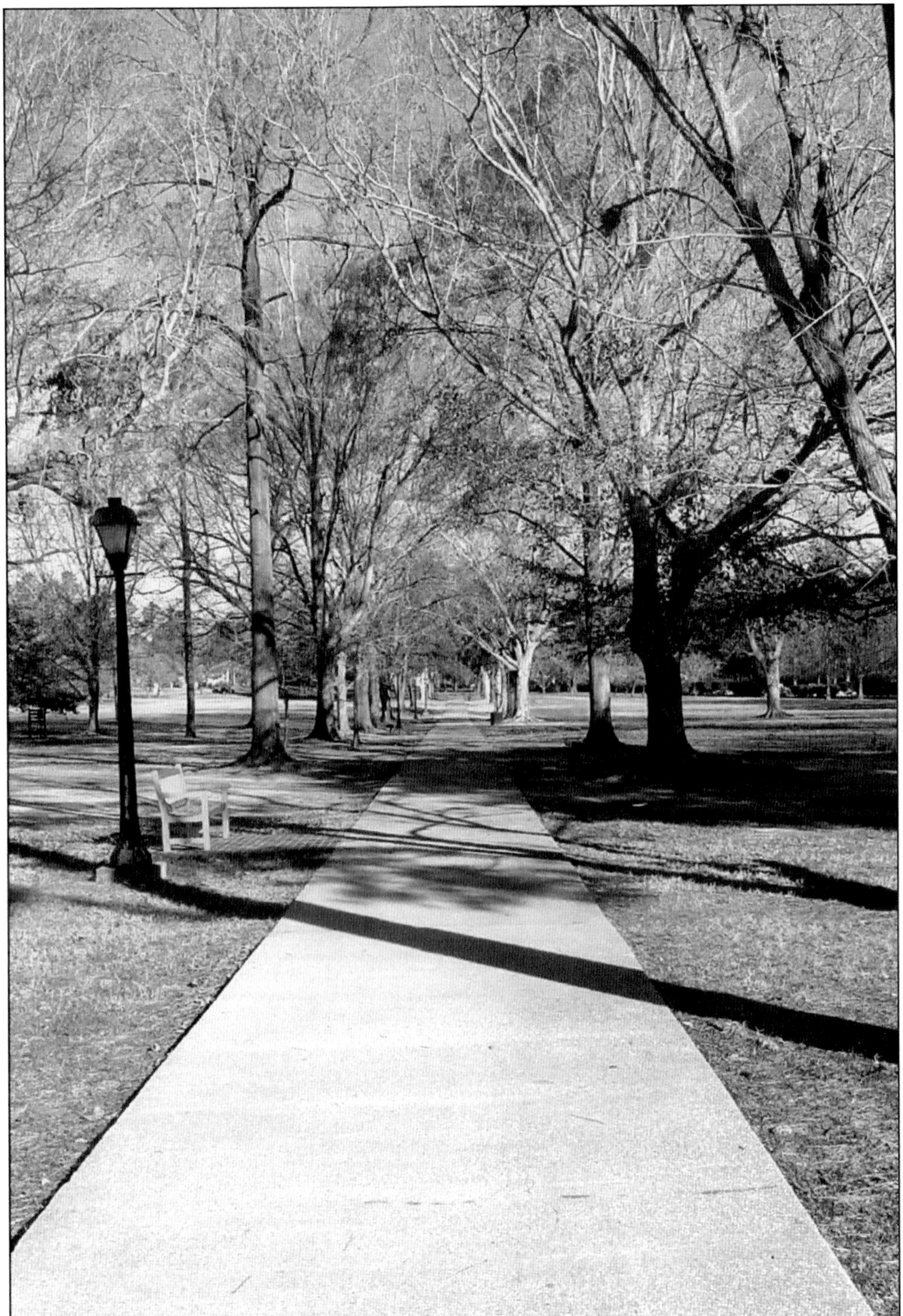

This is a 2004 view of the center front walk looking from the Columns Building outward. The front campus, including the center front walk, has lost a number of its original trees over the years from weather-related causes. Hurricane Floyd in 1999 and Hurricane Isabelle in 2003 were especially damaging.

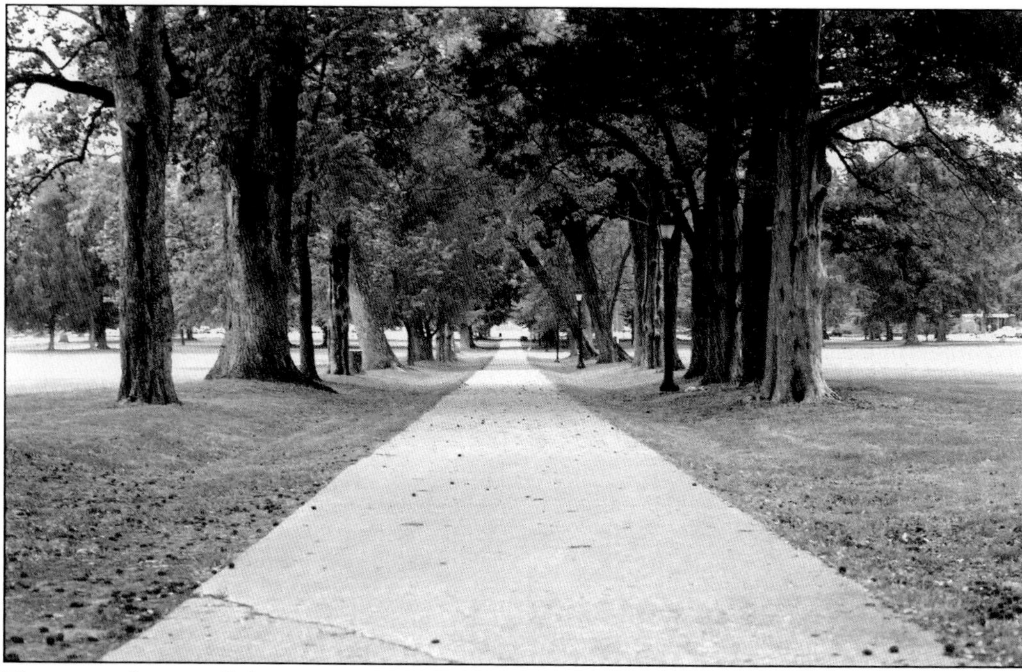

The center front walk has seen many transformations through the years. This view was taken in the summer of 1999 and looks inward towards the Columns Building.

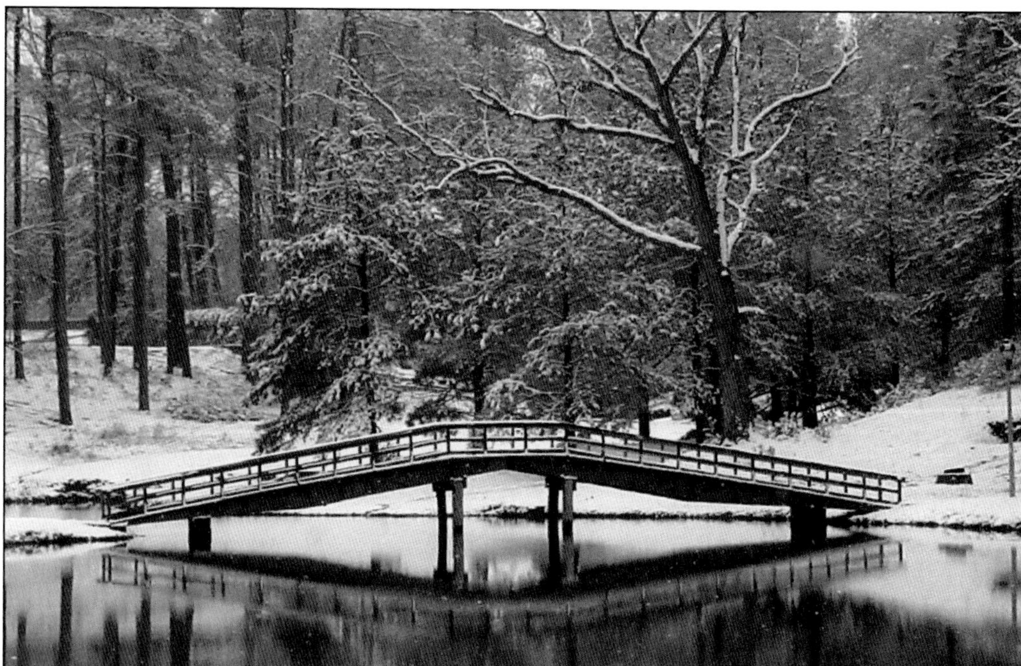

A January 2004 winter storm turned this lake and bridge below Parker Hall into a picture postcard.

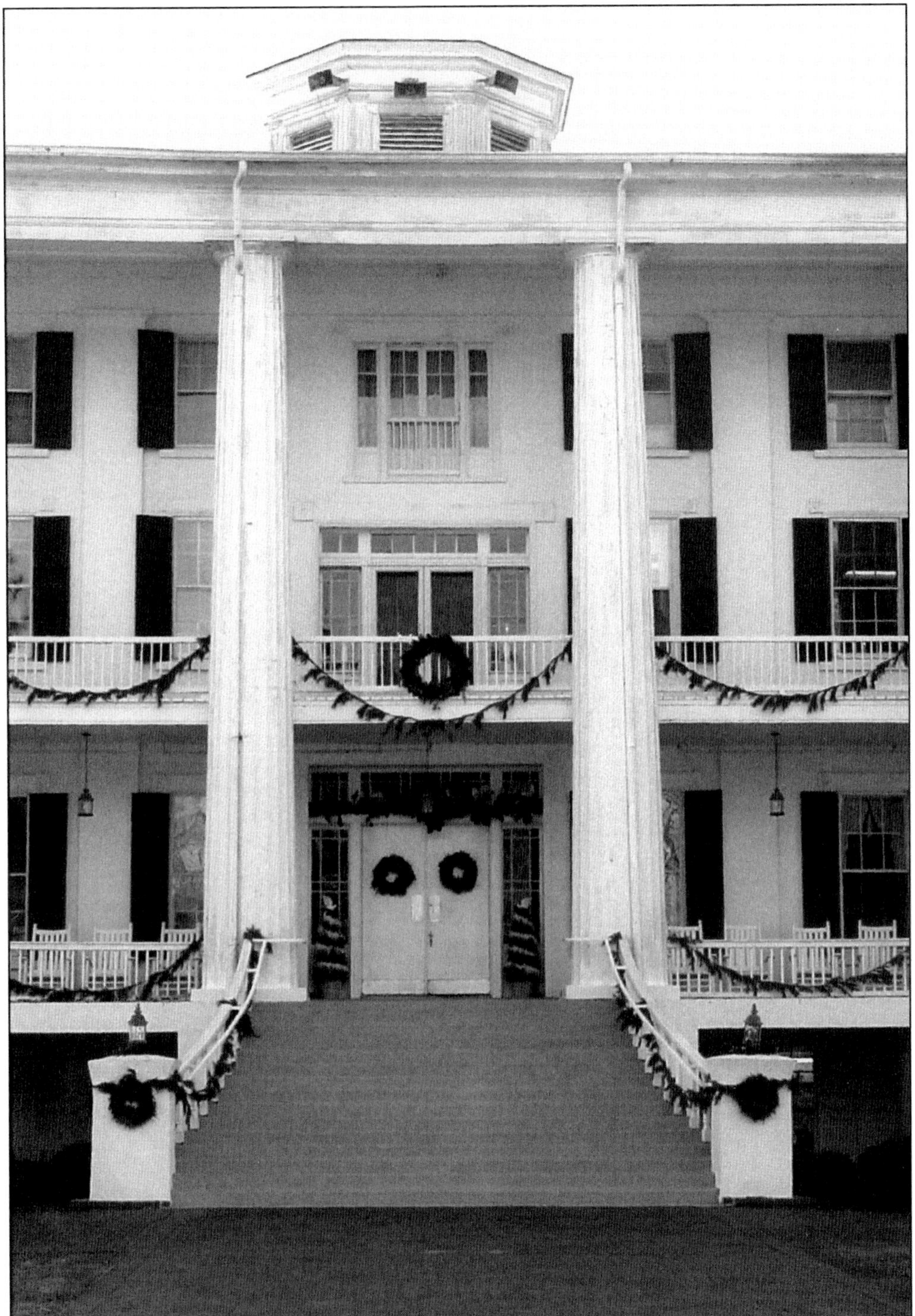

Holiday decorations adorn the 1851 McDowell Columns Building during the 2003 Christmas season. Holiday decorations for the 1851 McDowell Columns Building and the Ella Camp Cobb President's Home are made yearly on campus by the Christmas Decorating Committee, composed of members of the faculty and staff.

Chowan, Mother Dear

A song in thy praise, O mother dear,
Doth rise to lips from loyal hearts.
We do greet thee !
We do greet thee !
As out the darkness thou thy way
Dost break thro' night to perfect day.
We salute thee !
We salute thee !
Mother dear ! Mother dear !

Our hearts rejoice in thy wisdom and strength
And to God be thanks for thy fostering care.
We do praise thee !
We do praise thee !
Thy name—so fair—we love and adore,
So treasured with hopes and mem'ries of yore.
We adore thee !
We adore thee !
Dear Chowan ! Dear Chowan !

The thrill of thy beauty—kind Nature's own skill—
Doth surge thro' our souls, and brighten our way.
We adore thee !
We adore thee !
The beech, the magnolia, the longleaf rare
Each season doth rival to make more fair.
We do love thee !
We do love thee !
Mother fair ! Mother fair !

M. E. Mac C.

This song of praise can be found in the 1929 Chowan College yearbook.

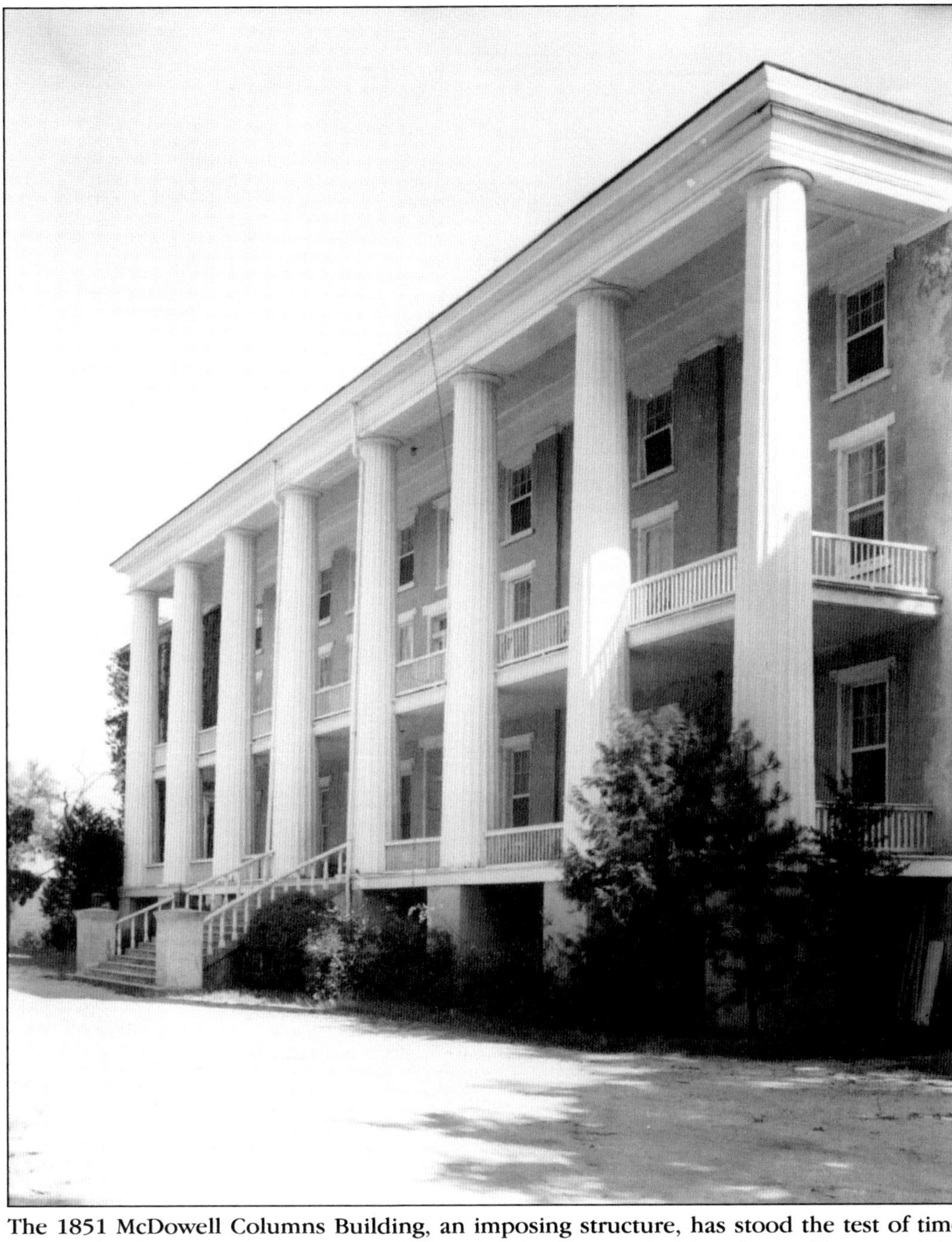

The 1851 McDowell Columns Building, an imposing structure, has stood the test of time and has held as a steadfast beacon of education for thousands of students. (Photograph by Joel C. Holland in 1949.)

Alma Mater

On the plains of Carolina,
'Neath her skies so blue,
Stands our noble Alma Mater,
Glorious to view.

With her classic walls and columns
Looks she proudly down,
Reared against the arch of heaven
With the stars for crown.

By Meherrin's rippling waters
Where the sungleams play,
We, her loyal friends and daughters,
Pledge our love for aye.

Praise to her! God grant His blessing;
May He give rich store.
Chowan we will ever cherish,
Love her evermore.

ANNE ABERNATHY, '90.

Miss Annie Elberton Abernathy composed Chowan College's alma mater. She graduated from Chowan College in 1890.

Miss Abernathy graduated from Chowan College in 1890 and attended Columbia University in New York City. She taught at Peace College in Raleigh and other North Carolina institutions. She died in 1952 and is buried at her family's plot at Brown's Church in Warren County, North Carolina.

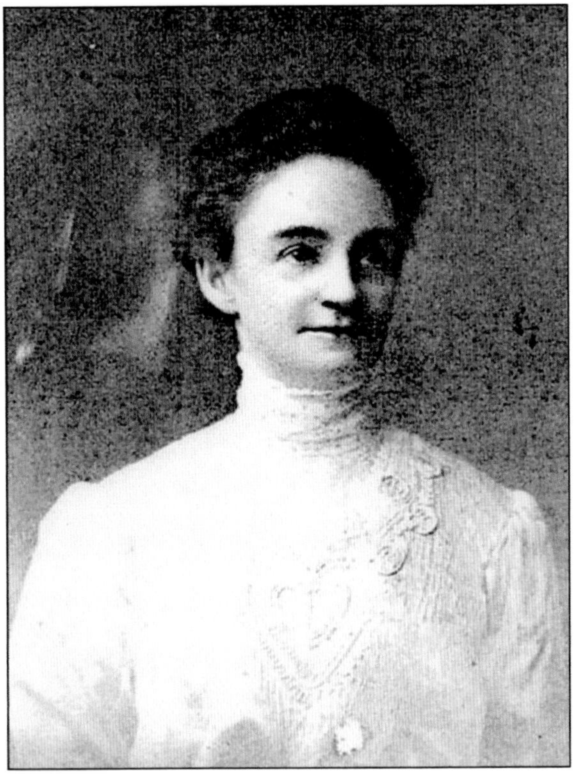

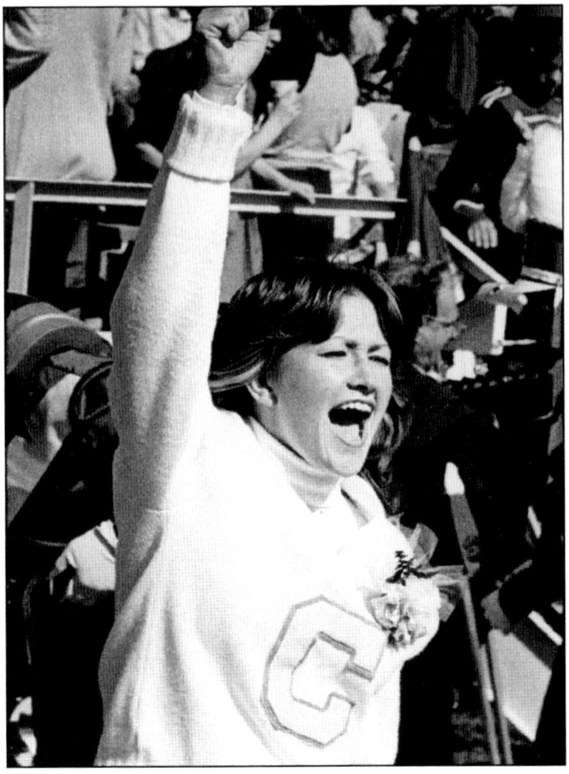

The spirit of Chowan College's founders is still alive and well among the students, faculty, and staff today. In 1993, Chowan made the transition from a junior college to a four-year institution. The true Chowan College spirit continues to be embodied in its students, who have selected a very special place to continue their education.

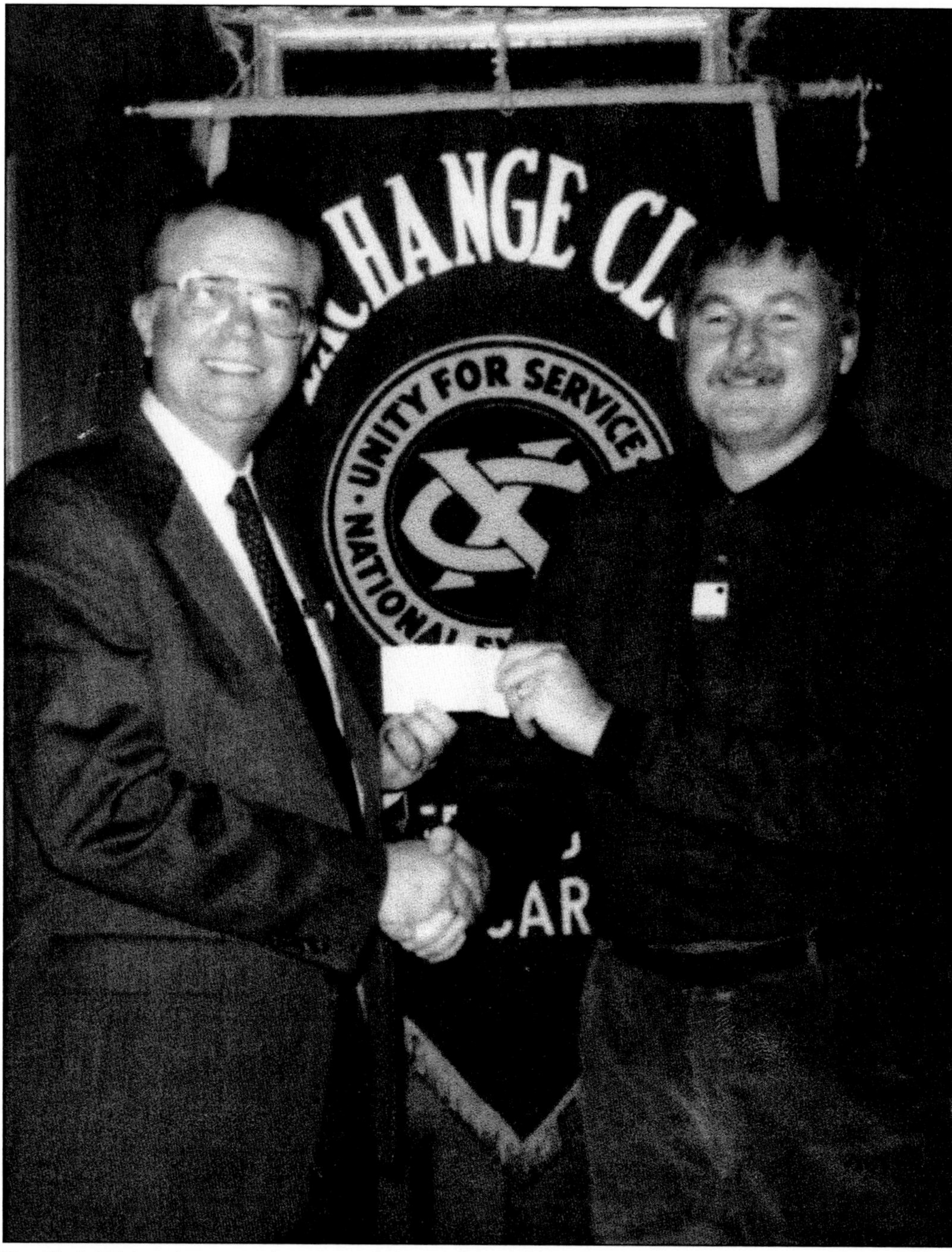

Dr. Chris White, the recently appointed president of Chowan College (left), and Murfreesboro Exchange Club president Danny Blowe are seen here renewing a special partnership started in 1949, when the Murfreesboro Exchange Club became a leading force in the reopening of Chowan College. When the college reopened in 1949, the Murfreesboro Exchange Club did not cease its strong support for the college, as shown by this scholarship check that President Blowe presented to President White on February 2, 2004. (Photograph courtesy of the Murfreesboro Exchange Club.)